Christmas 1947

Kingdom of Adventure: Everest

KINGDOM OF ADVENTURE: *EVEREST*

A chronicle of man's assault on the earth's highest mountain narrated by the participants and with an accompanying text by James Ramsey Ullman

WILLIAM SLOANE ASSOCIATES, Inc.

Publishers   *New York*

To my sons Jim and Bill
—and adventures yet to come

No end is visible or even conceivable
to this kingdom of adventure.

GEORGE LEIGH-MALLORY

Contents

Illustrations and Maps

ILLUSTRATIONS AND MAPS

Acknowledgments

Permission has been received to quote excerpts by:

Col. L. V. S. Blacker from *First Over Everest* by Col. Blacker and Col. P. T. Etherton, published by John Lane, England;

Gen. G. C. Bruce from *The Assault on Mount Everest: 1922*, published by Edward Arnold, England, with permission of the Mt. Everest Committee;

George C. Finch from *The Assault on Mount Everest: 1922*, published by Edward Arnold, England, with permission of the Mt. Everest Committee;

Lt. Col. C. K. Howard-Bury from *Mount Everest, the Reconnaissance, 1921*, published by Edward Arnold, England, with permission of the Mt. Everest Committee;

R. L. G. Irving from *Ten Great Mountains*, published by J. M. Dent, England, and E. P. Dutton, United States;

George Leigh-Mallory from *The Fight for Everest: 1924, Mount Everest, the Reconnaissance, 1921*, and *The Assault on Mount Everest: 1922*, published by Edward Arnold, England, with permission of the Mt. Everest Committee; and also published by Longmans, Green, United States;

Capt. John Noel from *The Story of Everest*, published by Little, Brown, United States;

Col. E. F. Norton from *The Fight for Everest: 1924*, published by Edward Arnold, England, with permission of the Mt. Everest Committee;

N. E. Odell from *The Fight for Everest: 1924*, published by Edward Arnold, England, with permission of the Mt. Everest Committee;

ACKNOWLEDGMENTS

Hugh Ruttledge from *Everest—the Unfinished Adventure*, published by Hodder & Stoughton, England; and from *Everest —1933*, published by Hodder & Stoughton, England (published in the United States by Robert McBride, copyright by the author, 1935, under title *Attack on Everest*);

Col. Robert L. Scott from *God Is My Co-Pilot*, published by Charles Scribner's, United States;

Eric Shipton from *Upon That Mountain*, published by and copyright by Hodder & Stoughton, England;

Frank S. Smythe from *Everest—1933* by Hugh Ruttledge, published by Hodder & Stoughton, England (published in the United States by Robert McBride, copyright by the author, 1935, under title *Attack on Everest*); from *Camp VI, Spirit of the Hills*, and *Adventures of a Mountaineer*, published by Hodder & Stoughton, England;

T. Howard Somervell from *After Everest*, published by and copyright by Hodder & Stoughton, England;

Sir Francis Younghusband from *Everest: the Challenge* by permission of Thomas Nelson & Sons, Ltd., Edinburgh and New York; from *The Assault on Mt. Everest*, published by Edward Arnold, with permission of the Mt. Everest Committee.

Excerpts by the following people first appeared in *The Alpine Journal*, England: Geo. C. Finch (1939); Lt. Col. C. K. Howard-Bury (1922); H. W. Tilman (1939); Eric Shipton (1936); Hugh Ruttledge (1936); and R. L. G. Irving (1924). *29,000 Feet* by Charles S. Houston is reprinted from *The American Alpine Journal* (Vol. VI, 1946).

Foreword

This book has been compiled and edited by a man who loves mountains and who is, therefore, strongly and unashamedly prejudiced in favor of his subject. One of my most memorable boyhood experiences was my first introduction to the Everest adventure (through Noel's *The Story of Everest*) at the age of, I think, sixteen. And one of my most genuine adult sorrows is that that adventure is to this day, among Americans at least, so little known. Virtually everyone has at least a nodding acquaintance with Peary, Scott, Amundsen, Byrd, and many of the other great explorers of modern times; but of the "Everesters," the men who in expedition after expedition, year after year, have done grim and gallant battle with the summit of the world, no one seems to know anything at all. . . . "Oh, yes, Mallory—" someone will perhaps recall. And the rest is silence.

This state of affairs, to be sure, is a perfectly agreeable one to the Everesters themselves, for mountaineers are a reticent and publicity-shunning breed. But it is also a deplorable thing that one of the world's great and valid adventure stories should be allowed to languish in comparative obscurity. If this volume should lead even a handful of newcomers into the kingdom of the highest mountain, I shall be a very happy guide indeed. And the guardians and champions of that kingdom will not, I think, consider us trespassers, provided only that we enter it in the same spirit as themselves.

The core of this book is a collection of the writings of many men—almost all of them actual participants in the struggle for Everest. It differs from most anthologies in that the selections have been made with an eye to telling a consecutive story, rather than on the basis of literary merit. And yet I am confident that merit will not be found wanting. A few of the Everesters—George Mallory for one, Frank Smythe for another —are writers of high professional accomplishment; and the rest, it seems to me, have risen magnificently to the greatness of their subject. They are all Englishmen and all mountaineers, which is a combination that makes for reticence; perhaps they do not always tell us quite everything that we would like to know. But that, I think, is a virtue of their story-telling, rather than a fault. What they have left unsaid is nonetheless *there*, clearer and more meaningful between the lines than if they had tried to set it down in actual words.

The forty-odd selections I have chosen from their writings are for the most part excerpts from longer pieces. The books or periodicals in which they first appeared are listed at the end of each excerpt, as well as, all together, in Appendix IV; and it is my hope that this bibliography will lead the reader on to a closer acquaintance with Everest and the Everesters than can be gained in the meager pages of this volume.

Many typographical inconsistencies (as in spelling, form of geographical names, and style of numerals) will be found in the pages that follow—as well as an occasional inconsistency in fact. As regards the first category, it is largely a matter of a mixture of nationalities, the original writers following the British usage and I, as interlocutor, the American. As to the second, the answer is simply that not all the facts about Everest and its surroundings are as yet known; and I have not seen fit to question the sometimes conflicting statements of the climbers, any one of whom, presumably, is as reliable an authority as the next.

By way of acknowledgment, I wish to express my thanks to

the American Alpine Club for the use of its library and other facilities, and in particular to the club's librarian, Miss Helen I. Buck, who was both patient and most helpful during the long period when I cluttered up her domain. My gratitude is due, too, to William Sloane, my publisher, whose idea this book was, and to Elizabeth C. Moore, my editor, for her painstaking work on text, proofs, and index.

And finally, and most obviously, of course, there must be my salute to the men who are at once the subjects and the authors of this volume—who have both lived and written the story of Everest. I believe that their adventure is one of the brightest, finest chapters in the sorry history of our century, and I am proud to be in their company, even if only vicariously in the pages of a book.

J. R. U.

CONTRIBUTING AUTHORS

L. V. Stewart Blacker
Charles G. Bruce
George I. Finch
Charles S. Houston
C. K. Howard-Bury
R. L. G. Irving
George Leigh-Mallory
John Noel
E. F. Norton
N. E. Odell
Hugh Ruttledge
Robert L. Scott, Jr.
Eric Shipton
Frank S. Smythe
T. Howard Somervell
H. W. Tilman
Francis Younghusband

Kingdom of Adventure: Everest

I

The High Road

Introduction

All the roads of our neighborhood were cheerful and friendly, having each of them pleasant
qualities of their own; but this one seemed different from the others in its masterful suggestion of a serious purpose, speeding you along
with a strange uplifting of the heart.

Kenneth Grahame: The Golden Age

James Ramsey Ullman:

In the early afternoon of June 8, 1924, two men crept slowly and painfully upward along a desolate skyline ridge. Below and on three sides of them were the blue depths of space. Ahead, a scant eight hundred feet above and perhaps a quarter of a mile away, the ridge ended in a steep, bleak pyramid of rock and snow. This pyramid was the summit of Everest, the highest mountain on earth.

What those two men thought and felt—what obstacles they encountered and how they sought to overcome them—no one knows. This much, however, we *do* know: that they were there. Two thousand feet below them on the mountainside one of their companions stood staring upward, watching. For five minutes—ten—he followed their progress: two tiny but clear-etched motes against the empty sky. Then presently the sky was no longer empty, but filled with moving mist, and he could see them only faintly through the gray pall. And soon the mist was so thick that they were blotted entirely from sight.

That was the last ever seen of George Leigh-Mallory, greatest of Everest climbers, and his young companion, Andrew Irvine. What happened to them is pure conjecture. And whether or not they reached the top before disaster overtook them—that is conjecture too. One thing only is certain: no man has yet climbed to the summit of the world and returned to tell the tale.

In its drama and mystery, in its almost classic pattern of struggle and tragedy, the expedition of 1924, on which Mallory

3

and Irvine vanished, remains today the most compelling, as it is the most famous, chapter in the story of Everest. But it is by no means the whole story. Nor is the Everest story the whole story of Himalayan climbing; nor Himalayan climbing more than a short, if spectacular, chapter of mountaineering history. This book is about Everest; about Mallory and Irvine; about —and by—the other "Everesters" who climbed with them and before them and after them. But it would do these men a great injustice, and give a false picture of the whole craft and spirit of mountaineering, to present them as in any sense stunt-men or irresponsible adventurers, engaged in an activity wholly apart and different from the activities of other men.

In difficult rock-climbing there is a standard technique, known by the French name of *courte-échelle*, whereby a climber reaches an otherwise inaccessible hold or stance by clambering up on the back, shoulder, or head of a companion. And the history of mountaineering is not unlike a long series of *courtes-échelles* up an immense and precipitous peak. The men who finally scale Everest will owe their triumph partly to their own determination and skill and fortitude, but partly, also, to the efforts, achievements, and failures of the men whose stories are told in the pages that follow. And these men, in turn, could not have done what they did if it had not been for *their* predecessors: the early explorers of the Himalaya; the climbers of the Alps, the Rockies, the Andes, the Caucasus; the men who year by year, range by range, peak by peak, inched their way up the earth's great mountain-masses and, in doing so, gradually developed the technique and spirit of modern mountaineering.

The long steep trail to the summit of the world does not begin at the Rongbuk Glacier, nor on the plateau of Tibet, nor even in the distant Indian foothills of Darjeeling. It begins at that point in history when men began at last to lose their primitive superstitious dread of the untrodden and unknown;

when, staring up at their mountains, they first said to one another: "They, too, are part of the earth—and the earth is ours."

Still it was not until comparatively recent times that the
exploration and ascent of the world's great ranges really began.
True, there was Moses on Sinai, Empedocles on Etna, and a
handful of other half-authentic, half-fabulous exploits in the
long ago. But, by and large, the man of ancient, medieval, and
even Renaissance times confined his interest in mountains to
the blazing of trails through their valleys for routes of trade
and war, and was content to leave the high desolation of the
peaks to the gods and demons who he believed inhabited them.

As in so many other fields of human activity, the first great
opening of horizons came during the years of the French
Revolution. Mont Blanc, the highest mountain of western
Europe, was first scaled in 1786 (and many times in the years
following), and the first half of the nineteenth century saw
the conquest of the Jungfrau, the Finsteraarhorn, the Ortler,
and several others of the more famous Alpine summits. But
activity remained unorganized and sporadic until the 1850's,
when, with the vast improvement in travel facilities and the
opening of Switzerland as a great continental resort, the Alps
were suddenly invaded in a campaign of almost military scale
and thoroughness. At the beginning of the decade a mere handful of the range's hundreds of peaks had been climbed. A scant
fifteen years later scarcely one was left *un*climbed, the so-called
"siege of the Alps" culminating in 1865 in Edward Whymper's
famous and tragic ascent of the reputedly invincible Matterhorn.

This wholesale invasion of the mountains added up to a great
deal more than the venturesome conquest of individual peaks.
Out of it came new knowledge and new skills, the development of climbing techniques, the formation of alpine clubs and
societies, and—most important of all—a new interest in the high

5

and far places of the world. No longer was a mountain merely an obstacle to be circumvented for trade or war. It was a thing worthy of knowing for its own sake: a laboratory, a lure, and a challenge.

As the explorers and navigators of earlier times moved gropingly out across continents and oceans, so have the mountaineers, during the past three-quarters of a century, pushed slowly outward and upward toward the last and highest frontiers of the physical earth. From the Alps to the Caucasus—to the Rockies—to the snowpeaks of Alaska and the firepeaks of the Andes—to the jungle-mountains of Africa and the glacier-mountains of Greenland and Antarctica. Mount Elburz, the highest peak in Europe, was first climbed in 1868, Africa's Kilimanjaro in 1889, South America's Aconcagua in 1897, our own McKinley in 1913, and before and after them a host of lesser, but often more formidable, peaks in almost every mountain area of the globe. Indeed, by the beginning of the First World War scarcely a major summit remained unclimbed anywhere, save only among the vast and all but unexplored ranges of Central Asia. Greatest among these—greatest of all mountains—are the Himalaya. And it was on these, in the years between the wars, that the world's ablest climbers concentrated their ambition and their skill.

Not, to be sure, that the Himalaya were wholly terra incognita before 1914. Rising in a vast two-thousand-mile arc along the northern frontiers of India, their principal subranges, peaks, and passes have been known to Western geographers almost since the earliest days of the British Raj. Throughout the nineteenth century surveyors and cartographers of the Indian Trigonometrical Survey were at work—measuring, triangulating, slowly and painstakingly filling in the blank spaces of the map. As early as 1852 Everest was recognized as the highest summit of the range—and therefore of the world—and

Summit of the world.

AFGHANISTAN

TIRICH MIR · 25,263
RAKAPOSHI · 25,550
HUNZA · 25,540
DISTAGHIL · 25,868
K-2 · 28,250
GASHERBRUM · 26,470
MUZTAGH · 23,890

KARAKORAMS

NANGA PARBAT · 26,660

Peshawar
Rawalpindi
Srinagar

INDUS RIVER
JHELUM RIVER
CHENAB RIVER
RAVI RIVER
SUTLEJ RIVER

I

Lahore
Kapurthala
Simla

N

Patiala

ALING KANGRI · 24,000
KAMET · 25,447
NANDA DEVI · 25,645
Gartok
API · 23,399
GURLA MANDHATA · 25,355

Delhi
New
Delhi

Rampur

D

JEMNA RIVER
GANGES RIVER
CHAMBAL RIVER

Lucknow
Cawnpore

Lashkar

N

0   50   100   200   300
MILES

palacios

East Rongbuk Glacier.

Glacier Camp.   *Ewing-Galloway*

shortly after was given the name by which it has since been known.*

But cataloguing mountains from afar was one thing; climbing them, or even reaching their bases, another. For not only were the Himalaya physically the loftiest and most formidable of all mountains, but they were also the most inaccessible politically. The approaches to most of the major peaks lay either in Tibet or in the independent Indian principality of Nepal, and both these isolated states of inner Asia consistently maintained—as, indeed, they still do—a policy of rigid exclusion toward the exploring and exploiting white man from the West. As a result, the early investigation of the range was a long, piecemeal process, only occasionally involving an officially sanctioned expedition and carried on for the most part in surreptitious secrecy by lone individuals in the service of the Trigonometrical Survey. Some of these adventurers were Englishmen, some Indian scouts. Almost always it was necessary for them to travel in disguise—as Nepalese herdsmen, Tibetan merchants, Buddhist pilgrims—and the hardships and hazards that they experienced were so fantastic as almost to pass belief. Many disappeared for years, and not a few forever. But always there were new adventurers to take the place of the old; and year by year, mile by mile, through their journeys and reports, the veil was gradually lifted from the theretofore unknown roof of the world.

Meanwhile, over the years, many of the lower and more accessible Himalayan peaks, abutting on the Indian plain, had been closely investigated, and a few of them even climbed. A mountain called Leo Pargyal, near Simla, was ascended to 19,000 feet as early as 1818; 23,000-foot Shilla, in the same region, in 1851; and Kabru, a 24,000-foot neighbor of Kan-

---

* For Sir George Everest, early Surveyor-General of India. The first reckonings fixed its height at 29,002 feet, but later observers amended this to 29,141—the currently accepted figure.

chenjunga, in 1883, this last establishing a record for the highest conquered peak that was to endure for almost fifty years.

Then, at last, around the turn of the century, came the first of the great expeditions into the very heart of the wilderness. England's Sir Martin Conway, the Italian Duke of the Abruzzi, and a remarkable American couple, Dr. and Mrs. William Hunter Workman, led successive exploring and climbing parties into the savage region of the Karakoram, in the northeast corner of the range; and the Abruzzi party, struggling almost to the summit of Bride Peak, established a world's altitude mark of 24,600 feet that was not broken until the second Everest Expedition of 1922. Alfred Mummery, perhaps the outstanding alpinist of his day, tried his skill—and lost his life —on the fearsome avalanche-slopes of Kashmir's Nanga Parbat. Douglas Freshfield, veteran of the Alps and Caucasus, made his famous pioneering circuit of Kanchenjunga, the glittering showpiece of the Himalaya that rises like a great white wave above the Indian hill-town of Darjeeling. Year by year the tide of the mountain-invaders swelled, advanced, ascended.

But Everest still remained aloof—unexplored and all but unknown. The greatest prize of all, it was also the most inaccessible, not only by virtue of its height and geographical remoteness, but also because its only approaches were through the jealously guarded domains of Tibet and Nepal, on whose frontiers it stands. The time for the unlocking of its mysteries, however, was now close at hand; and it is an interesting irony that the winning of the key was not achieved by exploration or mountaineering, but was wholly a political and military affair.

Through the 1890's and early 1900's friction had been growing between the British in India and their isolated and isolationist neighbors to the north. There were "incidents," claims and counterclaims, shots and raids across the border; and in the spring of 1904 matters reached a climax with the dispatching of a column of British troops into Tibet. Half military force, half diplomatic mission, this expeditionary force penetrated all the way to Lhasa, where it extracted various concessions from the Dalai Lama and his government, tending toward the at least partial opening up of the country. As an afterthought, permission was obtained for occasional British expeditions to explore and climb in the Tibetan Himalaya. Or, then again, perhaps it was not merely an afterthought, for Sir Francis Younghusband, the leader of the mission, was himself an ardent mountaineer and old Himalaya hand.

At all events, word presently reached England that the gate to Everest, if not precisely wide open, was at least invitingly ajar, and plans for an expedition were already well along, when the summer of 1914 arrived and, with it, the First World War. Everest, like the rest of men's goals and aspirations, had to wait.

The years before Sarajevo had been the period of preparation and reconnaissance in Himalayan climbing. The two decades between Versailles and Dunkirk were the time of assault and siege. As the English had been first, so they remained most numerous in the field, but their ranks were now swelled by the representatives of many other nationalities: Frenchmen, Germans, Italians, Swiss, even Russians and Poles, and in the later days Americans. With the shrinkage of global distances and the conquest of almost all the great ranges, climbers from many countries felt themselves ready for the biggest game of all, and during the twenties and thirties scarcely a year went by in which there were not one or more major expeditions active in the Himalaya.

Everest is our story in this book—and Everest was reconnoitered or actually attempted no fewer than seven times during this period. For a few moments, however, it may be useful to digress from our objective—as well as from strict chronology

—to review briefly the record of ascents and attempts at ascents in other parts of the range. The Everest story is not a thing distinct and complete in itself, but part of the larger story of modern Himalayan mountaineering. And even a king, be he man or mountain, can be seen in true perspective only against the background of his satellites and rivals.

Andean Aconcagua, slightly more than 23,000 feet in height, is the loftiest summit in the world outside of Central Asia. In the Himalaya there are uncounted hundreds of higher mountains, and even today only a handful have been climbed to the top. During the twenties a number of peaks in the 20- to 22,000-foot range were successfully ascended, but no new altitude record was set until 1930, when Jonsong Peak, a 24,340-foot snow-mountain near Kanchenjunga, was climbed by the members of a Swiss-organized international expedition. Two years later the record was broken by an English party on 25,447-foot Kamet, in Garhwal; and this, in turn, was bettered in 1936 with the ascent, by a British-American group, of nearby Nanda Devi, which, at 25,660 feet, remains today the highest mountain in the world that has been climbed to the top. In addition to these "highest yets," some fifteen to twenty other peaks of slightly lesser altitude have also been ascended, notable among them Siniolchu and Chomolhari in Sikkim, Mount Stalin in the Russian Pamirs, and Minya Konka in southeastern Tibet.

And that, by and large, is the meager record of Himalayan successes to date, if by "success" in mountaineering is meant setting out for the top of a mountain and getting there. Of the scores of still higher peaks—the giants among giants, ranging from 26,000 feet up to Everest's 29,141—not one has yet known the tread of conquerors' boots on its summit snows. Many have never been attempted, and several not even surveyed or approached, but a chosen few have been subjected to assault after assault. Pre-eminent among these—along with Everest—are Nanga Parbat, Kanchenjunga, and K2 (Godwin-Austen).

Of the three, Nanga Parbat, in the far northeastern corner of Kashmir, is the least in altitude—26,620 feet—but by no means in formidability. Indeed, it stands today, on its record, as the most murderous mountain in the world. Almost unvisited for thirty-seven years after Mummery's death, it was first actually attempted in 1932 by a German-American expedition, which not only succeeded in reaching the upper slopes but also performed the more remarkable feat (in the light of later events) of coming down from the mountain intact. Then, in 1934 and 1936, came two all-German attempts—and the two worst disasters in mountaineering history. The first expedition struggled to within a thousand feet of the summit, only to be overwhelmed by a great storm that took a toll of no fewer than eleven lives. The second was annihilated almost to a man by an avalanche that swept down upon the main camp while all the men were asleep. Mountaineers being the strange and stubborn breed they are, these disasters did not deter two subsequent expeditions from trying their luck in 1938 and 1939. Both escaped without loss of life, but neither succeeded in climbing as high as its predecessors.

Kanchenjunga, which at 28,146 feet is rated the third highest of all mountains, has been attempted three times. Two of the expeditions, in 1929 and 1931, were led by Karl Bauer of Munich and were composed of the finest German climbers of the day; the other, in 1930, was the Swiss-international party which later climbed Jonsong Peak. The Swiss did much important reconnaissance work, but suffered severe losses in an avalanche and did not get high on the mountain. The Germans, trying the peak from another side, succeeded on both occasions in reaching the summit ridge, only to fall short of their goal because of storms, exhaustion, and the depletion of their supplies. Even to reach the ridge, they had each time to cut what amounted to a three-mile vertical stairway in solid ice, and their two attempts, though failing of the objective, are universally conceded to be outstanding feats in mountaineering history. Indeed, their route was so formidable, their struggle so grim, that no one has since tried to follow in their footsteps, and since 1931 Kanchenjunga has been left to its savage and icebound solitude.

Both Nanga Parbat and Kanchenjunga have been attempted most often by German climbers. By the same token K2—28,250-foot monarch of the Karakoram and second in height only to Everest—is an "American" mountain. First challenged in 1909 by the Duke of the Abruzzi and declared by him unclimbable, it was surveyed and reconnoitered on various subsequent occasions, but never again actually attempted for almost thirty years. Then, in the summers of 1938 and 1939, expeditions from the United States, composed of different climbers but both sponsored by the American Alpine Club, launched two attacks on the peak, which, though failing of their goal, definitely proved Abruzzi to have been wrong. The first party, in a remarkable demonstration of skill and endurance, pioneered a way up the precipitous east ridge to a height of about 26,000 feet. The second, following their route, climbed even higher—to within a scant 750 feet of the top—but their achievement was marred by the loss of three lives.

Such, in brief outline, is the history to date of the major attempts on the higher Himalayan peaks. And on the highest of all the record is essentially the same. The Everest story, like the others, is a story of slow and painful effort; of hazard and hardship, courage and endurance; of hopes blasted, lives lost, the goal unattained. In short, a story of failure.

But what magnificent failure!

This is not the place to retell in detail the experiences of the various Everest expeditions and the men who participated in them. They will be told at first hand in the pages that follow. All that can profitably be done here is to present in broad outline the general nature of those experiences; to fill in a certain amount of historical and geographical background; and to indicate something of the climbers' problems, their methods, and —perhaps most mysterious of all to the nonclimber—their motives.

There have been seven expeditions to Everest, all told: in 1921, '22, '24, in '33, '35, '36, and finally in '38. Two of them, the ventures of '21 and '35, were purely reconnaissance parties, the rest actual attempts to climb. All were British—sponsored by the Mount Everest Committee, which was in turn composed of committees of the Alpine Club of London and the Royal Geographical Society.* In addition, there have been a few plane flights over and around the peak, and one abortive and suicidal climbing attempt by a lone English adventurer. And that is the sum-total to date of the Western World's contact with the highest mountain on earth.

As has been mentioned, plans for an expedition were already under way in 1914, when the First World War intervened. With the return of peace the Mount Everest Committee renewed its activity, and by 1921, with funds raised and the permission of the Tibetan government secured, was ready to launch the first attempt. Wisely, it was decided to spread the venture over two years: a reconnaissance party in '21, and an actual climbing attempt in '22 if the report of the advance guard held out any hope of success.

It did.

Historically, and in terms of accomplishing what it set out to do, this first of the many Everest expeditions was perhaps the most brilliant and successful of all. Composed of nine Englishmen and a large corps of Tibetan and Indian helpers, it

---

* The expeditions were financed partly by these organizations and partly by private subscription. Also, substantial sums were received for newspaper rights and from subsequent lectures and moving-picture showings. For a discussion of these financial aspects, see page 359 ff.

first pioneered the long trail across unknown terrain to the base of the mountain, and then, in three months of intensive surveying and exploration, pieced together the first detailed picture of Everest itself. The southern, or Nepalese, face, it was discovered, was utterly unclimbable—a sheer wall of rock and ice rising more than three vertical miles from the glacier below.* The northern and western sides of the peak offered little more hope. But on the northeast, and on the northeast only, there appeared to be a weakness in its armor. Here, bordering the ten-thousand-foot precipice of the north face, a steep but apparently climbable ridge descended from a great rocky shoulder near the summit to a high snow-saddle on the east of the Rongbuk Glacier. This saddle, the explorers believed, might well hold the key to the mountain. And they were right. Known to the Tibetans as the Chang La and to all subsequent climbers as the North Col, it has since served as the avenue of approach for every attempt on the heights of Everest.

Led by George Leigh-Mallory,† who was later to become the foremost of all Everesters, three members of the 1921 party reached the foot of the ice-wall below the col and inched their way up its 1500 precipitous feet to the col itself. The summit of the mountain was now a mere 6000 feet above them and some two and a half miles away, and the northeast ridge, slanting toward it, seemed to present no insuperable difficulties. The reconnoiterers were equipped to go no higher and after a day on the col descended to the glaciers. But they had fulfilled their mission with singular success, for the world now knew that Everest at least *might* be climbed.

And that *might* was all that mountaineers needed.

---

* Furthermore, this Nepalese side of the mountain was politically forbidden territory. To this day, so far as is known, no white man has ever seen Everest, close up, from its southern base.
† The correct form of the name, though he is commonly referred to as Mallory, and usually called himself by this shortened form.

The two great expeditions that followed, in 1922 and 1924, remain today among the most famous of all climbing exploits. Following the route pioneered the previous year, the 1922 party established a string of camps on the Rongbuk and the East Rongbuk glaciers, won and held a foothold on the North Col, and sent two teams of climbers to a height of about 27,000 feet. This was, to be sure, still a full 2000 feet short of the goal, but a remarkable record nevertheless and almost half a mile higher than men had ever climbed before on any mountain. The venture, however, was doomed to end not only in defeat but in disaster. Rallying their forces for still another attempt after storms and exhaustion had driven them down to the glaciers, the climbers sought to reoccupy their North Col camp, only to be overwhelmed by an avalanche that took the lives of seven native porters.

The 1924 expedition climbed even higher than its predecessor and, like it, culminated in tragedy. Sparked by Mallory—back for his third go at Everest—and Lt. Col. E. F. Norton, the climbers succeeded in establishing two camps on the mountainside above the North Col, and from the higher, at 26,800 feet, launched two mighty attempts at the summit. The first, by Norton and T. Howard Somervell, carried to the very base of the summit pyramid at more than 28,100 feet. The second, by Mallory and Andrew Irvine, ended in death—and mystery. Last observed from below on a skyline ridge a scant 800 feet from the top, their minute figures were presently obscured by mist, and they were never seen again. To this day no one knows whether or not they reached their goal or how they met their end.

Nine years were then to pass before Everest was again attempted, and then in 1933 a fourth expedition, composed of a new generation of British mountaineers, set out once more to climb and achieve—and fail. The route was the same, the struggle the same, and the two summit attempts bogged down at almost the identical point at which Norton had turned back in 1924. It seemed almost as if Everest were ringed by a magic and invisible wall a thousand feet beneath its pinnacle, beyond which no man could venture and live.

In 1933, too, came the first plane flight over Everest—a remarkable aeronautical feat for that time. The many photographs taken confirmed the belief of mountaineers that the topmost reaches of the peak present no insuperable climbing difficulties. But no hint of the fate of Mallory and Irvine was disclosed.

The year 1934 saw one short-lived attempt on the mountain —an attempt so hapless and hopeless that it appears less an actual climbing venture than an elaborate suicide. The would-be climber was Maurice Wilson, an eccentric young Englishman who had steeped himself in oriental mysticism and believed it to be his unalterable destiny to ascend to the summit of the world. Smuggling himself into Tibet, he hired a handful of natives to pack his supplies and launched a one-man assault on the mountain. Somehow he succeeded in struggling up the glaciers, but cold and exhaustion caught up with him before he had even reached the ice-cliffs beneath the North Col. His body was discovered and buried the following year.

In 1935 and 1936 the real Everesters returned to the wars. Because of delay in gaining the sanction of the Tibetan government only a reconnaissance was undertaken the first year, but in the spring of '36 a full-fledged climbing party was again at the Rongbuk base camp, ready for battle. Bad luck with the weather is the common fate of all Everest expeditions, but this one had no luck at all. Winds, blizzards, and avalanches beat down on the climbers from the first day on, and—crowning blow—the summer monsoon blew up from the Indian plains a month earlier than usual. After a few close calls on the crumbling and melting snow-slopes of the North Col, the expedition was forced to withdraw without having even set foot on the mountain itself.

In 1938 came still another party—the seventh and the last to date. Favored by moderate weather, the climbers reached the North Col in short order (ascending it for the first time by its western instead of its eastern wall), worked their way up the northeast ridge, and pitched their highest camp at 27,000 feet. But above it the inevitable pattern reasserted itself: two summit attempts; two failures; the last thousand feet of the mountain still unclimbed. Then, before a third try could be organized, the monsoon struck, putting an end to the venture.

During the years of the Second World War, of course, there were no expeditions, to Everest or elsewhere. Many airmen based in India and China had occasion to view the great peak from a distance, and one American pilot, Col. Robert L. Scott, emulated the pioneers of 1933 by flying directly over the summit. But that was all. Today, nine years after the last climbing attempt, the summit of the world still rises in lonely grandeur . . . and waits.

So stands the fight for Everest up to the present time. Seven great expeditions have come and challenged, struggled and failed.

The question remains: Why have they failed?

It is not an easy question to answer, because there is no one obvious and inclusive reason. Most nonclimbers are apt to think of mountaineering as consisting merely of two strenuous (and slightly insane) activities: putting one foot laboriously in front of the other in an endless uphill grind, or swinging dizzily at rope's end over mile-high precipices. On Everest, however, the sheerly mechanical climbing problems are so small as to be almost negligible, and the briefest glance through the pages that follow will give ample evidence that its challengers bear no resemblance, accidental or otherwise, either to plodding robots or to soaring acrobats. There are beyond doubt a great many men, in and out of the world's mountaineering clubs, who are athletically capable of reaching the summit. But athletic capability is only a small—and surprisingly small—part of the game.

In understanding the problems of Everest it is helpful to think of the various expeditions not only as pure climbing, but as almost military, ventures. The mountain is the objective—and the enemy; the mountaineers are the attacking force. Strategy, tactics, logistics: all of these are essential parts of the campaign, simplified, perhaps, by the fact that the antagonist is not a thinking one, but complicated by necessarily far different standards of safety and justifiable risk. As in war, there is first and foremost the question of manpower and organization. There are the problems of route, of weather, of health and morale, of supply and transport. Lastly, and ironically, there is the problem of politics, which, on Everest as on Anzio and Okinawa, pulls the strings that make the actors move. If all these aspects of the venture were not considered, labored over, and at least partially solved, no expedition would have the ghost of a chance, be it composed of the finest climbing-men on earth.

The expeditions to date have varied greatly in size. Those of '22, '24, and '33 were among the largest and most elaborately equipped that have ever been sent against a mountain; the later ones, notably that of '38, have been much smaller, with both personnel and equipment reduced to a compact and mobile minimum. Each kind appears to have its advantages and drawbacks, with the climbers themselves sharply divided in their opinions. In general, however, it is obvious that the party should not be either so large as to be unwieldy or so small that the injury or illness of one or two members would ruin the whole enterprise. Thus far every actual summit attempt has been made by teams of two men, but if the sleeping capacity of the highest camps can be enlarged this number might well be increased to three or four. Based on experience, it would seem that there should be six or eight potential high-climbers in an expedition. The rest of the personnel should include the party leader (making the major decisions from below, where his judgment will not be affected either by personal ambition or by extreme fatigue), a supply-and-transport officer, a geologist-meteorologist, and a physician. In short, ten to twelve men in all, plus, of course, the inevitable and indispensable porters.

As for the individual men who make up an expedition, it is obvious that they should possess stamina, courage, experience, and skill at their craft. Equally important, however, is it that they should get on well together and work well together—and this is an end not easily achieved in the rough, bitter, isolated routine of life at great altitudes. In this respect the Everest expeditions seem to have been singularly fortunate, for the climbers, throughout the seven expeditions, were a remarkably homogeneous group. There was, of course, great variation in individual personality: from Mallory's fire to Norton's calm; from Somervell's philosophic piety to Irvine's boyish impetuosity.* But they were all British. They were all, more specifically, what we have come to know as "public-school British" and very much alike in background, training, and point of view. Indeed, one is inclined to suspect that their very homogeneity was a strength turned into a weakness, and that a leavening of other nationalities, other temperaments and values, would have helped rather than harmed the chances for success.

No less important than the white climbers of Everest are the native porters who have accompanied them. Like primitive people everywhere, the vast majority of Indians and Tibetans look upon their mountains with awe and fear, and it has taken many years to develop even a small corps of men who are willing to so much as set foot on a great peak. Pre-

* For brief biographies of the most important Everest climbers, see Appendix II.

19

eminent among these few are the Sherpas, a hardy breed of hillmen from Nepal and the region around Darjeeling in northern India, who have served as the "high porters" on every Everest venture from 1921 on. Occasionally superstitious and temperamental, but far more often dogged and cheerful, they carried their loads up the mountain to heights where no man had ever stood before. All Everesters agree that without their Sherpa "Tigers" the highest camps could never have been pitched, nor the summit even attempted. Whatever the other plans for organization and personnel, it is safe to prophesy that coming expeditions, like those past, will be accompanied by these sturdy and faithful helpers. They will be of a new generation, to be sure, but so will the climbers themselves.

So much for the men. But there is still the mountain: two vertical miles of rock and ice rising out of the high desolation of the Rongbuk Valley.

The experiences of all the expeditions have borne out Mallory's original judgment that, in the strict climbing sense, Everest is not a particularly difficult peak. The by-now traditional Rongbuk-North Col-northeast ridge route presents few of the obstacles of rock and ice that climbers have encountered on Kanchenjunga, Nanga Parbat, and K2, and the unscaled top thousand feet seem also to present no major physical difficulties. Paradoxically, it is not even a very high mountain in terms of climbing. Based on the 17,000-foot Tibetan plateau, its northern face rises only some 12,000 feet in vertical height, whereas such lesser "lowland" mountains as Nanga Parbat and even our own McKinley measure 20,000 feet from base to summit. To date there has been no attempt on the peak from any direction save the northeast, and this approach will undoubtedly be the path of future expeditions. The only disagreement among old Everesters lies in the choice of routes for the actual summit attempt, some favoring Mallory's way along the crest of the east ridge and others preferring the traverse below it, as performed by Norton, Somervell, and others. The probability is that future climbers will have a try at both.

Far more serious than the problem of route is that of weather. Certain expeditions have had more luck than others, but, by and large, it is safe to say that there is no such thing as "good" weather on Everest, but merely degrees of bad.* Under winter conditions, which at high Himalayan altitudes prevail until May, the mountain is wholly unapproachable because of wind, cold, and storm; and in summer the warm, wet monsoon, blowing up from the south, turns it into a death-trap of crumbling ice-walls and thundering avalanches. Only two brief seasons remain in which Everest is even theoretically climbable—the late spring and early fall—and, except for the reconnaissance of 1921, the latter has not been tried. Moreover, even during these "possible" periods, the heights are guarded by cold and wind, blizzard and avalanche, and experience has shown that there are seldom more than two or three consecutive days of practicable climbing weather. Not only to reach the top, but simply to survive, an expedition must be equipped to keep itself fed and warm when the inevitable and paralyzing Himalayan storms swoop down upon it. For the rest, in the struggle against the elements, there can be only patience, perseverance—and luck.

To keep fed—to keep warm: storm or no storm, these are the two great fundamental problems of all high mountaineering, and more than one ambitious expedition has met defeat, and even disaster, because of failure in its system of supply and transport. On Everest there is obviously no possibility of living off the land. Food, tents, utensils, clothing, climbing gear, medicines, scientific instruments—literally *everything*—must first be

---

* It is generally agreed that the only expedition to date to encounter better-than-average conditions was that of 1924; and in that year the strongest climbers had already worn themselves out before they reached the high camps.

transported for hundreds of miles across wild, inhospitable terrain and subsequently carried up the mountain itself to the high and inaccessible camps. All the climbers are agreed on the importance of placing the topmost camp as close to the summit as is humanly possible. It is doubtful if any man could survive a night in the open on the upper slopes of Everest, and time and again the summit challengers have had to turn back, not only because of exhaustion or unfavorable weather, but also so that they might be sure of reaching shelter before darkness set in. To date, the highest altitude at which a camp has been placed is 27,400 feet. The establishment of an even higher one depends on two factors: the finding of a suitable site, and the ability of the porters to reach it. And on both counts the Everesters are confident that it can be done.

In the past the expeditions have used only two kinds of burden-carriers: pack animals to the base camp, and porters beyond. But it is highly probable that future parties will make use of planes (as has already been done on several Alaskan mountains) to drop supplies at the base, and even at strategic points on the actual peak. Many mountaineers, to whom the scaling of Everest is an adventure rather than a practical end, look askance at such mechanization of their sport and point out that the next logical step would be to drop not only supplies but men on the mountaintop and have done with climbing altogether. To such sentiments this vicarious Everester heartily subscribes. But it is unlikely that mountaineering, any more than other human activities, will be able to buck the inevitable tide of "progress"; and the purists of the craft may have to resign themselves to the presence of an air arm in the next campaign against the summit of the world.

Manpower, organization, routes, weather, supplies, and transport—all these are part of the problem of Everest. Beyond them, however, remains one further and fundamental problem related to them all. This is, quite briefly: Can the human body

Loading at Dochen.

The Monastery at Shakar Dzong.

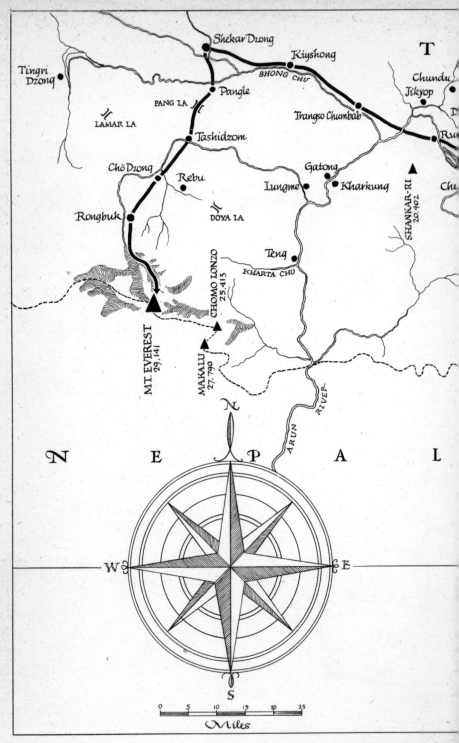

The long trail.

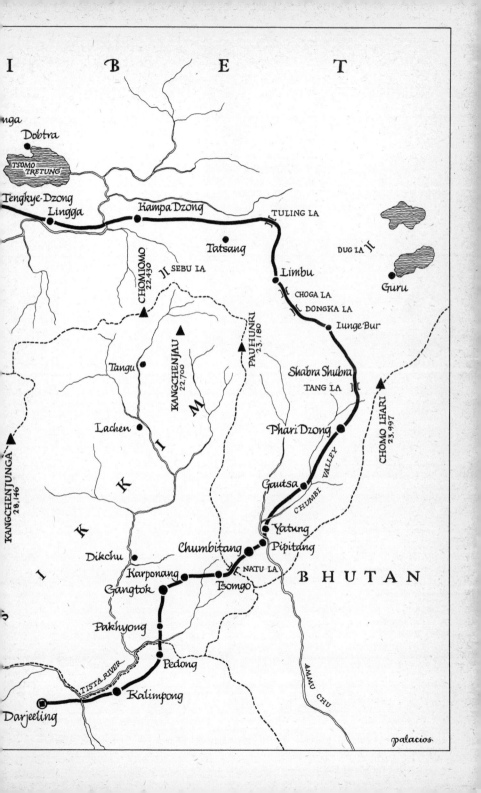

The Kama Valley.

The Rongbuk Monastery. Everest in the background.

do it? It is one of the most fascinating aspects of Nature's immense plan that the highest elevation on earth almost exactly coincides with the highest elevation at which man, without artificial aids, can live. Exactly? Or not quite? The final answer, to be sure, is for the future. On each of the highest summit attempts to date the climbers have reached the end of their tether at about 28,100 feet. In each case it was as if the mountain—and their own limbs and lungs and hearts—had said to them: "Thus far and no farther." Yet no fewer than seven men have reached that high, and it is hard not to believe that eventually there will be other men who can put themselves up that extra thousand feet—that scant three-and-a-fraction percent—to the top.

Many physiological factors enter into the problem, and, as we shall see in the pages that follow, many psychical ones as well. On the one hand, men must undergo a gradual period of acclimatization before their organs can function properly at great heights; but on the other, it has been found that if a man spends too long a period at high altitudes, severe bodily deterioration sets in. Individuals vary greatly in their speed and degree of acclimatization, and neither age, strength, nor general physical condition has proved a particularly reliable criterion of performance. Even more unpredictable are the mental reactions of men transplanted from their natural lowland habitat to the bitter and rarefied heights of the substratosphere. Perception becomes dulled, judgments faulty, the will atrophied. And extinction itself sometimes seems preferable to the next gasping, stumbling step.

In 1922 and 1924 and again in 1938 some of the high climbers used oxygen. Opinions differed as to its efficacy, but the consensus was that a thoroughly satisfactory carrying apparatus —sufficiently light and yet dependable—had yet to be devised. The war, of course, has brought about enormous improvements in such devices, and it is probable that the next expedition will make at least one of its attempts with artificial breathing aids. Like the supply-carrying plane, oxygen is a highly controversial subject among mountaineers. The conquest of Everest with its help would admittedly be a triumph for science. But conquest without it would be a still greater triumph—for man.

That the world's highest mountain will some day be climbed is inevitable—as inevitable as the crossing of the oceans, the spanning of the continents, the discovery of the poles. Perhaps the victory will be won on the next attempt; perhaps not for generations. But still men will try, and more men, and at last the day will come when the weather is right and the mountain is right and the men are right, and those men will get to the top.

But the road will still be long and arduous. Even with the physical aids of an ever-advancing science, climbers will find Everest an immense and implacable antagonist, and in one fundamental aspect—that of gaining political permission even to approach the mountain—the obstacles promise to be more formidable than ever. For one thing, there is the gradual British withdrawal from India; for another, the traditional Tibetan suspicion of the outside world, which—understandably—has not decreased in the past decade. India itself, China on the east, Russia to the north and west—all three, and other nations as well, have their eyes fixed on the high Asiatic heartland and will look distrustfully upon any alien attempts at penetration. It is a hard and discouraging thing to realize that such a wholly nonpolitical human activity as mountaineering has been caught up in the web of power politics and quarreling governments. But such is the sorry pattern of our mid-twentieth-century world, and even its remote and ice-sheathed summit is not exempt.

Already, in the brief period since the end of the war, climbing organizations in various Western countries have been actively trying to secure diplomatic permission for another Everest attempt. Thus far the permission has not been forthcoming; but mountaineers are a stubborn and persistent lot and they will doubtless find techniques for handling foreign offices and ambassadors no less than for cliffs and glaciers. One thing that remains to be seen is whether future expeditions—when and if—will be exclusively British, and on this score an impartial observer is apt to find his sentiments divided. On the one hand, the record to date, filled with struggle and hardship, great achievement and bitter tragedy, makes it fitting and dramatically just that an English party should eventually be the conquerors. But on the other, the goal seems almost too great, Everest too worldwide a symbol, for it properly to remain the private preserve of any one nationality.

In addition to political uncertainties another great and ambiguous shadow lies across the future of Everest. To wit: *Is* it earth's highest mountain? . . . For many years now there have been recurrent reports of a great range in the remote and all but unknown border-country of Tibet and western China, and of a peak, called Amne Machen, rising from it, which may be higher than the highest of the Himalayas. Until recently these reports were generally regarded as legends. During the war, however, there were several accounts by airmen, flying the India-China "Hump," of being blown off their course at 29,000 feet and more and looking *up* at a vast and uncharted mountaintop. The conditions of observation were not such that their reports can be accepted as established fact, or even as strong probability; but they have at least opened wide the door of speculation.

An exploring and surveying expedition to Amne Machen will undoubtedly be organized during the next few years. The prospect is a fascinating one, and if the mystery-mountain is indeed higher than Everest, its discovery will rank as the most important geographical event of modern times. Yet there are many —and in particular many mountaineers—who cherish the hope that Amne Machen, when measured, will be found wanting.

Call it sentimentality. Call it standpattism or old-fogeyism or what you will. The fact remains that Everest has for almost a hundred years stood up before the world as "the highest," that it has gathered about it a tremendous wealth of human associations—of courage and struggle, vision and aspiration—that make it far more than a mere mass of rock and snow; and it would be a bitter and unhappy irony if in the end it were relegated to second-best.

Whatever the final verdict, Amne Machen and its claims remain in the realm of the future. Both in proved fact and as a symbol Everest still stands today as the highest mountain on earth. That is what its gallant and great-hearted challengers believed. And that is what this chronicler chooses to believe, until the bleak and implacable patterns of trigonometry prove otherwise.

Everest climbed . . . Everest unclimbed . . .

What is the difference? asks the skeptic. What is the gain or loss? For what reason do men deliberately turn their backs on the hard-won security of their usual lives to face storm and cold, hardship, danger, and often death itself on lonely and savage heights?

WHY?

That, of course, is the inevitable question—the eternal blank-faced uncomprehending question that every climber must for-ever try to answer to every nonclimber. Why do you do it? Why do you *want* to do it? Why walk when you can ride, and climb when you can walk? Why go up Nob Hill, Old Baldy, Storm King, Washington, Rainier, the Matterhorn, Mc-Kinley, Aconcagua, Nanda Devi, Everest? Old Baldy and Everest are scarcely the same thing, to be sure, and yet in a strange and very fundamental way they *are* the same thing, and if you understand one you understand the other. George Mallory, who was not only a great mountaineer but also a deeply serious and thoughtful man, had his own answer, and it is given in the last excerpt in this book. To me it remains, after a quarter of a century, the best, as it is the briefest, of all answers.

The one basic fact that must be understood about the Everest ventures—or any mountaineering ventures worth the doing—is that their motives and ends are not "practical." In the first place, it is obviously not money that lures the climbers, for no fortune was ever made on the mountaintops. Nor is it fame, for even the greatest of peaks are still a closed world, God be praised, to the high-powered press agent. It is not power, nor prestige, nor—except on Hollywood mountains—the hand of a fair lady. And on a peak of the dimensions of Everest it is assuredly not recreation nor exercise nor "the view." Indeed, the diaries and records of most past climbers indicate that they spent a good part of the time wondering how they got themselves into such a plight and devoutly wishing they were at sea level, or below.

In recent years there has been much made of the scientific knowledge to be gained from high-mountain expeditions. To a degree, of course, this is a valid point, for specialists accompanying the various parties have brought back much useful information on such matters as the weather, geological structures, and the effects of high altitudes on the human system. But to say that the *raison d'être* of the Everest ventures was primarily to secure data of this sort is like claiming that the motive for the Normandy invasion was to test equipment and observe the reactions of men under fire. That the Everesters themselves have felt rather strongly on the subject is indicated by the unofficial slogan of one of the climbing parties: "No damned science." This was, perhaps, treating the most revered of modern sacred cows a bit too rudely; but if it does not quite reveal what the driving motives were, it at least shows very clearly what they were *not*. Scientific research has been a useful by-product of the Everest adventure and given it a cloak of respectability in the eyes of "practical" onlookers. One may be very sure, however, that any man who aspires, struggles, and suffers as did the men whose story is told in this book is driven by far deeper and more human forces than a lively interest in rock strata, wind velocities, or pulse rates.

In one form or another—in its place, one might say—science "belongs" on the mountaintops. There is another aspect of the modern world, however, that has recently intruded itself and that does not belong there at all. This is nationalism. Let it be said at once that this is a taint from which the past Everest expeditions were signally free. True, they were all British—rather clubbily British, perhaps, in the traditional Empire style —and the climbers, as well as their countrymen at home, cherished a natural hope that Englishmen would be the first on the summit of the world. But there was no jingoism about them, no blatant flag-waving or doing-and-dying for St. George. As might be expected, it was the Germans—and, aping them, the Italians—who introduced rabid nationalism into mountaineering, during the years preceding the last war. For *Führer* and *Vaterland* or *Duce* and *Patria*, as the case might be, brown- and black-shirted young climbers began vying with each other in what they considered to be feats of courage and skill. All or nothing was their watchword—victory or death; and the accounts of the famous German expeditions to Kanchenjunga and Nanga Parbat read less like the stories of sportsmen and adventurers than like the rantings of political demagogues.

Happily, avowedly Nazi and Fascist enterprises are now a thing of the past. But nationalism is all too obviously still rampant in the world, and one of the greatest future threats to the whole practice and spirit of mountaineering is that it will become simply another pawn in man's endless and feckless pattern of rivalries, jealousies, and fears.

A few pages back we expressed the opinion that the highest

mountain *can* be conquered. It could, and would, have been by now, if mountaineering were primarily a practical and pragmatic activity. Put an army in the field against it, equipped with the power and resources of a modern task force and prepared for losses on a wartime scale, and those last untouched thousand feet would yield in very short order indeed. But no army has ever attacked Everest, and probably none ever will, for the good and obvious reason that the venture would be a useless one.

And that, when all is said and done, is the very essence of mountaineering. That it *is*, by materialistic standards, useless. That its end is neither money nor power nor fame nor knowledge nor even victory. That it is one of those rare and precious human activities that man performs for their own sake, and for that alone. The organization, strategy, and tactics of an Everest expedition may, as has been indicated, have many resemblances to a military campaign; but in its end, its purpose, its motive it is utterly different. "Have we vanquished an enemy?" George Mallory once asked himself, standing with his companions upon a high, hard-won summit and looking down at the long way they had come. And there was only one answer: "None but ourselves."

As recounted in the pages to come, the story of Everest will appear principally in the guise of physical adventure. It will be told in terms of where and when and how, of practical men and their practical problems, of rock and snow, ropes and axes, cold and storms and avalanches. And, indeed, it is of these things that the ventures largely consisted. But they consisted of something else besides, and without that "something else" the exploits would not have been worth the doing nor their story worth the telling. Mallory and Irvine disappearing forever into the mists; Norton and Smythe turning back within a thousand feet of victory; Odell's lonely vigil at the high camps, and Somervell's rescue of his porters in an avalanche; man after man, group after group, expedition after expedition trying, struggling, failing, and returning to try and struggle again: all these are not merely scenes from an exciting melodrama of hazard and derring-do but part of a profound experience of the human spirit and the human heart.

The men in this book climbed because they needed to climb; because that was the way they were made. Lifting their eyes to their mountain, they saw more than rock and ice and snow and the immense blue emptiness of the sky. They saw, too, a great challenge to their own qualities *as men;* a chance to conquer their own weakness, ignorance, and fear; a struggle to match achievement to aspiration and reality to dream. Over and above everything else, the fight for Everest has been an act of faith and affirmation. That the high road is the good road. That man is never so much a man as when he is striving for what is beyond his grasp. That the game is worth the candle and the victory worth the fight.

That men will some day reach the summit of the world means little. That they should want to reach it and try to reach it means everything. Meanwhile, there is something better than victory—something that should make us almost thankful that the goal has not been reached. For, until the day when it is climbed, Everest is more than the highest mountain. It is one of the great unfinished adventures of mankind.

2

The Unknown

Discovery and Approach

Something hidden. Go and find it. Go and look behind the Ranges—
Something lost behind the Ranges. Lost and waiting for you. Go!

Rudyard Kipling: The Explorer

JAMES RAMSEY ULLMAN:

Geologically the history of Everest begins many millions of years ago when, together with the rest of the Himalayan Range, it began slowly and monstrously to rise from the floor of the prehistoric sea. But in human terms its story is less than a century old.

True, it has been known to men far longer than that: for uncounted thousands of years it has stood as a landmark and a symbol to the nomadic tribes of south-central Asia. But it had no history. An inorganic mass of rock and ice, the imagined dwelling place of gods and demons, it lay beyond the horizon of human knowledge and experience until the advent, in modern times, of the restless and questing white man from the West.

No sooner had the British taken hold in India during the early 1800's than they began a far-flung and systematic survey of their new domain. And as the years passed, their investigations pressed even beyond the frontiers of India proper into the great unknown wilderness of the Himalaya that loomed above it to the north. It was not mountains or mountaineering, to be sure, in which the early explorers were primarily interested. Rather was it the old familiar lure of trade, conquest, and colonial expansion that urged them on. But with expansion, inevitably, came knowledge, and, with knowledge, the thirst for more knowledge. Where Empire led, Science followed; and along with them both went something more fundamentally human and important than either: the spirit of discovery and adventure.

Indeed, the early exploration of the high Himalayas held no less of romance and high enterprise than did the later famous expeditions to Everest itself. Nor is it any less an integral part

33

of the Everest story; for the road to the mountain had to be found before the mountain could be attempted, or even known. In the first chapter of that story, therefore, Captain John Noel, photographer, explorer, and member of two Everest expeditions, tells of the first searching, groping steps which men made in the long and still unfinished struggle toward the summit of the world.

CAPT. JOHN NOEL:

The first scene in the series of dramas which together constitute the story of Everest, has for its setting prosaic Indian Government offices where one day in 1852 the Bengali Chief Computer rushed into the room of the Surveyor General, Sir Andrew Waugh, breathlessly saying, "Sir, I have discovered the highest mountain in the world!"

The office of the Trigonometrical Survey had been long engaged on a series of observations of the peaks of Nepal from the plains of India. Native names had been officially adopted where native names were known, but many of these mountains, so numerous, massed together and towering one above the other, were nameless even to natives. Numbers therefore had to be given to distinguish them. Among these unnamed peaks was one "Peak XV." Observations of it were recorded in 1849, but were not worked out for some three years afterwards.

Then, leisurely working over the accumulated data, the Computer made his dramatic discovery and immediately hastened to his chief with the news.

Excited as he was, he could have had no conception of the adventures to which his mathematical calculations were destined to lure men. The sequel was to be a struggle with gods and demons—existing only in the minds of the dwellers in the remote country of the mountain, but none the less real opponents. It was to be a contest with Nature in her cruellest moods, waged where the earth, surging upwards, thrusts herself—stark, bleak, and lonely—through her enveloping atmosphere into the Great Void.

Immediately the officials got busy. Carefully the observations from all six stations, whence this Peak XV had been observed, were checked, and the mean height of 29,002 feet was arrived at. The measurement was in later years carefully rechecked and raised to 29,145 feet.* Sir Andrew Waugh named the mountain after Sir George Everest, his predecessor, the Surveyor General of India, under whose directions the triangulations had been started, but afterwards the Everest Expeditions discovered that the Tibetan name is Chomo Lungma, which means "The Goddess Mother of the World."

All sorts of people have from time to time told stories of mountains higher than Everest; but it is definitely known that there is no higher mountain,† and it became the dream and goal of explorers and mountaineers. But nobody could reach it, although it was so tantalizingly near. It was computed to be only one hundred and ten miles, as the crow flies, from Darjeeling, and to be situated on the borders of Nepal and Tibet; but the Tibetans refused, as also did the Nepalese, to give permission to approach it.

Access to the giant peak was not to come for many years. The mountain land of the Himalaya that bounds India on the north like a huge wall of rock and stretches beyond to the east and the west, might be called the backbone of Asia. There are two thousand miles of giant mountains, one hundred peaks each twenty-four thousand feet in height, higher than any mountains in other parts of the world; twenty giants, twenty-six thousand feet in height; six super-giants of twenty-seven thousand feet; and finally the culminating summit of Mount Everest,

* The currently accepted figure is 29,141.—*Editor.*
† Noel's book was written in 1925, long before the recent war-fliers' reports on Amne Machen. (See Introduction.)—*Editor.*

twenty-nine thousand one hundred and forty-five feet—five and a half miles high. This mountain range is one of the youngest in the world, and is still being pushed up, so geologists tell us, by the pressure of the oceans on the crust of the earth.

There were secrets guarded by these colossal natural ramparts. Now we know the geography, but it is not long since Central Asia from the Pamirs to Tibet and the Gobi Desert as far as the steppes of Siberia, were white spaces on the best of maps, except where dotted lines marking the routes taken by rare explorers, such as the Abbé Huc, Bogle, Turner, Manning, and some Russians from the other side, stretched tenuously.

The position of Lhasa, the mysterious home of Buddhism in the heart of Tibet, was only guessed at. Such data as its latitude and longitude were unknown. Only vague knowledge existed of the Tsampo, the great river of Tibet which becomes the Brahmaputra in India, and of the great Indus which comes down from Tibet, carving its way through a series of terrific gorges in the mountains.

All this geographical knowledge had to be sought. But how? The Himalayan passes were walled, barricaded, and guarded by hostile Tibetan soldiery. Beyond the passes the lamas in the fortress-monasteries ceaselessly spied the land for foreigners, and captured and tortured any they found. It was hopeless for any white man to attempt to go.

How the prayer wheels and rosaries of the Tibetans, instruments of piety, were cunningly turned to use against them, is one of the most fascinating romances of Asiatic exploration.

In 1860 Captain Montgomery, an active officer of the Indian Survey, hit upon the idea of training certain intelligent Indians in the use of scientific instruments. They became known as the "Pundit Explorers." They were not all Hindoos, although styled pundits. Some were Mohammedans, like Ata Mahomed "The Mullah," who explored the gorge of the Indus. Another was a Persian, the intrepid Mirza Shuja, who found his way through North Afghanistan and the Pamirs, but in later years was foully murdered in his sleep at Bokhara. Because of the secrecy of their explorations, the names of these men were not published until later years. They were known by two letters, Kalian Singh becoming "A.K."; Hari Ram, who explored towards Mount Everest, "M.H."

They were trained in the making of route traverses by compasses and the pacing of steps. They traveled in disguise and were allowed a free hand, earning only a few rupees a month. They were rewarded only when they returned—if they returned!

What perseverance in the face of danger and what skill they showed in their scientific observations! "A.K." from his traverse fixed the longitude of Yarkand as 77° 15′ 55″ and years later, this was checked by wireless telegraphy and found to be actually 77° 15′ 46″.

They would leave their journeys and disappear sometimes for years, reappearing unexpectedly with the geographical knowledge so laboriously collected. They counted their every step by the revolution of their prayer wheels, or by the beads on their rosaries. At night they would write their notes on a roll of paper hidden inside the prayer wheel. They recorded compass bearings of mountains and rivers passed, by means of little compasses cleverly disguised as amulets worn round their necks. They carried boiling-point thermometers inside hollow walking sticks for the measurement of altitudes. Some pretended to be pilgrims and others traders, carrying medicines in order to ingratiate themselves with the lamas and officers they met in Tibet.

The physical hardships and nerve-racking effects of such travels told heavily upon them, and not more than two or three journeys could any one explorer accomplish in his lifetime. If he survived these he was withdrawn and employed to teach and train other men to continue the work. Time after time they suffered robbery by bandits, or desertion by companions and caravans to which they had attached themselves; as in the case of "A.K." who, after he had been away for four years and had been given up as lost, made his way back through China —destitute except for the knowledge gained of another two thousand miles of the Forbidden Land.

One of the most romantic of all these adventures was that of the pundit, Kintup. He was sent to trace the course of the great Tibetan river, the Tsampo, and find out if it was the same stream as the Brahmaputra which pours into India from the Himalayas through the impenetrable forests of the Abor savages.

For two whole years, every day and night, Captain Harman of the Indian Survey, who sent Kintup on his hazardous mission, had the river watched in India for the special blocks of wood that Kintup was to cut and throw into the river in Tibet. But never a block was seen. Then Captain Harman fell seriously ill, left India, and the watch was abandoned. So also was hope that Kintup would ever return.

Kintup meanwhile had fallen a prisoner in Tibet, and been sold as a slave. Four years later, however, he gained his freedom and then—such was the amazing devotion to duty of the man —instead of making his way home, he set out to accomplish the work for which he had been sent. He followed the course of the Tibetan river into the unknown, within sixty miles of the plains. There he came to forest lands, where he cut logs and threw them into the river. But more than four years of dwindling hope had gone by and there was no longer any one watching for them.

Brave Kintup got back to India at length, and went to report to the survey officers and to ask who had found his logs. The story he gave of his wanderings was so romantic that many disbelieved him, but the Survey Department trusted his account officially; and, indeed, later his discoveries were proved true. Kintup received just reward for his devotion. The Geographical

Society honored him, while the Indian Government gave him the Order of the Commander of the Indian Empire and a gift of a prosperous village where he could spend the remainder of his days.

The Explorer Hari Ram, "M.H.," was sent in the direction of Everest. He made his way from India secretly, disguised as a pilgrim, by the Kosi, one of the great rivers of Nepal. He crossed a twenty-thousand foot pass, west of Everest, and reached Dingri, north of the mountain, in Tibet. He gained valuable knowledge of the surroundings of Everest, particularly to the north, but he found himself so blocked in by enormous peaks that he could not reach or identify his real objective. Vague rumors, however, he heard of the "Lamasery of the Snows."

This journey of "M.H." and that of Sarat Chandra Das in 1879 were the nearest foreign approaches made to Mount Everest. Sarat Chandra Das made a journey to satisfy a religious ambition, traveling from India to Lhasa. He was not a trained geographer and his account of the country along the eastern approaches to Mount Everest was vague, but interesting as showing the hardships of travel over high mountain lands. . . .

The plateau north of Everest was known as the Dingri Maidan. Besides the work of "M.H.," the Dingri Maidan had been crossed by the Capuchin Friars, who established a mission at Lhasa in the eighteenth century and who reached Tibet via Khatmandu in Nepal, where they had their headquarters. It is significant to observe the influence which these Roman Catholic monks had upon the Tibetan lamas as regards ritual and ceremony. The lamas copied from the friars many things now seen in their vestments, etc. But these Franciscans were permitted to remain for only a short while and then they were banished from Tibet.

The route they followed was far to the north of Everest and their writings contain no mention of the mountain. For Everest is shy and retiring. She hides behind a wall of other mountains, which are nearer and appear to be higher.

At the conclusion of Sir Francis Younghusband's military mission to Lhasa in 1904,* Captain Rawling and Major Ryder passed by Shigatse and surveyed the Tsampo valley and the mountains forming the watershed between the Tsampo and Dingri rivers. But owing to the lateness of the season and the length of the journey that they had to accomplish to Rudok, they did not deviate sufficiently far to the south to reconnoiter the Dingri Plain, and the northern approaches to Mount Everest. As late therefore as the early years of the present century, the journey of Sarat Chandra Das, who passed by the east, and the journey of the Explorer "M.H." who passed by the west, comprised the sum total of our knowledge of the approaches to Mount Everest. It was known that on the east side was a deep gorge, where the Arun River breaks through from the plains of Tibet; while on the west side there appeared to be no river breaking the chain of mountains, and only high and difficult passes lay between Nepal and Tibet, with no practicable pass anywhere near the mountain. No explorer had penetrated to Everest's glacier valleys. Surrounding the great summit, which had been plotted by observation from India, was a blank white space on the map. The mountain stood, stupendous, seen through telescopes; its slopes untrodden by human beings as far as we know.

From *The Story of Everest.*

JAMES RAMSEY ULLMAN:

Out of ignorance, very slowly, came knowledge; out of darkness, light.

The "pundits" were followed by Younghusband, Rawling, and Ryder, and they in turn by other Western explorers and

---

* See Introduction.—*Editor.*

adventurers, pushing ever farther and higher into the mountain fastnesses of inner Asia. Gen. C. G. Bruce and Lt. Col. C. K. Howard-Bury, of the Indian Army, who were later to be Everest expedition-leaders, ranged far and wide over the Himalayan plateaus and passes during the early 1900's. An indefatigable Scotsman, Dr. A. M. Kellas, who lived a remarkable double life as London research chemist and explorer-mountaineer, climbed and investigated in theretofore unknown regions, began the training of a corps of native Sherpa guides and porters, and patiently plotted out the first tentative routes from northern India to Everest. And Capt. Noel himself, in 1913, traveled in disguise through Tibet to within forty miles of the mountain's base—the closest that any white man had approached up to that time.

Meanwhile, in faraway London, all this long-range activity was bearing fruit in the formulation of plans for a full-scale and officially sanctioned expedition. War intervened; but no sooner was it over than the project was revived, and after protracted negotiations Sir Charles Bell, the British envoy to Lhasa, secured the permission of the Tibetan government for two exploratory and climbing parties to approach Everest in 1921 and 1922. The political obstacles surmounted, the Royal Geographical Society and the Alpine Club combined forces in the Mount Everest Committee and, with Sir Francis Younghusband as chairman and prime mover, began the complex work of planning and organization.

The 1921 reconnaissance expedition which they assembled was composed of the flower of British mountaineers and explorers. The leader was Lt. Col. Howard-Bury, who, though not primarily a climber, knew Tibet as well as any white man living; and next in command were Dr. Kellas and A. F. R. Wollaston, another celebrated veteran mountaineer. Others were Harold Raeburn, an experienced Himalayan climber; Dr. A. M. Heron, a geologist; and Major Morshead and Captain

Wheeler, Army surveyors who had known and traveled among the great Asiatic peaks for years. And to these mature and experienced hands were added two younger men with brilliant, if briefer, records: G. H. Bullock, of the Consular Service, and George Leigh-Mallory, master at Charterhouse School, Cambridge.

Assembling at the northeastern Indian hill-town of Darjeeling in early May, the expedition busied itself with its final preparations, and presently the great caravan of explorers, porters, pack animals, and supplies was ready for the start. In a direct line the distance from Darjeeling to Everest is only a hundred miles, but they were to journey more than three hundred, threading their way slowly into the unknown through the great passes and gorges of the eastern Himalaya.

Lt. Col. C. K. Howard-Bury:

On May 18 and 19 the expedition left Darjeeling in two parties, with fifty mules and twenty coolies in each party. Major Morshead had left on May 13, travelling up the Teesta Valley, with his surveyors, and was to meet us at Kampa Dzong. We were unable to take all our stores at once, and left part of them behind, intending to make use of the Government mules in bringing them on later. Throughout the journey across Sikkim the weather was very wet, with heavy rain each day; the mountain tops and ridges were all covered with clouds and prevented our obtaining any views. Owing to its heavy rainfall Sikkim is a country with a lavish growth and a marvellous vegetation; the path that leads across to the Tibetan frontier is a very trying one, as it is a series of steep climbs followed by equally steep descents into steaming tropical valleys. Wonderful butterflies of every shade and hue flitted across the path, scarlet clerodendrons made brilliant patches of colour in the dark green of the luxuriant forest among huge tree ferns.

Creepers and ferns hung from every tree; white, orange, mauve, or purple orchids grew among the mosses and ferns on the branches of the trees, and showed up in lovely clumps of colour. We passed big hedges of daturas on the way, 15 to 20 feet in height and covered with hundreds of great white trumpet-shaped blooms, quite 8 inches in diameter and fully a foot in length. At night they gave out a strangely sweet scent and seemed to gleam in the darkness with a curious kind of phosphorescence.

Ever since leaving Darjeeling our mules had been giving trouble, and two or three from each party had to be left behind after each march. After travelling for four days we stopped at Rongli, hoping they might recover after a day's rest. Ten mules had already been left behind and one had died. The next march to Sedonchen was a short one of only 9 miles, but the path climbed from 2700 feet to 7000 feet and this completely finished the mules. For one party alone we had already hired twenty-two ponies to take some of the loads, and after Sedonchen we should have had to hire ponies to carry their own line-gear as well as all our loads, so that there was now nothing to be done except to send the mules back and rely on what local transport we could get. The marches ahead of us were longer and the climbing steeper than anything we had yet done. We were, however, on the main trade route to Tibet, and had passed hundreds of Tibetan mules coming down from Tibet laden with bales of wool and others returning with rice, grain, and cloth bought in exchange. We were, therefore, able to pick up sufficient mules to carry us to Yatung; if we had taken the shorter route up the Teesta valley this would have been impossible, as villages there are small and there is practically no transport passing along that route.

The path is really only a steep stone causeway up the mountain side, a regular *via dolorosa* and most unpleasant to walk upon; but probably anything else would be washed away by the torrential rain that falls here during most of the year. Leeches abounded here, sitting up at the end of every leaf and fern and waving at the passers-by. From Sedonchen to Gnatong the path climbs 5000 feet in the first 5 miles, and as we rose higher we entered into the rhododendron forests after passing through the zone of oaks and magnolias. The rhododendrons at this time of the year were a glorious sight. No photograph could do justice to the scene—it needed a painter at least. The hillside was a blaze of colour—rhododendrons, orange, red, deep crimson, pink, white, cream-coloured, formed a glorious mixture of colours. Every yard of the path was a pure delight. Now appeared grassy fields carpeted with primulas and many others of the purely Alpine plants. Gnatong was a very wet and cold spot with a rainfall of 180 inches, and on the next day we crossed the Jelep La, 14,390 feet, in pouring rain. This was the frontier between Sikkim and Tibet, and on going a few hundred feet down on the Tibetan side we emerged into fine weather with blue skies, having left the rain behind us on the Sikkim side. Everywhere were primulas and rhododendrons, the former appearing the moment the winter snow had melted from the ground. It was a steep and a stony descent of over 5000 feet into the Chumbi Valley, but the rhododendrons in the great forest of fir trees showed up splendidly, the big pink blooms of *Auckiandi*, the orange bells of *cinnabarinum*, and many a white and yellow one too, in striking contrast to the dark green of the firs. We now met birch, sycamore, and willows, all pale green, with the tender green of early spring, white spiræas and clematis, yellow berberis, white and pink roses, purple iris, and a mass of other wild flowers.

The Chumbi Valley is one of the most fertile and prosperous valleys in all Tibet; the houses are large and well built, reminding one very much of Tirolese villages. The rainfall here is but a quarter of that which falls on the other side of the Jelap La; potatoes, barley, wheat, apples and pears all grow well here. The air everywhere at this time of the year was scented by the wild roses. From Yatung to Phari was 28 miles, two days' easy march up the Chumbi Valley. We visited the Galinka and Donka monasteries on the way, both containing enormous prayer-wheels in which they said there were over one million prayers. Each time the wheel is turned a bell rings, and one million prayers have ascended to heaven. In other places we met prayer-wheels turned by water brought down in irrigation channels, and again in other parts the wind was used to do the same work, a kind of anemometer being fitted up to catch the wind. This latter was, perhaps, the most constant, as the wind blows both summer and winter in Tibet, whereas for six months in the year the water is frozen, and the water-wheel is silent and can offer up no prayers. In the Donka monastery was a famous oracle, a regular Delphic oracle who was consulted far and wide, and his oracles had a great reputation for truth. Here we were given the usual Tibetan tea, poured out into agate and silver teacups and made with salt, tea, and butter, all churned up together. On a cold day this was a warming drink, but I never took to it as a beverage, though I had to take many cups of it during the next few months and had to pretend to enjoy it.

Phari is a very dirty village, with a stone fort, and is situated at a height of 14,300 feet. It is always a cold windy spot, but it is an important trade mart, both to India and across the Tremo La to Bhutan. It lies at the foot of the sacred peak of Chomo-lhari—a very beautiful mountain, just under 24,000 feet, which stands at the entrance to the real Tibet, where the great plains and rolling downs begin with their far distant views. We left Phari on May 31 with a most marvellous collection of transport animals, comprising donkeys, bullocks, mules, ponies, and yaks. There is a short way from Phari to Kampa Dzong which takes only three days, but we were told that it was too early in the season to use that road, and that we would have to take the long way round. We afterwards found out that this was a lie, and that they had sent us the long way round in order to be able to charge us more. We had not yet got accustomed to Tibetan ways.

From Phari to Kampa Dzong by the long route took us six days. For the first two days we followed the ordinary trade route to Gyantse, over the Tang La, 15,200 feet, through Tuna to Dochen, keeping at a height of 14,800 all the way. Chomo-lhari was a magnificent sight the whole time, with its 7000 feet of precipices descending right on to the Tuna plain. Near Dochen was the large shallow lake of Bam-tso, a lake with the most lovely colours, the shades varying from deep blue through purple to a light blue-green. In other parts of it the waters were quite red from a weed that grew in it, and in the still morning light the whole of the range of glacier-covered mountains that formed the background to the picture were reflected in its calm waters and formed a charming picture. Many bar-headed geese were seen swimming about, also some Brahmany duck and a few terns. On the plains roamed herds of Kiang, the wild horse of Tibet, and many Goa, the Tibetan gazelle, were feeding there, but the latter were very wary and would not allow us to get within 500 yards of them. It was at Dochen that our cook tried to boil a tin of fish without opening it first, and when he tried to open it afterwards when it was hot, to his surprise and fright, it exploded like a bomb in his face, and he and all his assistants in the kitchen were covered with small pieces of fish.

From Dochen we crossed the Dug Pass, 16,400 feet, to Khe, which was the site of the once-important town of Khe-tam. In those days the Kala-tso must have extended right up to it, but everywhere were traces of rapid desiccation. Ruins extended for more than a mile in every direction, and some of the buildings must have been of considerable size, but now there is no water in the valley, and all we could get that night came from a very dirty and muddy pond that was nearly dried up. From here we marched to Kheru, and camped at 15,700 feet with some nomads who were very friendly. The days were very warm, but at nights there were still sharp frosts. From Kheru there was a longer march of 16 miles to Tat-sang, crossing two small passes of 16,450 and 17,100 feet. Tat-sang lies at a height of 16,000 feet on the edge of a broad plain, where there were some excellent springs full of fish, and below a small nunnery, which stands on a commanding rock. That night, again, there was a sharp frost. The next day's march to Kampa Dzong led for 12 miles along a barren and dry valley to a pass 17,300 feet, and then gradually descended through a curious limestone gorge to Kampa Dzong, whose walls suddenly appeared towering above us on the cliffs. We passed many iris, light and dark blue, growing in the valley, and a curious pink trumpet-shaped flower that came straight out of the sand. Game was plentiful along the route, and I shot a gazelle and an *Ovis Ammon* (*Hodgsoni*) on the way. Here we met Morshead and his surveyors, who had come up the Teesta Valley and over the Serpo La.

Several of us, ever since leaving Phari, had not been feeling well, and had had stomach troubles owing to the change of climate and bad cooking on the part of our cooks. It took most of us some time to get acclimatized to the changed conditions. Dr. Kellas, however, instead of getting better, gradually grew worse and weaker every day, until on the last march before reaching Kampa Dzong, while being carried in a litter over a 17,000-feet pass, his heart failed him, and he passed quietly away. The following day we buried him at Kampa Dzong, within sight of the three great mountains he had climbed in Sikkim—Pawhunri, Kinchenjhow, and Chomiomo, and in view of Mount Everest, which he had so longed to approach. Mr. Raeburn, too, had been gradually getting worse, and there was no other alternative but to send him down with Mr. Wollaston to Lachen and put him under the care of the missionaries there until he could recover. This was a very serious blow to the expedition, the loss of two members of the climbing party.

After Kampa Dzong our route lay across broad plains and along the flat and swampy valley of the Yaru with the snowy chain of the Himalayas to the south of us; from these heights, for we were about 15,000 feet, they did not appear nearly as imposing as they do from the south, and for the most part the northern slopes were not as steep as those on the south. Game was plentiful all the way to Tinki Dzong, and we passed many ponds covered with teal, duck, and bar-headed geese. In these flat valleys, the midges were very troublesome all day, surrounding us in clouds. Tinki Dzong was a picturesque old fort, situated on the banks of a large pond that swarmed with bar-headed geese, Brahmany duck, and teal. They were wonderfully tame and came waddling round our tents, knowing no fear of man, for they had never been shot or killed here. For some years a Lama, who had been sent from Lhasa, had lived here and made it his special object to tame all the wild animals around. The Jongpen rode out to meet us and escorted us to tents which had been pitched for us, where he had ceremonial tea, sweetmeats, and chang—Tibetan beer—all ready for us. The Jongpen was very Mongolian in appearance, was dressed in fine embroidered Chinese silks, and proved a most obliging and courteous host, presenting us with a couple of hundred eggs and four sheep. There were several large monasteries and prosperous-looking villages tucked away all around in the recesses of the hills. The barley was just beginning to come up, for in Tibet it can be grown and ripened at heights of over 15,000 feet, and during the summer months I saw some of the finest crops that I have seen anywhere. It is nearly all irrigated, as they do not seem to put much faith in the rain.

On June 11 we left Tinki, and had the usual trouble in starting. Some forty-five families were supplying us with transport, and as each wanted the lightest loads for their animals, there was a babel of noise and nothing was done. The headman eventually settled the squabbling by taking a garter from each family, and after mixing them up, laid one on each load, and whoever was the owner of the garter had to take the load. Crossing the Tinki Pass, we descended again into the Yaru Valley at Chusher Nango, passing on the way a curious dwarf gorse which carpeted the valley with yellow. Our yaks here proved very wild, and the plain was soon strewn with loads flung off by them as they careened away, tail in air, in every direction. We forded the Yaru here by a ford 3 feet deep and some 80 yards wide, and soon afterwards came to the fine country house of Gyanga Nangpa, which was the home of the Phari Jongpen. He rode out to meet us, and provided us with a very solid meal of soup and Tibetan dumplings with a chillie sauce. As we were given fifteen dumplings apiece we found some difficulty in making room for these. Europeans had never been seen before in any of these parts since leaving Kampa Dzong, so everywhere we were objects of the greatest interest to all the inhabitants who flocked out to see us.

Our next march proved a more exciting one, as after fording the Yaru again we had to cross a wide sandy plain full of shifting quicksands. When we arrived there a violent sandstorm was blowing, which our guides said would make the crossing easier. So off we started, dressed as though for a gas attack, with goggles over the eyes and with mouth and nose covered with handkerchiefs and mufflers. The sand was blowing in great clouds from off the sand-dunes, through which we wound our way, and under one we found some of our coolies halted and quite lost. After leaving the sand-dunes we had some wide stretches of wet sand to cross, over which the dry sand was blowing in smoke-like wisps, so that the whole ground appeared to be moving. In places where the wet sand shook and quivered we hurried on as fast as possible, and eventually we got everything over in safety. It was too late now to go on, so we camped in a howling gale among the sand-dunes, and it was many days afterwards before we got rid of the sand which had penetrated everywhere.

Close to this camp the Bong Chu and Yaru rivers meet and flow south, cutting their way through the great Himalayan mountain range. Much to our surprise, there suddenly appeared just before sunset, and far away down the valley over the clouds, a lofty and very beautiful peak. This we eventually decided must be Mount Everest, and the next morning we were able to prove this was so by climbing one of the hills to the west of the camp, from which we could see the whole range of the Himalaya to the south of us. Our drivers called this peak Chomo-uri, the Goddess of the Turquoise Peak, but this can only be a very local name, as Everest is known and called by the Tibetans Chomo-lungma, Goddess Mother of the country.* This is the official name in Lhasa, and this name was known throughout the country, so that this is apparently the correct Tibetan name for Mount Everest. From this point we now entered the valley of the Bhong Chu, and this we followed up to Tingri. Major Morshead and his surveyors were kept very busy all the time, mapping the country as they went along, for they were travelling now in unsurveyed country. From one peak to the north of the Bhong Chu we had a very extensive view, stretching from the snowy ranges beyond Chomolhari and 120 miles to the east of us to Kanchenjunga, and then on to Makalu and Everest, and from there passing on to the high snow peaks west of Everest and to Gosainthan, a range of some 250 miles of snow peaks; but above them all towered Mount Everest, several thousand feet above its neighbours.

Three days' march brought us to Shekar Dzong, where was

* It is interesting to note the varying translations which the Everesters supply: Goddess Mother of the *World*, of the *Country*, of the *Snows*. —*Editor*.

the headquarters of the district with two Jongpens. There was also a large monastery here containing 400 monks. Shekar was a most remarkable place, on a rocky hill like a gigantic St. Michael's Mount. The town is at the base of the hill, but the monastery, consisting of innumerable buildings with narrow streets, was literally perched on stone terraces built out from the rocky sides of the hill and connected by walls and towers with the fort, which was built still higher up, and this again was connected by turreted walls with a Gothic-like structure at the summit, where incense was freely burnt every morning. Immense crowds came to see us and were most embarrassing in their attentions. While we were here we visited the monastery, which was a very rich one. In the largest temple, which, like all Buddhist structures, was very dark, were several life-sized gilded statues of Buddha, covered with precious stones and turquoises, and behind these was a colossal statue of Buddha fully 50 feet high. Round the temple were eight curious figures, about 10 feet in height, and dressed in quaint flounce dresses, which were the guardians of the shrine.

From the entrance to the temple we climbed up a steep staircase, almost in complete darkness, until we came out on a platform almost opposite the gilded face of the great Buddha. Here were offerings of grain and butter and some exquisitely carved bowls and teapots of silver. The abbot of this monastery was the reincarnation of a former abbot, and was looked upon as an extremely holy man. He had spent sixty-six years of his life in this monastery, and all the monks seemed to adore him for his gentle and charming personality. His attendants with much difficulty persuaded him to be photographed, as they wanted to have some picture of him, for they said that his time on earth could now only be short. They dressed him up in some beautiful gold brocades and priceless silk hangings were put up for a background. This photograph proved afterwards most useful, and people hundreds of miles away used to beg for a print of it, as they put it in their shrines and worshipped it and burnt incense before it, and I could not give any one a more welcome present than the picture of the old abbot of Shekar-chöde.

Two days' march from here brought us to Tingri, which was a large village and trading centre, situated on a small hill in the middle of the great Tingri plain. This was to be our first base while reconnoitring the north-western approaches to Mount Everest. We could get no information about the country to the south of us, so that it was necessary to send out parties in different directions. Information on any subject was always hard to get in Tibet. Most of the people knew nothing beyond their own village, and of those that had travelled further no two would tell you the same story. It was the same with distances; they would have no real measure of distance or time. It would be a long day's journey or a short one, and for short distances it was expressed by cups of tea, which means the time it would take to drink one, two, or three cups of tea. The representative of the Depon received us at Tingri, and put at our disposal the old Chinese Rest Home, where we made ourselves quite comfortable. We had rooms in which to put away our stores, and another room we turned into a dark room to develop all the photographs that we were taking. It had taken the expedition just one month to get to Tingri from Darjeeling.

From *The Alpine Journal*, vol. 34, 1922.

JAMES RAMSEY ULLMAN:

The long journey was sometimes fascinating, sometimes tedious and grueling; but the explorers' thoughts were on the future rather than the present, their eyes fixed on the horizon to the west and south. And at last, out of that horizon, rose the great shape which they had come so far to see.

Hemmed in by other, lesser peaks, Everest did not burst into their vision in a single gesture but revealed itself gradually, piece by piece. In the three excerpts that follow, George Mallory describes his first views of the mountain as the expedition pressed on toward its goal.

GEORGE LEIGH-MALLORY:

It may seem an irony of fate that actually on the day after the distressing event of Dr. Kellas' death we experienced the strange elation of seeing Everest for the first time. It was a perfect early morning as we plodded up the barren slopes above our camp and rising behind the old rugged fort which is itself a singularly impressive and dramatic spectacle; we had mounted perhaps a thousand feet when we stayed and turned, and saw what we came to see. There was no mistaking the two great peaks in the West: that to the left must be Makalu, grey, severe and yet distinctly graceful, and the other away to the right— who could doubt its identity? It was a prodigious white fang excrescent from the jaw of the world. We saw Mount Everest not quite sharply defined on account of a slight haze in that direction; this circumstance added a touch of mystery and grandeur; we were satisfied that the highest of mountains would not disappoint us. And we learned one fact of great importance: the lower parts of the mountain were hidden by the range of nearer mountains clearly shown in the map running North from the Nila La and now called the Gyanka Range, but it was possible to distinguish all that showed near Everest beyond them by a difference in tone, and we were certain that one great rocky peak appearing a little way to the left of Everest must belong to its near vicinity.

* * *

We were now able to make out almost exactly where Everest should be; but the clouds were dark in that direction. We gazed at them intently through field glasses as though by some miracle we might pierce the veil. Presently the miracle happened. We caught the gleam of snow behind the grey mists. A whole group of mountains began to appear in gigantic fragments. Mountain shapes are often fantastic seen through a mist; these were like the wildest creation of a dream. A preposterous triangular lump rose out of the depths; its edge came leaping up at an angle of about 70° and ended nowhere. To the left a black serrated crest was hanging in the sky incredibly. Gradually, very gradually, we saw the great mountain sides and glaciers and arêtes, now one fragment and now another through the floating rifts, until far higher in the sky than imagination had dared to suggest the white summit of Everest appeared. And in this series of partial glimpses we had seen a whole; we were able to piece together the fragments, to interpret the dream. However much might remain to be understood, the centre had a clear meaning as one mountain shape, the shape of Everest.

It is hardly possible of course from a distance of 57 miles to formulate an accurate idea of a mountain's shape. But some of its most remarkable features may be distinguished for what they are. We were looking at Everest from about North-east and evidently a long arête was thrust out towards us. Some little distance below the summit the arête came down to a black shoulder, which we conjectured would be an insuperable obstacle. To the right of this we saw the sky line in profile and judged it not impossibly steep. The edge was probably a true arête because it appeared to be joined by a col to a sharp peak to the North. From the direction of this col a valley came down to the East and evidently drained into the Arun. This was one fact of supreme importance which was now established and we noticed that it agreed with what was shown on the map; the map in fact went up in our esteem and we were inclined hereafter to believe in its veracity until we established the contrary. Another fact was even more remarkable. We knew something more about the great peak near Everest which we had seen from Kampa Dzong; we knew now that it was not a separate mountain; in a sense it was part of Everest, or rather Everest was not one mountain but two; this great black mountain to the South was connected with Everest by a continuous arête and divided from it only by a snow col which must itself be at least 27,000 feet high. The black cliffs of this mountain, which faced us, were continuous with the icy East face of Everest itself.

A bank of cloud still lay across the face of the mountain when Bullock and I left the crest where we were established. It was late in the afternoon. We had looked down into the gorge and watched our little donkeys crossing the stream. Now we proceeded to follow their tracks across the plain. The wind was fiercely blowing up the sand and swept it away to leeward, transforming the dead flat surface into a wriggling sea of watered silk. The party were all sheltering in their tents when we rejoined them. Our camp was situated on a grassy bank below which by some miracle a spring wells out from the sand. We also sought shelter. But a short while after sunset the wind subsided. We all came forth and proceeded to a little eminence near at hand; and as we looked down the valley there was Everest calm in the stillness of evening and clear in the last light.

*   *   *

It was a day of brilliant sunshine, as yet warm and windless. The memory of Alpine meadows came into my mind. I remembered their manifold allurements; I could almost smell the scent of pines. Now I was filled with the desire to lie here in this "oasis" and live at ease and sniff the clean fragrance of mountain plants. But we went on, on and up the long valley winding across a broad stony bay; and all the stony hillsides under the midday sun were alike monotonously dreary. At length we followed the path up a steeper rise crowned by two chortens between which it passes. We paused here in sheer astonishment. Perhaps we had half expected to see Mount Everest at this moment. In the back of my mind were a host of questions about it clamouring for answer. But the sight of it now banished every thought. We forgot the stony wastes and regrets for other beauties. We asked no questions and made no comment, but simply looked.

It is perhaps because Everest presented itself so dramatically on this occasion that I find the Northern aspect more particularly imaged in my mind, when I recall the mountain. But in any case this aspect has a special significance. The Rongbuk Valley is well constructed to show off the peak at its head; for about 20 miles it is extraordinarily straight and in that distance rises only 4,000 feet, the glacier, which is 10 miles long, no more steeply than the rest. In consequence of this arrangement one has only to be raised very slightly above the bed of the valley to see it almost as a flat way up to the very head of the glacier from which the cliffs at Everest spring. To the place where Everest stands one looks along rather than up. The glacier is prostrate; not a part of the mountain; not even a pediment; merely a floor footing the high walls. At the end of the valley and above the glacier Everest rises not so much a peak as a prodigious mountain-mass. There is no complication for the eye. The highest of the world's great mountains, it seems, has to make but a single gesture of magnificence to be lord of all, vast in unchallenged and isolated supremacy. To the discerning eye other mountains are visible, giants between 23,000 and 26,000 feet high. Not one of their slenderer heads even reaches their chief's shoulder; beside Everest they escape notice—such is the pre-eminence of the greatest.

Considered as a structure Mount Everest is seen from the Rongbuk Valley to achieve height with amazing simplicity. The steep wall 10,000 feet high is contained between two colossal members—to the left the North-eastern arête, which leaves the summit at a gentle angle and in a distance of about half a mile descends only 1,000 feet before turning more sharply downwards from a clearly defined shoulder; and to the right the North-west arête (its true direction is about W.N.W.), which comes down steeply from the summit but makes up for the weaker nature of this support by immense length below. Such is the broad plan. In one respect it is modified. The wide angle between the two main arêtes involves perhaps too long a face; a further support is added. The Northern face is brought out a little below the North-east shoulder and then turned back to meet the crest again, so that from the point of the shoulder a broad arête leads down to the North and is connected by a snow col at about 23,000 feet with a Northern wing of mountains which forms the right bank of the Rongbuk Glacier and to some extent masks the view of the lower parts of Everest. Nothing could be stronger than this arrangement and it is nowhere fantastic. We do not see jagged crests and a multitude of pinnacles, and beautiful as such ornament may be we do not miss it. The outline is comparatively smooth because the stratification is horizontal, a circumstance which seems again to give strength, emphasising the broad foundations. And yet Everest is a rugged giant. It has not the smooth undulations of a snow mountain with white snow cap and glaciated flanks. It is rather a great rock mass, coated often with a thin layer of white powder which is blown about its sides, and bearing perennial snow only on the gentler ledges and on several wide faces less steep than the rest. One such place is the long arm of the North-west arête which with its slightly articulated buttresses is like the nave of a vast cathedral roofed with snow. I was, in fact, reminded often by this Northern view of Winchester Cathedral with its long high nave and low square tower; it is only at a considerable distance that one appreciates the great height of this building and the strength which seems capable of supporting a far taller tower. Similarly with Everest; the summit lies back so far along the immense arêtes that big as it always appears one required a distance view to realise its height; and it has no spire though it might easily bear one; I have thought sometimes that a Matterhorn might be piled on the top of Everest and the gigantic structure would support the added weight in stable equanimity.

From Mount Everest: the Reconnaissance, 1921.

JAMES RAMSEY ULLMAN:

At last, late in June, the expedition arrived at the Rongbuk Monastery, where an isolated colony of lamas and hermits dwelt, some twenty miles due north of Everest. Here they were already at an altitude of 18,000 feet—far higher than the highest summit in the Alps or Rockies—and the slightest exertion set their lungs to burning and their hearts to pounding. The world around them was a trackless wilderness of peaks, ridges, and glaciers, and wind and snow roared down from the heights with hurricane fury. And there still remained two vertical miles of mountain soaring above them into the sky.

Working slowly around Everest's northern and western flanks, Mallory and Bullock investigated, one after another, the various possible approaches and painstakingly pieced together the immense architectural plan of the peak. During these days, too, they had their first experiences of both the rigors and the rewards of life in the high, frozen world into which they had penetrated.

GEORGE LEIGH-MALLORY:

Ou August 6 the Whymper tents were taken up, and a camp was made under a moraine at about 17,500 feet, where a stream flows quietly through a flat space before plunging steeply down into the valley. In this sheltered spot we bid defiance to the usual snowstorm of the afternoon; perhaps as night came on and snow was still falling we were vaguely disquieted, but we refused to believe in anything worse than the heavens' passing spite, and before we put out our candles the weather cleared. We went out into the keen air; it was a night of early moons. Mounting a little rise of stones and faintly crunching under our feet the granular atoms of fresh fallen snow we were already aware of some unusual loveliness in the moment and the scenes. We were not kept waiting for the supreme effects; the curtain was withdrawn. Rising from the bright mists Mount Everest above us was immanent, vast, incalculable—no fleeting apparition of elusive dream-form: nothing could have been more set and permanent, steadfast like Keats's star, "in lone splendour hung aloft the night," a watcher of all the nights, diffusing, it seemed universally, an exalted radiance.

It is the property of all that is most sublime in mountain scenery to be uniquely splendid, or at least to seem so, and it is commonly the fate of the sublime in this sort very soon to be mixed with what is trivial. Not infrequently we had experience of wonderful moments; it is always exciting to spend a night under the stars. And such a situation may be arranged quite comfortably; lying with his head but just within the tent a man has but to stir in his sleep to see, at all events, half the starry sky. Then perhaps thoughts come tumbling from the heavens and slip in at the tent-door; his dozing is an ecstasy: until, at length, the alarm-watch sounds; and after? . . . Mean considerations din it all away, all that delight.

On the morning of August 7 the trivial, with us, preponderated. Something more than the usual inertia reigned in our frozen camp at 2 A.M. The cook was feeling unwell; the coolies prolonged their minutes of grace after the warning shout, dallied with the thought of meeting the cold air, procrastinated, drew the blankets more closely round them, and—snored once more. An expedition over the snow to the outlying tents by a half-clad Sahib, who expects to enjoy at least the advantage of withdrawing himself at the last moment from the friendly down-bag, is calculated to disturb the recumbency of others; and a kick-off in this manner to the day's work is at all events exhilarating. The task of extricating our frozen belongings, where they lay and ought not to have lain, was performed with alacrity if not with zeal; feet did not loiter over the slippery boulders as we mounted the moraine, and in spite of the half-hour lost, or gained, we were well up by sunrise. Even before the first glimmer of dawn the snow-mantled, slumbering monsters around us had been somehow touched to life by a faint blue light showing their form and presence—a light that changed as the day grew to a pale yellow on Everest and then to a bright blue-grey before it flamed all golden as the sun hit the summit and the shadow crept perceptibly down the slope until the whole mountain stood bare and splendid in the morning glory.

From *Mount Everest: the Reconnaissance, 1921.*

JAMES RAMSEY ULLMAN:

Mallory and Bullock's investigations presently led them to the conclusion that the one feasible route to the upper slopes of the mountain was by way of the Chang La, or North Col —a great snow-saddle abutting from the northeast ridge of the peak onto the eastern flank of the Rongbuk Glacier. The Rongbuk side, however, had too much the appearance of an avalanche-slope to be to Mallory's liking, and, having reason to believe that the other, or eastern, side would prove more promising, he set out to find a way to its base.

A way was found, but the finding required two long months of planning and toil. The Rongbuk Glacier was a narrow avenue of ice, walled in by tremendous mountain masses in

which no break appeared to exist. Actually there was a break
—a narrow defile leading into an eastern tributary glacier—
and if the explorers had found it, they would have been able to
reach the far side of the col in a day or two. But it was so tiny
and obscure a passage that they missed it. The result was a cir-
cuitous journey of more than a hundred miles, back across the
plateau and passes which they had traversed before and then
south and west again toward the base of Everest.

The long trek, however, held rich compensations, for it
brought them, in its last stages, to the Kharta and Kama valleys—a mountain wonderland such as few men have ever been
privileged to see.

LT. COL. C. K. HOWARD-BURY:

We had not been able to gather much information locally
about Mount Everest. A few of the shepherds said that they
had heard that there was a great mountain in the next valley
to the South, but they could not tell us whether the Kharta
River came from this great mountain. The easiest way to get
to this valley, they told us, was by crossing the Shao La, or
the Langma La, both of which passes were to the South of
the Kharta Valley, and, they said, led into this new valley.
They called this valley the Kama Valley, and little did we
realise at the time that in it we were going to find one of the
most beautiful valleys in the world. Mallory and Bullock had
already left Kharta on August 2 to explore this route, which
we thought would lead us to the Eastern face of Mount Everest. As Wollaston and Morshead had now arrived at Kharta,
there was nothing to prevent my following the others and
learning something about the geography of the country. Eleven
mule-loads of rations, consisting of flour, potatoes, sugar and
rations for the surveyors, had just arrived; there was therefore now no cause for me to worry about shortage of supplies.

These had been sent off from Yatung on June 15, but had only arrived at Kharta on August 2. Learning that I was about to start off, Hopaphema, the old Zemindar, hurriedly came round with a large basket full of spinach, potatoes, and turnips, which he insisted on my taking with me.

On August 5, taking with me Chheten Wangdi and a dozen coolies, I started off in the tracks of Mallory and Bullock. For the first few miles we travelled up the Kharta Valley, through rich fields of barley, by far the best that I had seen so far in Tibet. The crops were very even and everywhere quite 3 feet in height. The valley was thickly inhabited, containing villages nearly every mile, and many monasteries, some of which were surrounded by fine old gnarled juniper trees. Our local coolies made very poor progress, taking six hours to cover the first 6 miles, as they stopped at every village for a drink. After passing the last village, there was a steep climb of 1,000 feet. Here our coolies were very anxious to stop and spend the night, but I pushed on ahead, and they came on behind very slowly and reluctantly. Seeing that it was impossible to get over the Langma La, I stopped at the limit of firewood and camped at a height of 16,100 feet. Poo, who was acting as my cook, had forgotten to bring any matches with him, and I watched him with much interest lighting a fire of damp rhodo-dendron bushes with the flint and tinder that he always carried. The day had been clear and very warm; and on the way up we had had some fine views of the great snowy peaks on the Eastern side of the Arun River. The villagers had told us that this pass was impossible for ponies, and I accordingly left mine behind at Kharta, though we found out that ponies could quite well have crossed the pass. Opposite our camp was a peak of black rock with a glacier just below it. During the night there was a little rain and the morning was unfortunately cloudy. As our coolies had informed us that there were three passes to be crossed in the next march, I had them all started off by 5.30 a.m., after which I left with my coolies Ang Tenze and Nyima Tendu, who always accompanied me carrying a rifle, a shot-gun and three cameras of different sizes. Above the camp there was a steep climb of 1,000 feet on to a broad, rocky shelf in which was a pretty turquoise-blue lake. This was followed by another steep climb of 500 feet on to another great shelf, after which a further climb of 500 feet brought us to the top of the Langma La, 18,000 feet. The three steps up to this pass were evidently the three passes that the coolies had told us about, as from the top we looked down into the next valley. All the coolies who were carrying loads complained of headaches, due no doubt to the steep climb and the high elevation of the pass. To the East there was a curious view looking over the Arun towards some high snow peaks. Clouds were lying in patches everywhere on the hillsides, as the air was saturated with moisture. To the West our gaze encountered a most wonderful amphitheatre of peaks and glaciers. Three great glaciers almost met in the deep green valley that lay at our feet. One of these glaciers evidently came down from Mount Everest, the second from the beautiful cliffs of Chomolönzo, the Northern peak of Makalu, of which we unfortunately could only get occasional and partial glimpses, an ice or rock cliff peeping out of the clouds every now and then at incredible heights above us. The third glacier came from Kama Changri, a fine peak to the North of the Kama Valley which later on we climbed. The clouds kept mostly at a height of about 22,000 feet, and prevented us from seeing the tops of the mountains.

After waiting for an hour at the top of the pass in hopes of the clouds lifting, I started the descent catching on the way a very pretty Marmot rat, with huge eyes and ears for his size, and a pretty bluish grey fur. Meeting shortly afterwards some of Mallory and Bullock's coolies, I gave this animal to them to take back to Wollaston. We now descended through grassy uplands for nearly 3,000 feet, past another beautiful blue lake called Shurim Tso, and came to a curious long and narrow terrace about 1,000 feet above the bottom of the valley. Here there was a tent belonging to some yak herds; and as wood and water were plentiful I determined to stop and spend the night with them. They called the place Tangsham. It was certainly a most glorious place for a camp, for it overlooked three great valleys and glaciers. Opposite us, on the other side of the valley, were the immense cliffs of Chomolönzo, which towered up to nearly 26,000 feet, while Mount Everest and its great ridges filled up the head of the valley. I spent the whole afternoon lying among the rhododendrons at 15,000 feet, and admiring the beautiful glimpses of these mighty peaks revealed by occasional breaks among the fleecy clouds. The shepherds were able to give me much information about the district, which proved very useful to us afterwards. They come up here every year for a few months in the summer and in the winter cross over to the valley of the Bong-chu.

After a slight frost during the night, we had one of the few really perfect days that fell to our lot in the Kama Valley. As soon as I had finished breakfast I climbed up 1,000 feet behind the camp; opposite me were the wonderful white cliffs of Chomolönzo and Makalu, which dropped almost sheer for 11,000 feet into the valley below. Close at hand were precipices of black rock on which, in the dark hollows, nestled a few dirty glaciers. Mount Everest being some way further off, did not appear nearly as imposing. Our object now was to get as close to it as possible; we therefore descended into the valley, a steep drop of nearly 1,000 feet, through luxuriant vegetation. A very beautiful blue primula was just beginning to come out. This Wollaston had already discovered a fortnight before near Lapchi-Kang. We then crossed the Rabkar Chu, a stream which came out of the Rabkar Glacier, by a very rickety bridge over which the water was washing. Beyond this was a very fertile plain covered with rhododendrons, juniper, willow and mountain ash. On it were a couple of small huts which were occupied by some yak herds. From here we had to follow along the edge of the Kang-do-shung Glacier which, coming down from Chomolönzo, plunges across the valley until it strikes against the rocks of the opposite side. Between the glacier and these cliffs was an old water-course up which we travelled, but stones kept frequently falling from the cliffs above and the passage was somewhat dangerous. This had evidently been the old channel of the stream that has its source in the glaciers of Mount Everest, but owing to the advance of the Kang-do-shung Glacier, is now compelled to find its way through this glacier and hurls itself into a great ice cavern in it. Opposite this ice cavern we had a steep climb for 500 feet, and found ourselves among pleasant grassy meadows, after a few miles of which we came to a place called Pethang Ringmo, where we found some yak herds living.

We found that Mallory and Bullock had chosen this place to be their base camp. It was a most delightfully sunny spot at 16,400 feet, right under the gigantic and marvellously beautiful cliffs of Chomolönzo, now all powdered over with the fresh snow of the night before and only separated from us by the Kangshung Glacier, here about a mile wide. Great avalanches thunder down its sides all the day long with a terrifying sound. Everest from here is seen to fill up the head of the valley with a most formidable circle of cliffs overhung by hanging glaciers, but it is not nearly such a beautiful or striking mountain as Makalu or Chomolönzo. The shepherds would insist that Makalu was the higher of the two mountains and would not believe us when we said that Mount Everest was the higher. Next morning was foggy, but there was a glimpse of blue sky behind the mists, so after breakfast I hurried up the valley, intending to climb a ridge exactly opposite to Mount Everest which I had marked down the night before. After walking for an hour up the valley in a thick fog, by luck I struck the right ridge, which proved a very steep climb. Glimpses of blue sky and white peaks, however, gave us hopes of better views higher up. It took me two and a half hours to climb 3,000 feet, which at last brought me above the mists.

The top of the ridge was 19,500 feet high, and from it we had most superb views. Mount Everest was only 3 or 4 miles away from us. From it to the South-east swept a huge amphitheatre of mighty peaks culminating in a new and unsurveyed peak, 28,100 feet in height, to which we gave the name of Lhotse, which in Tibetan means the South Peak. From this side the mountain appeared quite unclimbable, as the cliffs were all topped with hanging glaciers, from which great masses of ice came thundering down into the valley below all the day long. Between Mount Everest and Makalu, on the watershed between Tibet and Nepal, there stands up a very curious conical peak, to which we gave the name of Pethangtse. On either side of it are two very steep, but not very high, passes into Nepal; both of them are, however, probably unclimbable. To the South-east towered up the immense cliffs of Makalu, far the more beautiful mountain of the two. The whole morning I spent on this ridge, taking photographs whenever opportunity offered. The clouds kept coming up and melting away again and were most annoying, but they occasionally afforded us the most beautiful glimpses and peeps of the snow and rock peaks by which we were surrounded. At a height of over 19,000 feet, I had a great chase after a new kind of rat; but it finally eluded me, and I was not able to add it to our already large collection. Even at these heights I found both yellow and white saxifrages and a blue gentian. From the top of this ridge I had been able to see Kanchenjunga and Jannu, though nearly 100 miles away, but their summits stood up out of the great sea of clouds which covered Nepal.

From *Mount Everest: the Reconnaissance, 1921.*

James Ramsey Ullman:

The Kama Valley, on investigation, proved a blind alley, but the neighboring Kharta Valley gave the explorers access to the eastern slopes of Everest. Ascending it to its apex, they came out on a high wind-swept pass known as the Lhakpa La, to find, before and below them, the long white ribbon of the East Rongbuk Glacier and, beyond it, a steep snow-slope rising to the North Col.

As Mallory had hoped, this eastern side seemed to offer a much better route to the col than the western. Although the season was late, he was determined to have a go at it, and accordingly, on September twenty-third, he, Bullock, Wheeler, and a few porters set out from their camp on the Lhakpa La for the base of the col. The key to the mountain had been found, but whether it would turn in the lock remained to be seen.

George Leigh-Mallory:

There was no question of bustling off before dawn on the 23rd, but we rose early enough, as I supposed, to push on to Chang La if we were sufficiently strong. Morshead and I in a Mummery tent had slept well and I congratulated myself on an act of mutilation in cutting two large slits in its roof. The rest had not fared so well, but seemed fit enough, and the wonderful prospect from our camp at sunrise was a cheering sight. With the coolies, however, the case was different. Those who had been unwell overnight had not recovered, and it was evident that only a comparatively small number would be able to come on; eventually I gathered ten, two men who both protested they were ill casting lots for the last place; and of these ten it was evident that none were unaffected by the height and several were more seriously mountain-sick.* Under these circumstances it was necessary to consider which loads should be carried on. Bury, Wollaston and Morshead suggested that they should go back at once so as not to burden the party with the extra weight of their belongings, and it seemed the wisest plan that they should return. Certain stores were left behind at Lhakpa La as reserve supplies for the climbing party. I decided at an early hour that our best chance was to take an easy day; after a late start and a very slow march we pitched our tents on the open snow up towards the col.

It might have been supposed that in so deep a cwm and sheltered on three sides by steep mountain slopes, we should find a tranquil air and the soothing, though chilly calm of un-disturbed frost. Night came clearly indeed, but with no gentle intentions. Fierce squalls of wind visited our tents and shook and worried them with the disagreeable threat of tearing them away from their moorings, and then scurried off, leaving us in wonder at the change and asking what next to expect. It was a cold wind at an altitude of 22,000 feet, and however little one may have suffered, the atmosphere discouraged sleep. Again I believe I was more fortunate than my companions, but Bullock and Wheeler fared badly. Lack of sleep, since it makes one sleepy, always discourages an early start, and hot drinks take time to brew; in any case, it was wise to start rather late so as to have the benefit of warm sun whenever our feet should be obliged to linger in cold snow or ice steps. It was an hour or so after sunrise when we left the camp and half an hour later we were breaking the crust on the first slopes under the wall. We had taken three coolies who were suffi-ciently fit and competent, and now proceeded to use them for the hardest work. Apart from one brief spell of cutting when

---

* I use this expression to denote not a state of intermittent vomiting, but simply one in which physical exertion exhausts the body abnormally and causes a remarkable disinclination to further exertion.

we passed the corner of a bergschrund it was a matter of straightforward plugging, firstly slanting up to the right on partially frozen avalanche snow and then left in one long upward traverse to the summit. Only one passage shortly below the col caused either anxiety or trouble; here the snow was lying at a very steep angle and was deep enough to be disagreeable. About 500 steps of very hard work covered all the worst of the traverse and we were on the col shortly before 11.30 a.m.

By this time two coolies were distinctly tired, though by no means incapable of coming on; the third, who had been in front, was comparatively fresh. Wheeler thought he might be good for some further effort, but had lost all feeling in his feet. Bullock was tired, but by sheer will power would evidently come on—how far, one couldn't say. For my part I had had the wonderful good fortune of sleeping tolerably well at both high camps and now finding my best form; I supposed I might be capable of another 2,000 feet, and there would be no time for more. But what lay ahead of us? My eyes had often strayed, as we came up, to the rounded edge above the col and the final rocks below the North-east arête. If ever we had doubted whether the arête were accessible, it was impossible to doubt any longer. For a long way up those easy rock and snow slopes was neither danger nor difficulty. But at present there was wind. Even where we stood under the lee of a little ice cliff it came in fierce gusts at frequent intervals, blowing up the powdery snow in a suffocating tourbillon. On the col beyond it was blowing a gale. And higher was a more fearful sight. The powdery fresh snow on the great face of Everest was being swept along in unbroken spindrift and the very ridge where our route lay was marked out to receive its unmitigated fury. We could see the blown snow deflected upwards for a moment where the wind met the ridge, only to rush violently down in a frightful blizzard on the leeward side. To see, in fact, was enough; the wind had settled the question; it would have been folly to go on. Nevertheless, some little discussion took place as to what might be possible, and we struggled a few steps further to put the matter to the test. For a few moments we exposed ourselves on the col to feel the full strength of the blast, then struggled back to shelter. Nothing more was said about pushing our assault any further.

From *Mount Everest: the Reconnaissance, 1921.*

JAMES RAMSEY ULLMAN:

The ascent to the North Col was the climax of the 1921 reconnaissance, but one important discovery was subsequently made. This was that a passage from the main Rongbuk Glacier to the eastern side of the col actually did exist. It was now too late, of course, for it to be of any use to them that year, but all future expeditions were to approach the col by this Rongbuk-East Rongbuk route.

Their task accomplished, the expedition presently broke camp and started on the long journey home. Looking back on the four months of adventure and struggle, Mallory set down the salient features of what had been learned about Everest and his opinions of the obstacles and problems that remained for the future.

GEORGE LEIGH-MALLORY:

The reader who has carefully followed the preceding story will hardly have failed to notice that the route which has been chosen as the only one offering reasonable chances of success remains still very largely a matter of speculation. But the reconnaissance, unless it were actually to reach the summit, was obliged to leave much unproved, and its value must depend upon observations in various sorts and not merely upon the practice of treading the snow and rocks. Speculation in this case is founded upon experience of certain phenomena and a study of the mountain's features; and it is by relating what has been only seen with known facts that inferences have been drawn.

It may perhaps be accounted a misfortune that the party of 1921 did not approach Chang La by the East Rongbuk Glacier. The Lhakpa La proved a bigger obstacle than was expected. But in conditions such as we hope to find before the monsoon, this way would have much to recommend it. It avoids all laborious walking on a dry glacier, and with hard snow the walk up to the pass from the camp on stones at 20,000 feet should not be unduly fatiguing. Still the fact remains that the descent from the Lhakpa La on to the East Rongbuk Glacier is not less than 1,200 feet. Would it not be better to follow up this glacier from the Rongbuk Valley? The absence of wood on this side need not deter the party of 1922. For them plenty of time will be available sufficiently to provide their base with fuel, and the sole consideration should be the easiest line of approach; and though no one has traversed the whole length of the East Rongbuk Glacier, enough is known to choose this way with confidence. Here, as on other glaciers which we saw, the difficulties clearly lie below the limit of perpetual snow, and the greater part of them were avoided or solved by Major Wheeler, who found a practicable way on to the middle of the glacier at about 19,000 feet, and felt certain that the medial moraine ahead of him would serve for an ascent and be no more arduous than the moraines of the West Rongbuk Glacier had proved to be. The view of this way from the Lhakpa La confirmed his opinion, and though it may be called a speculation to choose it, whereas the way from the East has been established by experiment, it is a fair inference from experience to conclude that the untraversed section of the East Rongbuk Glacier, a distance which could be accomplished very easily in one march if all went well, will afford a simple approach to Chang La.

The Eastern wall, about 1,000 feet high, by which the gap itself must be reached, can never be lightly esteemed. Here reconnaissance has forged a link. But those who reached the col were not laden with tents and stores; and on another occasion the conditions may be different. There may be the danger of an avalanche or the difficulty of ice. From what we saw this year before the monsoon had brought a heavy snowfall it is by no means improbable that ice will be found at the end of May on the steepest slope below Chang La. In that case much labour will be required to hew and keep in repair a staircase, and perhaps fix a banister, so that the laden coolies, not all of whom will be competent ice-men, may be brought up in safety.

The summit of Mount Everest is about 6,000 feet above Chang La; the distance is something like 2½ miles and the whole of it is unexplored. What grounds have we for thinking that the mountaineering difficulties will not prove insuperable, that in so far as mere climbing is concerned the route is practicable? Two factors, generally speaking, have to be considered: the nature of the ground and the general angle of inclination. Where the climber is confined to a narrow crest and can find no way to circumvent an obstacle, a very small tower or wall, a matter of 20 feet, may bar his progress. There the general angle may be what it likes: the important matter for him is that the angle is too steep in a particular place. But on a mountain's face where his choice is not limited to a strict and narrow way, the general angle is of primary importance: if it is sufficiently gentle, the climber will find that he may wander almost where he will to avoid the steeper places. Long before we reached Chang La Mr. Bullock and I were fairly well convinced that the slope from here to the North-east Shoulder was sufficiently gentle and that the nature of the ill-defined ridge connecting these two points was not such as to limit the choice of route to a narrow line. Looking up from the North Col, we learnt nothing more about the angles. The view, however, was not without value; it amply confirmed our opinion as to the character of what lay ahead of us. The ridge is not a crest; its section is a wide and rounded angle. It is not decorated by pinnacles, it does not rise in steps. It presents a smooth continuous way, and whether the rocks are still covered with powdery snow, or only slightly sprinkled and for the most part bare, the party of 1922 should be able to go up a long way at all events without meeting any serious obstacle. It may not prove a perfectly simple matter actually to reach the North-east arête above the shoulder at about 28,000 feet. The angle becomes steeper towards this arête. But even in the last section below it, the choice of a way should not be inconveniently restricted. On the right of the ascending party will be permanent snow on various sloping ledges, an easy alternative to rocks if the snow is found in good condition, and always offering a détour by which to avoid an obstacle.

From the North-east Shoulder to the summit of the mountain the way is not so smooth. The rise is only 1,000 feet in a distance of half a mile, but the first part of the crest is distinctly jagged by several towers and the last part is steep. Much will depend upon the possibility of escaping from the crest to avoid the obstacles and of regaining it easily. The South-east side (the left going up) is terribly steep, and it will almost certainly be out of the question to traverse there. But the sloping snow-covered ledges on the North-west may serve very well; the difficulty about them is their tendency to be horizontal in direction and to diverge from the arête where it slopes upwards, so that a party which had followed one in preference to the crest might find themselves cut off by a cliff running across the face above them. But one way or another I think it should be possible with the help of such ledges to reach the final obstacle. The summit itself is like the thin end of a wedge thrust up from the mass in which it is embedded. The edge of it, with the highest point at the far end, can only be reached from the North-east by climbing a steep blunt edge of snow. The height of this final obstacle must be fully 200 feet. Mr. Bullock and I examined it often through our field-glasses, and though it did not appear insuperable, whatever our point of view, it never looked anything but steep.

To determine whether it is humanly possible to climb to the summit of Mount Everest or what may be the chances of success in such an undertaking, other factors besides the mere mountaineering difficulties have to be considered. It is at least probable that the obstacles presented by this mountain could be overcome by any competent party if they met them in the Alps. But it is a very different matter to be confronted with such obstacles at elevations between 23,000 and 29,000 feet. We do not know that it is physiologically possible at such high altitudes for the human body to make the efforts required to lift itself up even on the simplest ground. The condition of the party of 1921 in September during the days of the Assault * cannot be taken as evidence that the feat is impossible. The long periods spent in high camps and the tax of many exhausting expeditions had undoubtedly reduced the physical efficiency of Sahibs and coolies alike. The party of 1922, on the other hand, will presumably choose for their attempt a time when the climbers are at the top of their form and their powers will depend on the extent of their adaptability to the condition of high altitude.

Nothing perhaps was so astonishing in the party of reconnaissance as the rapidity with which they became acclimatised and capable of great exertions between 18,000 and 21,000 feet. Where is the limit of this process? Will the multiplication of

* Mallory is here referring to the climbing of the North Col during the reconnaissance.—*Editor.*

red corpuscles continue so that men may become acclimatised much higher? There is evidence enough to show that they may exist comfortably enough, eating and digesting hearty meals and retaining a feeling of vitality and energy up to 23,000 feet. It may be that, after two or three days quietly spent at this height, the body would sufficiently adjust itself to endure the still greater difference from normal atmospheric pressure 6,000 feet higher. At all events, a practical test can alone provide the proof in such a case. Experiments carried out in a laboratory by putting a man into a sealed chamber and reducing the pressure say to half an atmosphere, valuable as they may be when related to the experiences of airmen, can establish nothing for mountaineers; for they leave out of account the all-important physiological factor of acclimatisation. But in any case it is to be expected that efforts above 23,000 feet will be more exhausting than those at lower elevations; and it may well be that the nature of the ground will turn the scale against the climber. For him it is all important that he should be able to breathe regularly, the demand upon his lungs along the final arête cannot fail to be a terrible strain, and anything like a tussle up some steep obstacle which would interfere with the regularity of his breathing might prove to be an ordeal beyond his strength.

As a way out of these difficulties of breathing, the use of oxygen has often been recommended and experiments were made by Dr. Kellas, which will be continued in 1922.

Even so there will remain the difficulty of establishing one or perhaps two camps above Chang La (23,000 feet). It is by no means certain that any place exists above this point on which tents could be pitched. Perhaps the party will manage without tents, but no great economy of weight will be effected that way; those who sleep out at an elevation of 25,000 or 26,000 feet will have to be bountifully provided with warm things. Probably about fifteen, or at least twelve loads will have to be carried up from Chang La. It is not expected that oxygen will be available for this purpose, and the task, whatever organisation is provided, will be severe, possibly beyond the limits of human strength.

Further, another sort of difficulty will jeopardise the chances of success. It might be possible for two men to struggle somehow to the summit, disregarding every other consideration. It is a different matter to climb the mountain as mountaineers would have it climbed. Principles, time-honoured in the Alpine Club, must of course be respected in the ascent of Mount Everest. The party must keep a margin of safety. It is not to be a mad enterprise rashly pushed on regardless of danger. The ill-considered acceptance of any and every risk has no part in the essence of persevering courage. A mountaineering enterprise may keep sanity and sound judgment and remain an adventure. And of all principles by which we hold the first is that of mutual help. What is to be done for a man who is sick or abnormally exhausted at these high altitudes? His companions must see to it that he is taken down at the first opportunity and with an adequate escort; and the obligation is the same whether he be Sahib or coolie; if we ask a man to carry our loads up the mountain we must care for his welfare at need. It may be taken for granted that such need will arise and will interfere very seriously with any organisation however ingeniously and carefully it may be arranged.

In all it may be said that one factor beyond all others is required for success. Too many chances are against the climbers; too many contingencies may turn against them. Anything like a breakdown of the transport will be fatal; soft snow on the mountain will be an impregnable defence; a big wind will send back the strongest; even so small a matter as a boot fitting a shade too tight may endanger one man's foot and involve the whole party in retreat. The climbers must have above all things, if they are to win through, good fortune, and the greatest good fortune of all for mountaineers, some constant spirit of kindness in Mount Everest itself, the forgetfulness for long enough of its more cruel moods; for we must remember that the highest of mountains is capable of severity, a severity so awful and so fatal that the wiser sort of men do well to think and tremble even on the threshold of their high endeavour.

From *Mount Everest: the Reconnaissance, 1921.*

3

First Assault

The Expedition of 1922

This wall of eagle-baffling mountain,
Black, wintry, dead, unmeasured; without herb,
Insect, or beast, or shape or sound of life . . .

Shelley: *Prometheus Unbound*

James Ramsey Ullman:

No sooner had the reports of the reconnaissance party reached England than the Mount Everest Committee set about its organizational work in earnest; and in late March of 1922 the first climbing expedition set out on the long trail from Darjeeling to the base of the mountain. It was composed of thirteen Englishmen, sixty hillmen from Nepal and Northern India, a hundred-odd Tibetan helpers, and more than three hundred pack animals—a veritable army in miniature.

In the previous year the purpose had been to explore, reconnoiter, and learn. Now, however, all else was to be subordinated to one great purpose: to reach the top of Everest. To this end, the personnel of the party had been almost completely changed, only Mallory and Morshead remaining from the original group. The new leader was Brig. Gen. Charles G. Bruce, a veteran of the British Army in India and a far-ranging Himalayan explorer over a period of many years. Col. E. T. Strutt, another noted mountaineer, was second in command, and Dr. T. E. Longstaff, one of the most celebrated of the older generation of British climbers, was on hand to lend the benefit of his wide experience. The others included Lt. Col. E. F. Norton, Dr. T. Howard Somervell, and Dr. Wakefield; Capts. Geoffrey Bruce, George Finch, and C. G. Morris; C. G. Crawford, of the India Civil Service; and, as photographer, Captain John Noel. Of these, Norton, Somervell, and Finch were climbers in the prime of their careers and were expected, together with Mallory, to make the strongest bid for the summit.

On the first of May the expedition pitched its base camp near the snout of the Rongbuk Glacier, sixteen miles from the base of the mountain. Close by was the fantastic Rongbuk Monastery with its hermit lamas, devoted to the guardianship of Chomolungma, Goddess Mother of the World. And here the climbers paused before launching out on their great enterprise.

CAPT. JOHN NOEL:

For weeks we had toiled through desolation of mountain and plateau. At last we sighted our goal and gazed spellbound at the sheer cliffs of rock draped with ice which seemed to form part of the very heavens above us.

We stood at sixteen thousand feet above the sea. The valley, a mile wide, ran straight ahead for nearly twenty miles. At its farther end, stretching across, closing the valley, rearing its imposing head of granite and ice, was Everest. Some colossal architect, who built with peaks and valleys, seemed here to have wrought a dramatic prodigy—a hall of grandeur that led to the mountain.

A spectacle of astounding beauty and strangeness, for me it evoked singular remembrances and emotions; I could look back ten years upon an adventure to which this experience came as a climax and completion.

Many stories had been heard, yet few believed, of this region of the Rongbuk, called Chamalung, "The Sanctuary of the Birds," where indeed all wild creatures, because they are considered to be the reincarnated spirits of former human lives, may live unharmed and untouched. Who would there be to hurt them? There are no inhabitants save the hermit monks who dwell in solitude and meditation in the rock-hewn cells we saw dotted over the hillsides.

In the heart of this sacred valley these hermits live their

entire lives, gaining merit so that when they die their souls may escape from the affrighting cycle of reincarnation which they believe to be the inevitable and eternal sequel to the lives of ordinary men. One can be oppressed with a sense of mystery in this lifted hidden world, in the solitude and in the impressive majesty of the surroundings.

There is one tremendous reputed saint, who has been sealed up in a rock cell beneath Mount Everest, dwelling in darkness for fifteen years, meditating, sitting motionless, year after year. Once a day brother monks bring a cup of water and a handful of barley meal to this self-isolated priest. I myself watched, and saw through a hole in the wall of the hermit's cell a hand steal out and take in the water and the bread. Even the hand was muffled, because not only must no one see him, not even the light of day may touch his skin.

On the left at the entrance of the valley lay the monastery. Certainly no architectural pains had been expended on it. That, indeed, would have been futile labor, with Everest straight down the gigantic corridor. It was a collection of low, flat buildings, and in front stood an immense chorten, a cupola-like monument built in terraces and crowned by emblems of the sun and moon, symbolizing the light of Buddha's teaching illuminating the world.

This is the highest monastery in the world—the Rongbuk lamasery, where the venerable Rongbuk Lama, one of the holiest hermit monks of Tibet and the incarnation of the god Chongraysay, lives and contemplates. The monastery is the shrine dedicated to Everest; and the Lama is the High Priest of the mountain, who communes with the Goddess Mother of the World. Here was the reality of that which had been merely vague legend from the time of the Pundit explorers.

Our handful of white men and band of Tibetan and Nepalese carriers advanced into this secret place with feelings of awe, the white men scarcely less than the natives.

According to Tibetan historical legend, the monastery was built or possibly rebuilt over two thousand years ago. In a later time, a Chinese princess of the Tsang dynasty that ruled China, then in one of the most exalted ages of her culture and civilization, had married the King of Tibet, Srong-Tsan-Gampo; and she had persuaded her king to invite the Indian Buddhist Saint, Padma Samblava, to teach the religion of Buddha to the people of Tibet, then possessed only of the devil-worship of Bom. Padma Samblava came miraculously across the Himalaya by the sky, and rested awhile at the monastery beneath Mount Everest to subjugate those evil spirits —the Zhidag—that had opposed his saintly advent, conjuring up the anger of the storms and the poisons of the air against him, but without avail.

The chief of the devil-worshipping lamas, who dwelt in this monastery, challenged the Buddhist to prove which was the more powerful—the teachings of Buddha, or the ancient faith of the people. To decide the matter they would hold a race to the top of Mount Everest, each calling on his gods or devils. During the night the Bombo Lama, determined to steal a march on his adversary, started off in the dark, riding on his magical drum.

The disciples of the other came to wake him, and cried anxiously that the Bombo Lama was already half way up the mountain. But Padma Samblava said, "Fear not, because just as soon as the sun's rays come, so shall I start."

When the sun appeared, he was conveyed by a beam to the very top of the mountain, while sitting in his chair. There he sat awhile, enthroned on the steeple of the world. When he descended he left the chair behind. The wicked Bombo Lama perished; and the spirits of the mountain kept his drum. So now, when the rumble of rock avalanche is heard, the Tibetans say the spirits are beating the drum.

Tibetans always had difficulty in understanding why we had

come, and why we wanted to climb the mountain. They had no conception of the idea of sport, and they were certain that the reasons we gave were lies. They decided that what we were really seeking was the magical chair which the Buddhist apostle had left on the mountain. They were convinced that the spirits of Everest would see to it that we did not get to the top. Probably they would even punish us severely for our impiety —beliefs which, I admit, after events seemed to bear out.

From the outer world we had found our way to this rallying place of demons and deities, along the pilgrim paths marked with chortens and mani walls, structures that must be passed right-handed, and with religious lifting of the hat to the flying prayer flags that wing to heaven with every flutter of the wind the Mantra:

"Om mani padme hum!"

("Hail! Jewel of the Lotus Flower!")

Many pilgrims seek for merit here in this valley of the Rongbuk. These devout and simple people travel sometimes two thousand miles, from China and Mongolia, and cover every inch of the way by measuring their length on the ground. They prostrate themselves on their faces, marking the soil with their fingers a little beyond their heads, arise and bring their toes to the mark they have made and fall again, stretched full length on the ground, their arms extended, muttering an already million-times-repeated prayer.

Thus they spend their lives. They live upon the hospitality of villagers and shepherds, who themselves merit spiritual reward by giving hospitality to them. There are other places of pilgrimage: the Holy Lake of Manasarowar of South Central Tibet, where the great Indus and the Brahmaputra rivers both rise together, to flow, in exactly opposite directions, to the gorges by which they break through the Himalaya to the Indian Ocean; the shrine of Chorten-Nyim, and others; but the pilgrimage to the Rongbuk and Mount Everest is one of the most sacred in Southern Tibet.

We Western men who had entered this strange land were pilgrims, but unlike the pilgrims who came measuring their length on the ground. We were pilgrims only of adventure. We had our camp with our horses and our tents and our servants and our machines. Our business was to fight the mountain, not to worship it.

We visited the lamasery. In dramatic contrast to all expectation, our visit was an intrusion into a place of joy. I can describe it best as a mixture of pious religion and uproarious laughter —and a little dirt. Mystical peace and contemplation is not entirely a solemnity. Divine service was brightened by the music of drums, with plentiful food and buttered tea served by attendants. We heard laughter on all sides from the boys, dozens and dozens of them, little fellows with shaven heads and slanting yellow eyes and long claws, clad in robes of yellow and maroon. They played much as children in any land. One of them will, by spells and incantations, perhaps be found to be the reincarnation of a saint or god. There was laughter from the grown-up monks too who swarmed about. Laughter is universal in Tibet, especially when a white man comes round. The white man is a strange object to Tibetans. They kill themselves laughing at him. You can please yourself whether you feel humbled or not about it. Personally, I think that it is the laughter of pleasure and wonder at meeting; a happy polite laugh that conceals no derision. They are indeed a most cheerful and happy people although they lead as hard a life as any of the human race.

Our way being opened by the passports and letters of friendship given our expedition by the Dalai Lama of Lhasa, we were accepted as honored guests, although the lamas were all a little appalled at our hardihood in proposing to brave the mysterious dangers of Everest.

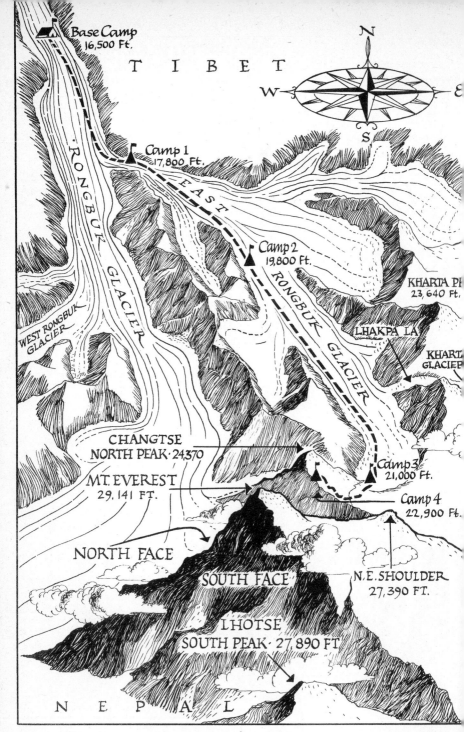

The route toward the summit.

One thing about the lamas that catches your immediate sympathy is their gentleness. On the whole they and the Tibetans at large are extremely kind. They are almost fantastically humane towards animals, especially wild creatures, although there is the inconsistency of their harshness with their beasts of burden. This, however, is to be observed among all people throughout the world who depend upon pack trains for their transportation. They are cruel at times towards human beings, although much less so than the Chinese.

You might imagine that they would be theologically argumentative and inclined to proselytize, even to the point of trying to convert us. But they could seldom be persuaded to say anything about either their gods or their devils. A lama once, however, condescended to make a few confidences. It was not matter of idle disputation, but quite practical.

The hairy men, he explained, were most malignant. They lived high up on Everest, and at times came down and wrought havoc in the villages. They carried off women and yaks, and killed all men. I was a trifle annoyed at the solemn fantasy.

"But," I replied, "I want to meet the hairy men."

He could not understand that, but then he thought we were quite mad anyway.

The Tibetan monk believes in a most incredible collection of devils and takes his beliefs with the most matter-of-fact seriousness.

Everywhere you go, you see endless chortens erected to keep the evil spirits in the ground. If a Tibetan encounters a mishap, falls or breaks his leg, the explanation is that the goblin —they are called Yi-dag or Preta—has risen from the lower world within the earth at that point and has caused the trouble, whether it be the work of Srin-Po, who devours the limbs of men, or Srul-Po, a female demon who causes all the illnesses of children, or Brjed-Byed, who causes forgetfulness, or Snyo-Byed, who causes people to go mad. Thereupon a chorten is erected to keep that spirit down; and the stonemasons carve phrases on the slabs. Passers-by add stones to the pile and mutter *"Om mani padme hum"* as they pass on by the left.

A fascinating legend of the monastery, which all good Tibetans believe in, is one that tells of the Nitikanji, or Snow Men. That is the name the lamas give them because they are dread beings who inhabit the snows. One must speak of them with great respect, otherwise they will bring bad luck and perhaps even come down and raid and kill, because they are known to kill men, carry off women, and to bite the necks of yaks and drink their blood. The ordinary Tibetan peasant calls these beings Sukpa, and tells of their strange rovings in the snow, of the long hair which falls over their eyes, so that if you are chased by the Sukpa you must run downhill; then the long hair will get into his eyes and you can escape from him.

What are they? Man? Ape? Bear? Nobody can tell. But there must be some reason for this legend, because it is an accepted fact in these valleys of Tibet. An ape perhaps, which once strayed from the forests of India and found a home in the snow. The King of the Sukpas is supposed to live on the very top of Everest, whence he can look down upon the world below, and choose upon which herd of grazing yaks he will descend. Yak-herds say that the Sukpa can jump by huge bounds at a time; that he is much taller than the tallest man; and that he had a hard tail upon which he can sit. The men he kills he will not eat. He just bites off the tips of their fingers, toes and noses, and leaves them.

Before taking our departure from the monastery we were allowed to visit the Chief Lama of the Rongbuk, the great god-lama, who is the god Chongraysay reincarnate. He consented to give us an audience.

We found ourselves trudging up a narrow dark stairway to a shrine in the upper part of the monastery buildings. A long deep trumpet note began and continued on and on without a break, and the sound of cymbals came clashing with a regular rhythm. When any ceremony was under way, a party of trumpeters and cymbal beaters on the roof sounded a proclamation. The trumpeters held the note sustained while the ritual proceeded, blowing in relays so that the blare of the instruments overlapped unceasingly. We came into a small, simply furnished room. A few holy pictures and inscriptions in Chinese fashion were on the wall. Before us we saw two lamas holding a screen of cloth. Our Tibetan bearers, who had come with us, prostrated themselves, with their faces pressed to the floor. Behind that screen, we understood, was the Saint.

We waited silently for a moment. The white men were allowed to remain standing. Then the two lamas slowly lowered their screen. A figure sat with crossed knees in the Buddha posture. There were draperies of costly Chinese silks. The figure sat absolutely motionless and silent. Not a soul spoke a word, or even whispered in the room. Somehow we did not dare to interrupt the weird suspense. We stood with our hats in our hands. Outside the blare of the trumpets persisted in a monotonous, unceasing blare as if announcing the occasion to remote powers. Within the room, there was an intoxicating smell from the juniper burning by the peacock's feathers in the urn before the figure.

Looking closely, we saw the face of an elderly man of extraordinary personality. The Mongolian features had a singular cast of thought and expression. It is said that each year he himself also retires for three months to the darkness of a hermit's cell.

He looked at us, but did not speak or move. Rather he seemed to look over us, through us. There was something vastly observant and yet impersonal in his gaze. The screen of cloth was raised and our audience was at an end and we filed out. Not a word had been spoken. I felt absolutely hypnotized, it was so weird. Then out in the sunlight and fresh air again, on the way back to our tents, we all recovered ourselves and somebody—I forget who it was now—said:

"Gee—that chap is either the holiest saint or the greatest actor on earth."

It had been a meeting between the East and the West. We were pilgrims but we had come to wrestle, not with bogeys and demons, but against not less real and powerful opponents, against blizzards and tempests holding revel amid chasms and rocks, for a prize for which we perhaps would—as we actually did—have to pay a price of human lives.

Can I give you a better contrast between ourselves and the strange people we found living here, or give you a better proof that no physical obstacle of nature, or any immaterial obstacle of superstition can ever beat the spirit of modern man, or prevent him winning any victory he may set himself to win—than by reminding you of a little incident that happened in 1922, when Captain Geoffrey Bruce, of the 6th Gurka Rifles, standing at the world's record altitude of twenty-seven thousand two hundred and thirty-five feet, forced to give up the struggle against the icy blasts blowing at a hundred miles an hour across to Himalaya, looked up to Everest above, and said:

"Just you wait, old thing, we will get you yet."

By that little incident alone the ultimate fate of Everest was sealed.

From *The Story of Everest.*

JAMES RAMSEY ULLMAN:

With the monastery behind it, the expedition bent its efforts to the immense task ahead. The route to the mountain was to be a new one. The 1921 party had approached the North Col from the high pass of the Lhakpa La; but the present plan was to reach it by way of the Rongbuk and the East Rongbuk glaciers, passing from one to the other through the narrow defile which Mallory had missed the previous year. Three camps were to be set up on the glaciers, not more than four or five hours' march apart, and the highest of them must be as close under the col as it was possible to get it.

BRIG. GEN. C. G. BRUCE:

Now began in earnest our race against the monsoon. I have often been asked since my return, whether we should not have done better if we had started sooner. I think none of us would have cared to have arrived at our Upper Rongbuk camp a fortnight earlier in the year, nor, having done so, would any good purpose have been served. As it was, the temperature and the coldness of the wind was as much as any of us could keep up with and still keep our good health. This was to be our Base Camp at a height of 16,500 feet. We made suitable dumps of stores, pitched our mess tents, put all our porters in tents at their own particular places, and made ourselves as comfortable as circumstances allowed, strengthening the tents in every way to resist the wind. Noel also pitched his developing tent near the small stream that issues from the Rongbuk Glacier. On our arrival water was hardly available; all the running streams were frozen hard, and we drove the whole of our animals over them. Where the glacier stream flowed fastest in the centre, we got sufficient water for drinking purposes.

The establishment and support of such a large party (for we were thirteen Europeans and over sixty of what may be termed other ranks) in a country as desolate and as bare as Tibet is a difficulty. There is, of course, no fuel to be found, with the exception of a very little scrubby root which, burnt in large quantities, would heat an oven, but which was not good enough or plentiful enough for ordinary cooking purposes.

Our first work, beyond the establishment of the Base Camp,

was immediately to send out a reconnaissance party. Strutt was put in charge of this and chose as his assistants Norton, Longstaff, and Morshead. The remainder of the party had to work very hard dividing stores and arranging for the movement up to the different camps we wished to make on the way up to the East Rongbuk Glacier to the North Col. It was pretty apparent from Major Wheeler's map that our advance up the East Rongbuk to the glacier crossed by Mr. Mallory in 1921, which is below the Chang La, would not be a very difficult road. But it was a very considerable question how many camps should be established, and how full provision should be made for each? We were naturally very anxious to save our own porters for the much more strenuous work of establishing our camp at the North Col, and perhaps of further camps up the mountain. I had, therefore, on our march up, made every possible endeavour to collect a large number of Tibetan coolies in order that they should be employed in moving all the heavy stuff as far up the glacier as possible; in fact, until we came to ground which would not be suitable to them, or, rather, not suitable to their clothing. They were perfectly willing to work on any ground which was fairly dry, but their form of foot-covering would certainly not allow of continual work in snow. We had a promise of ninety men.

We further had to make full arrangements for a regular supply of yak-dung, the whole of which, as in fact everything to burn in Tibet, is called "shing," which really means wood; all our fuel, therefore, from now on, will be referred to as "shing." All tzampa,* meat, and grain for the men had to be procured as far down as Chobu, Tashishong, and even from other villages still further down the Dzakar Chu; that is to say, very often our supplies were brought up from at least 40 miles distant. We required a pretty continuous flow of everything.

* Flour.

It is wonderful how much even seventy men can get through.

The preliminary reconnaissance had fixed an excellent camp as our first stage out. Geoffrey Bruce and Morris, with our own porters went up, and, so as to save tents, built a number of stone shelters and roofed them with spare parts of tents. This camp was immediately provisioned and filled with every kind of supply in large amounts in order to form again a little base from which to move up further. Strutt returned with his reconnaissance on May 9, having made a complete plan for our advance and having fixed all our camps up to the flat glacier under the North Col. During this period Finch had also been very active with his oxygen apparatus, not only in getting it all together, but continuing the training of the personnel and in making experiments with the Leonard Hill apparatus as well. He also gave lectures and demonstrations on the use of our Primus stove, with which everybody practised. Primus stoves are excellent when they are carefully treated, but are kittle cattle unless everything goes quite as it should, and are apt to blow up.

Longstaff suffered considerably on the reconnaissance, and was brought down not too fit. We also had a real set-back— our ninety coolies did not eventuate, only forty-five appearing, and these coolies only worked for about two days, when they said that their food was exhausted and they must go down for more. We took the best guarantee we could for their return by keeping back half their pay. They went for more food, but found it in their houses and stopped there; we never saw them again. However, it is not to be wondered at. If ploughing in the upper valleys is to be done at all, it is to be done in May. They were, therefore, very anxious to get back to their homes. Ninety men is a big toll for these valleys to supply, but their behaviour left us rather dispirited. We had to turn every one to work, and then we had to make every possible exertion to collect further coolies from the different villages. The Chongay

La who came with us, and who understood our needs, was frantic, but said he could do nothing. However, we persuaded him to do something, at any rate, and further offered very high prices to all the men who had come. He certainly played up and did his very best. Men came up in driblets, or rather men, women, and children came, as every one in this country can carry loads, and they seem to be quite unaffected by sleeping out under rocks at 16,000 or 17,000 feet.

For the whole time we remained at the Rongbuk Base Camp the equipping and supply of our first and second camps up the East Rongbuk was mostly carried out by local coolies, and the supply of these was very difficult to assure. We never knew whether we should have three or four men working, or thirty; they came up for different periods, so that we would often have a dozen men coming down and four or five going up, and in order to keep their complete confidence, they were received and paid personally by myself or the transport officers. By degrees their confidence was restored, and a very fair stream of porters arrived. Not only that, but many of the men's own relations came over from Sola-Khombu, which is a great Sherpa Settlement at the head of the Dudh Kosi Valley in Nepal. To reach us they had to cross the Ngangba La, sometimes called the Khombu La, which is 19,000 feet in height. Often the men's relations came and were willing to carry a load or two and then go off again. The mothers often brought their children, even of less than a year old, who did not apparently suffer. It is evidently a case of the survival of the fittest.

We had brought also large stores of rice, sugar, tea, and wheat grain, both for the use of the officers of the Expedition and of the porters, for fear we should run short of grain, and this proved a great stand-by. The very rough tzampa of Tibet is often upsetting even to those most accustomed to it. It was found to be an excellent policy to feed our porters on the good grain when they came down to the Base Camp, and to use the tzampa, which is cooked and ready for eating, at the upper camps. Meat also had to be bought low down, sheep killed low down in the valleys, and brought up for the use of the officers and men, and often fresh yak meat for the porters. The Gurkhas got the fresh mutton. Dried meat was brought up in large quantities for the porters, and proved of the greatest use.

On the return, having received a full report from the reconnaissance party, we tackled in earnest the establishment of the different camps.

Camp III, which was under the North Col, was first established in full. This was to be our advance base of operations; and Mallory and Somervell established themselves there, their business being to make the road to the North Col while the rest of the Expedition was being pushed up to join them.

From *The Assault on Mount Everest: 1922.*

JAMES RAMSEY ULLMAN:

It was not until May tenth that Mallory and Somervell started out from the base camp. Considered the strongest climbers in the expedition, they had wisely been kept in reserve during the long grind of supply-packing, so that they might be fresh and fit when the time came for the real thing. Proceeding quickly and easily, they reached Camp I and pushed on up the East Rongbuk toward II and III.

GEORGE LEIGH-MALLORY:

By this time we had seen a good deal of the East Rongbuk Glacier. As we came up the moraine near its left bank we looked northwards on a remarkable scene. From the stony surface of the glacier fantastic pinnacles arose, a strange, gigantic company, gleaming white as they stood in some sort of order, divided by the definite lines of the moraines. Beyond

and above them was a vast mountain of reddish rock known
to us only by the triangulated height of its sharp summit,
marked in Wheeler's map as 23,180. The pinnacles became
more thickly crowded together as we mounted, until, as we
followed the bend southwards, individuals were lost in the
crowd and finally the crowd was merged in the great tumbled
sea of the glacier, now no longer dark with stones, but exhibit-
ing everywhere the bright surfaces of its steep and angry waves.
At Camp II we were surrounded on three sides by this amazing
world of ice. We lay in the shelter of a vertical cliff not less
than 60 feet high, sombrely cold in the evening shadow, daz-
zlingly white in the morning sun, and perfectly set off by the
frozen pool at its foot. Nothing, of course, was to be seen of
Mount Everest; the whole bulk of the North Peak stood in
front of it. But by mounting a few steps up some stony slopes
above us we could see to the south-east, over the surface of
the ice, the slopes coming down from the Lhapka La, from
which high pass we had looked down the East Rongbuk Glacier
in September, 1921, and observed the special whiteness of the
broken stream, at our own level now, and puzzled over its
curious course. We had yet another sight to cheer us as we
lay in our tents. On the range between us and the main Rongbuk Glacier stood, in the one direction of uninterrupted vision,
a peak of slender beauty, and as the moon rose its crests were
silver cords.

Next morning, May 12, according to Colonel Strutt's directions, we worked our way along the true left edge of the
glacier and the stones of its left bank. The problem here is to
avoid that tumbled sea of ice where no moraine can be continuously followed. Probably it would be possible to get
through this ice almost anywhere, for it is not an ice-fall, the
gradient is not steep, the pinnacles are not seracs, and there
are few crevasses: but much time and labour would be wasted
in attempting such a course. Further up the surface becomes

more even, and the reconnaissance party had reached this better surface by only a short and simple crossing of the rougher ice. We easily found the place, marked by a conspicuous cairn, where they had turned away from the bank. Their tracks on the glacier, though snow was lying in the hollows, were not easy to follow, and we quickly lost them; but presently we found another cairn built upon a single large stone, and here proceeded with confidence to cross a deep and wide trough of which we had been warned; and once this obstacle was overcome we knew no difficulty could impede our progress to Camp III. The laden porters, however, did not get along very easily. Their nails, for the most part, were worn smooth, and they found the ice too slippery. As I had never seen in the Alps a glacier-surface like this one I was greatly surprised by the nature of the bare ice. In a sense it was often extremely rough, with holes and minute watercourses having vertical sides 6 inches to 13 inches high; but the upper surfaces of the little knobs and plateaus intervening were extraordinarily hard and smooth and the colour was very much bluer than the usual granular surface of a dry glacier. It was also surprising to find at most a thin coating of fine snow as high as 20,500 feet; for in 1921 we had found, even before the first heavy snowfall, plenty of snow on the glaciers above 19,000 feet. For my part, with new nails in my boots, I was not troubled by the slippery surfaces. But we decided to supply the porters with crampons,* which they subsequently found very useful on this stage of the journey.

The situation of Camp III when we reached it early in the afternoon was not calculated to encourage me, though I suppose it might be found congenial by hardier men. We had turned the corner of the North Peak so that the steep slopes of its Eastern arm rose above us to North and West. Our tents were to be pitched on the stones that have rolled down these

* See Glossary, p. 398.—*Editor.*

slopes on to the glacier, and just out of range of a stone fall
from the rocks immediately above us. A shallow trough divided
us from the main plateau of the glacier, and up this trough the
wind was blowing; since the higher current was hurrying the
clouds from the normal direction, North-west, we might pre-
sume that this local variation was habitual. But wind we could
hardly expect to escape from one direction or another. A more
important consideration, perhaps, for a mountain camp is the
duration of sunshine. Here we should have the sun early, for
to the East we looked across a wide snowy basin to the comparatively low mountains round about the Lhakpa La; but we
should lose it early too, and we observed with dismay on this
first afternoon that our camp was in shadow at 3.15 p.m. The
water supply was conveniently near, running in a trough, and
we might expect it to be unfrozen for several hours each day.

Whatever we might think of this place it was undoubtedly
the best available. Very little energy remained among the
party, most of whom had now reached 21,000 feet for the first
time in their lives. However, a number soon set to work level-
ling the ground which we chose for two tents. It was necessary
to do this work thoroughly, for, unlike the smooth, flat stones
at Camp I, these, like those at Camp II, of which we had obtained sufficient experience during the previous night, were extremely sharp and uncomfortable to lie on. After it was done
we sent down the main body of the porters, keeping only one
man for cook and each the man specially attached to him as
servant by Geoffrey Bruce's command long ago in Darjeeling.
With these we proceeded to order our camp. The tents were
pitched, some sort of a cookhouse was constructed from the
wealth of building material, and we also began to put up walls
behind which we could lie in shelter to eat our meals. Perhaps
the most important matter was the instruction of Pou, our cook,
in the correct use of the Primus stove; with the purpose of giving him confidence a fine fountain of blazing paraffin was ar-

ranged and at once extinguished by opening the safety valve; for the conservation of our fuel supply we carefully showed him how the absolute alcohol must be used to warm the burner while paraffin and petrol were to be mixed for combustion. Fortunately his intelligence rose above those disagreeable agitations which attend the roaring or the failure to roar of Primus stoves, so that after these first explanations we had never again to begrime our hands with paraffin and soot.

In our tent this evening of May 12, Somervell and I discussed what we should do. There was something to be said for taking a day's rest at this altitude before attempting to rise another 2,000 feet. Neither of us felt at his best. After our first activities in camp I had made myself comfortable with my legs in a sleeping-bag, Somervell with his accustomed energy had been exploring at some distance—he had walked as far as the broad pass on the far side of our snowy basin, the Rápiu La, at the foot of Everest's North-east ridge, and had already begun a sketch of the wonderful view obtained from that point of Makalu. When he returned to camp about 5.30 p.m. he was suffering from a headache and made a poor supper. Moreover, we were full of doubts about the way up to the North Col. After finding so much ice on the glacier we must expect to find ice on those East-facing slopes below the Col. It was not unlikely that we should be compelled to cut steps the whole way up, and several days would be required for so arduous a task. We decided therefore to lose no time in establishing a track to the North Col.

It was our intention on the following morning, May 13, to take with us two available porters, leaving only our cook in camp, and so make a small beginning towards the supply of our next camp. But Somervell's man was sick and could not come with us. We set out in good time with only my porter, Dasno, and carried with us, besides one small tent, a large coil of spare rope and some wooden pegs about 18 inches long. As we made our way up the gently sloping snow it was easy to distinguish the line followed to the North Col after the monsoon last year—a long slope at a fairly easy angle bearing away to the right, or North, a traverse to the left, and a steep slope leading up to the shelf under the ice-cliff on the skyline. With the sun behind us we saw the first long slope, nearly 1,000 feet, glittering in a way that snow will never glitter; there we should find only blue ice, bare and hard. Further to the North was no better, and as we looked at the steep final slope it became plain enough that there and nowhere else was the necessary key to the whole ascent; for to the South of an imaginary vertical line drawn below it was a hopeless series of impassable cliffs. The more we thought about it the more convinced we became that an alternative way must be found up to this final slope. We had not merely to reach the North Col once: whatever way we chose must be used for all the comings and goings to and from a camp up there. Unless the connection between Camps III and IV were free from serious obstacles, the whole problem of transport would increase enormously in difficulty; every party of porters must be escorted by climbers both up and down, and even so the dangers on a big ice slope after a fall of snow would hardly be avoided.

Endeavouring to trace out a satisfactory route from the shelf of the North Col downwards, we soon determined that we should make use of a sloping corridor lying some distance to the left of the icy line used last year and apparently well covered with snow. For 300 or 400 feet above the flat snowfield it appeared to be cut off by very steep ice-slopes; nevertheless the best hope was to attempt an approach more or less direct to the foot of this corridor; and first we must reconnoitre the steepest of these obstacles, which promised the most convenient access to the desired point could we climb it. Here fortune favoured our enterprise. We found the surface slightly cleft by a fissure slanting at first to the right and then directly upwards. In the disintegrated substance of its edges it was hardly necessary to cut steps, and we mounted 250 feet of what threatened to be formidable ice with no great expenditure of time and energy. Two lengths of rope were now fixed for the security of future parties, the one hanging directly downwards from a single wooden peg driven in almost to the head, and another on a series of pegs for the passage of a leftward traverse which brought us to the edge of a large crevasse. We were now able to let ourselves down into the snow which choked this crevasse a little distance below its edges, and by means of some large steps hewn in the walls and another length of rope a satisfactory crossing was established. Above this crevasse we mounted easy snow to the corridor.

So far as the shelf which was our objective we now met no serious difficulty. The gentle angle steepened for a short space where we were obliged to cut a score of steps in hard ice; we fixed another length of rope, and again the final slope was steep, but not so as to trouble us. However, the condition of the snow was not perfect; we were surprised, on a face where so much ice appeared, to find any snow that was not perfectly hard; and yet we were usually breaking a heavy crust and stamping down the steps in snow deep enough to cover our ankles. It was a question rather of strength than of skill. An East-facing slope in the heat and glare of the morning sun favours the enemy mountain-sickness, and though no one of us three was sick our lassitude increased continually as we mounted and it required as much energy as we could muster to keep on stamping slowly upwards.

From *The Assault on Mount Everest: 1922.*

JAMES RAMSEY ULLMAN:

Mallory, Somervell, and Dasno reached the col without mishap, and during the succeeding days long files of porters followed the trail that they had blazed, carrying up loads for the establishment of Camp IV, near the crest. Now the time for the assault on Everest proper had at last arrived. Mallory, Somervell, Norton, and Morshead were selected for the first attempt, and on May seventeenth the four climbers occupied Camp IV and busied themselves with their final preparations. The cold was almost unendurable; the wild west wind roared down upon them like an invisible avalanche; and their goal was still 6000 feet above them, remote and tantalizing in the sky. But their hopes and hearts were high. "No end," wrote Mallory in his diary, "is visible or even conceivable to this kingdom of adventure."

T. Howard Somervell:

At length, the camp on the North Col at 23,000 feet was established. There were four tents, each capable of holding two people, and a few porters' tents besides. In fact, it was a quite considerable encampment. But we had already taken a long time. The North Col was not hospitable enough, and not sufficiently equipped, to permit of any attempts on the climbing of the mountain until May 20th.

Life at No. 3 Camp had become irksome. Mallory and I had made two expeditions with carrying parties to the North Col, including the actual blazing of the trail thither. Of this last, my chief recollection is of pounding through deep snow, taking turns with Mallory to go first and do the donkey-work. While on this job I remember breathlessness, fatigue, and a longing that my demeanour should not betray my feelings—to an extent to which I have never felt it before or since, not even whilst actually climbing Everest itself.

We were at first insufficiently acclimatised, but a few rather wearisome days, of lying in the tent awaiting the next meal, or going short walks and ski-runs on the glacier, soon put this right. We were really pretty fit when we started in earnest to do the actual climbing, exactly one week after we had felt so breathless on the way up to the North Col.

We had decided, on the advice of Strutt, that Mallory, Morshead, Norton, and I should make the first attempt on the peak, and with hearts full of anticipation we trudged up the slopes of snow and ice which led to our camp at 23,000 feet. We spent a good night at this camp, with excellent and varied food, starting off on a fine, calm morning to get, if possible, 2,000 feet higher and there pitch a couple of small tents. We had filled half a dozen thermos flasks with hot coffee and other liquids, made from snow melted the previous night, and we had roused our porters, discovering that only four of them were fit to accompany us. However, these four stalwarts were sufficient to carry the required loads. We had no time to be pessimistic over the fact (which we hardly realized at the time) that all our reserves of porters were exhausted before we had set foot on the mountain itself.

We all carried rucksacks full of warm clothes, a little food and drink, and, in my case, sketching materials and a vest-pocket Kodak, with which all my photographs were obtained.

My first recollection of the actual ascent was the suddenness with which the west wind sprang up. We stepped onwards up the easy shoulder of the north-east ridge, which was covered in places with good, firm snow. On the lower part of this ridge we kicked steps, but on the upper and steeper portion it became necessary to use the axe; progress was rapid, a single chip or two being all that was required.

As soon as we were conveniently able to get off to the left (east) side of the ridge we did so to avoid the wind. At a height of some 24,500 feet we traversed on rough rocks and over snow-filled gullies to attain a stony slope (25,000 feet *)

* By now they were already higher than man had ever climbed before. —*Editor.*

at an angle of about thirty degrees. This could not be called an ideal camping ground; but everything else was steeper and more rocky. So we built two little platforms and pitched our tiny camp, weighting the tent-ropes with large stones, as pegs would have been useless, and here, after pemmican soup and coffee, we proceeded to spend the most uncomfortable of nights, two of us in each tent. Wherever we lay, and in whatever position, there were always a few sharp stones sticking into the tenderest parts of our anatomy. We obtained sleep in snatches of the most fitful and unresting variety, so much so that on the following morning we were quite glad to get up and stand on our less tender feet.

When we crawled out of our shelters we had a bitter disappointment. The wind was not too bad, but fresh snow had fallen during the night, and our chances of getting to the top seemed very doubtful. Moreover, we had gone only a hundred yards or so when Morshead announced that he was not feeling at all well, and could not come with us. We knew that it was unwise for him to overtax his strength, and we knew Morshead well enough to realize that if he complained of his health he must feel pretty bad; so we went on without him, leaving him to go back to his tent and there to await our return.

For six hours or more we climbed steadily on, taking the lead by turns, as we did on all our climbs, thus sharing the responsibility and fatigue in truly democratic manner. We could progress only some 300 feet* in an hour, and every attempt to go faster than this for a few yards was perforce followed by a rest for a minute or so in order to regain breath enough to proceed. Our tempers were getting a bit edgy, and though no actual quarrels broke out, we were each feeling definitely quarrelsome. Our intelligence, too, was not at concert pitch. When, at a height of just under 27,000 feet, we discussed

* Of vertical height.

whether we should go farther or not, we chose the course of wisdom and retreat with the minimum of regret at not having reached the top of the mountain.

It was obvious that we must get back to Morshead in time to take him back to the North Col before nightfall if possible. The decision to go down at 2.30, wherever we might be at that time, had been made without disappointment and without disagreement. It was the right decision. Another night at 25,000 feet might have made it well-nigh impossible for Morshead to walk at all. That meant a risk of his losing his life, for the active movement of body and limbs is the surest preventive of frostbite, and a certain prophylactic against being frozen to death. At 2.30 we had reached a sheltered ledge behind a large rock. Here we stopped for half an hour to eat, do a rapid sketch, and take some photographs.

Truly the view was magnificent, and the north peak of Everest, itself 1,000 feet higher than the highest summit previously attained by man, was almost another 2,000 feet below us. Away to the north, beyond the cloudy and unsettled weather of southern Tibet, was a range of snow-covered peaks, some 80 miles distant. In the foreground Cho Uyo and Gyachung Kang, only 10 miles from us and each over 26,000 feet high, were actually below the place where we stood. Of all the mountains we could see that day, only Everest, the one we were on, was higher than ourselves. However irritable and unintelligent we may have been rendered by the altitude, we were all enthralled by the magnificence of the view.

Yet we could not stay to enjoy it too long, and down we went, following our tracks, to the little camp 2,000 feet below. Morshead was not too bad—or so he told us with his wonted optimism; but he was by no means fit, and we started off right away in order to get back to No. 4 Camp at the North Col before nightfall. The fresh snow had obliterated our tracks of the previous day, and we made a mistake which almost cost us our lives in traversing back to the ridge at too low a level.

I was going last, and Mallory first, at a place where we had to cross the steep head of a long, wide couloir which swept down to the foot of the mountain, 3,000 feet below us. The man in front of me slipped at a time when I was just moving myself, and I, too, was jerked out of my steps. Both of us began sliding at increasing speed down the icy couloir. The second man checked our progress for a moment, but could not hold us. He, too, was dragged off his feet. But Mallory had had just enough time to prepare for a pull on the rope, digging his axe firmly into the hard snow. It held, and so did the rope, and the party was saved.

I remember having no thought of danger or impending disaster, but experimenting, as I slipped down, as to whether I could control my pace with the pick of my axe in the snow and ice of the couloir, and whether the rest of us could do so, too. I had just decided that my pace was constant, and was not accelerating, and was feeling rather pleased with myself when the rope pulled me up with a jerk. My experiment was stopped, for Mallory had saved my life and the lives of us all. It is strange how much of one's common sense and judgment is warped by the effects of high altitude; but, looking back on the incident, which we hardly noticed at the time, I am convinced that, by having the time and sense to do the right thing, Mallory prevented a serious disaster that day.

Chastened, and cursing at the effort required, those of us who had fallen kicked steps wearily in the snow and slowly ascended to join Mallory on his sound stance. From then onwards we were much more cautious. This was doubly necessary, for Morshead, though he stoutly endeavoured to appear normal, was obviously getting worse every minute, and we soon discovered that he had hardly the strength to walk. He kept suggesting a glissade or a slide, either of which might have spelt disaster to him, if not to us all. We had to use every possible persuasion to keep him moving and using his legs, and he was getting worse and worse. It was now dark and we were still some distance from the tents on the Col. A jump of 10 feet down an ice-cliff was successfully negotiated, Morshead being lowered on the rope. On we went through deeper snow, pushing and pulling our invalid, who persisted that he was all right, but was obviously not far from death.

We reached the tents at about ten o'clock—not a moment too soon. A great disappointment awaited us. We found all sorts of food, but no sign of stove or fuel. What had they done? Where had they put the stove before they left the camp in readiness for us to occupy? We were so indescribably thirsty that to eat a single morsel of food without a drink was unthinkable. And would Morshead last until the morning without sustenance?

A few spoonfuls of strawberry jam, to stave off danger of actual collapse from hunger, were all that we could manage without liquid refreshment, and on the next morning we hurried down to No. 3 Camp. Again we were forced to use the utmost caution, for in many places an avalanche of the newly fallen snow seemed almost inevitable. Fortunately it never occurred, and before noon the four of us trudged into the camp on the glacier, all alive, but one of us only just snatched from death and already badly frostbitten in all his fingers and toes.

The lesson we learned from this episode is that a camp to which a party is returning, or is likely to return, should never be left unsupported. Did the Nanga Parbat Expedition of 1934 realize this? * If they had acted upon it, the appalling disaster they underwent would most probably never have occurred.

What Morshead suffered during the next few weeks will never be known. Although outwardly and in company he was

* See Introduction, p. 11. Somervell's reminiscences of the 1922 Everest climb were written many years afterward.—*Editor.*

always cheerful, yet he used to get away by himself as often as he could, and cry like a child. After two months of torture his hands and feet cleared up, and though he lost portions of most of his fingers he was not seriously crippled. He was a stout fellow, an ideal member of a party of adventurers. Nevertheless, on the outing just recounted, he was at grips with death. Fortunately, we all realized it, or we might have been just a little careless or thoughtless, and given death the victory.

Anyway, we all arrived at No. 3 Camp alive—but with what a thirst! For thirty-six hours we had been struggling and panting in a dry, cold climate, losing pints of water from our lungs, and without any drink to repair the deficiency. I have never been so thirsty in my life; they tell me that I had seventeen large cups of tea without stirring from my seat. I expect we all did much the same.

From *After Everest.*

JAMES RAMSEY ULLMAN:

The campaign for Everest involved skill and courage, struggle and danger, but it included other, homelier ingredients as well: food, drink, sleep, and at least the rudimentary human amenities. Lest anyone labor under the misapprehension that these Everesters were either supermen who despised such matters, or robots who ignored them, the following excerpts from Mallory's accounts should help keep the record straight. The second objective on any mountain is to reach the summit. The first is to keep fed and warm—and sane.

GEORGE LEIGH-MALLORY:

Food

Morshead and Somervell had not long returned, after duly fixing the rope, before our meal was ready. As I have already referred to our table manners, the more delicate-minded among my readers may not relish the spectacle of us four feasting around our cooking-pots—in which case I caution them to omit this paragraph, for now, living up to my own standard of faithful narrative, I must honestly and courageously face the subject of victuals. As mankind is agreed that the pleasures of the senses, when it is impossible they should be actually experienced, can most nearly be tasted by exercising an artistic faculty in choosing the dishes of imaginary repasts, so it might be supposed that the state of affairs, when those pleasures were thousands of feet below in other worlds, might more easily be brought to mind by reconstructing the associated menus. But such a practice was unfortunately out of the question, for it would have involved assigning this, that, and the other to breakfast, lunch, and supper; and when, calling to mind what we ate, I try to distinguish between one meal and another, I am altogether at a loss. I can only suppose that they were interchangeable. The nature of our supplies confirms my belief that this was the case. Practically speaking, we hardly considered by which name our meal should be called, but only what would seem nice to eat or convenient to produce, when we next wanted food and drink. Among the supplies I classify some as "standard pattern"—such things as we knew were always to be had in abundance, the "pièce," as it were, of our whole ménage—three solid foods, two liquid foods, and one stimulant.

The stimulant, in the first place, as long as we remained at Camp III, was amazingly satisfactory, both for its kind, its quality, and especially for its abundance. We took it shamelessly before breakfast, and at breakfast again; occasionally with or after lunch, and most usually a little time before supper, when it was known as afternoon tea. The longer we stayed at this camp, the deeper were our potations. So good was the tea that I came almost to disregard the objectionable flavour of tinned milk in it. I had always supposed that General Bruce would keep a special herd of yaks at the Base Camp for the provision of fresh milk; but this scheme was hardly practicable, for the only grass at the Base Camp grew under canvas, and no one suggested sharing his tent with a yak. The one trouble about our stimulant was its scarcity as we proceeded up the mountain. It diminished instead of increasing to the climax where it was needed most. Fortunately, the lower temperatures at which water boils as the atmospheric pressure diminishes made no appreciable difference to the quality, and the difficulty of melting snow enough to fill our saucepans with water was set off to some extent by increasing the quantity of tea-leaves.

The two liquid foods, cocoa and pea-soup, though not imbibed so plentifully as tea, were considered no less as the natural and fitting companions of meat on any and every occasion. At Camp III it was not unusual to begin supper with pea-soup and end it with cocoa, but such a custom by no means precluded their use at other times. Cocoa tended to fall in my esteem, though it never lost a certain popularity. Pea-soup, on the other hand, had a growing reputation, and, from being considered an accessory, came to be regarded as a principal. However, before I describe its dominating influence on the whole matter of diet, I must mention the solid foods. The three of "standard pattern" were ration biscuits, ham, and cheese. It was no misfortune to find above the Base Camp that we had left the region of fancy breads; for while the chupatis and scones, baked by our cooks with such surprising skill and energy, were usually palatable, they were probably more difficult of digestion than the biscuits, and our appetite for these hard whole-meal biscuits increased as we went upwards, possibly to the detriment of teeth, which became ever more brittle. Ham, of all foods, was the most generally acceptable. The quality of our "Hunter's hams" left nothing to be desired, and the supply, apparently, was inexhaustible. A slice of ham, or several slices, either cold or fried, was fit food for any and almost every meal. The cheeses supplied for our use at these higher camps, and for expeditions on the mountains besides, were always delicious and freely eaten. We had also a considerable variety of other tinned foods. Harris's sausages, sardines, herrings, sliced bacon, soups, ox tongues, green vegetables, both peas and beans, all these I remember in general use at Camp III. We were never short of jam and chocolate. As luxuries we had "quails in truffles," besides various sweet-stuffs, such as mixed biscuits, acid drops, crystallized ginger, figs and prunes (I feel greedy again as I name them), and, reserved more or less for use at the highest camps, Heinz's spaghetti. More important, perhaps, than any of these was "Army and Navy Rations," from the special use we made of it. I never quite made out what these tins contained; they were designed to be, when heated up, a rich stew of mutton or beef, or both. They were used by us to enrich a stew which was the peculiar invention of Morshead. He called it "hoosch." Like a trained chef, he was well aware that "the foundation of good cooking is the stock-pot." But such a maxim was decidedly depressing under our circumstances. Instead of accepting and regretting our want of a "stock-pot," Morshead, with the true genius that penetrates to the inward truth, devised a substitute and improved the motto: "The foundation of every dish must be pea-soup." Or if these were not his very words, it was easy to deduce that they contained the substance of his culinary thoughts. It was a corollary of this axiom that any and every available solid food might be used to stew with pea-soup. The process of selection tended to emphasize the merits of some as compared with other solids until it became almost a custom, sadly to the limitation of Morshead's art, to prefer to "sliced bacon," or even sausages, for the flotsam and jetsam of "hoosch," Army and Navy Rations. It was "hoosch" that we ate at Camp IV, about the hour of an early afternoon tea on May 19.

More Food

Had we known what was yet in store for us, or rather what was not in store, we might have waited a little longer for so emphatic an exclamation.* We were in need of food, and no solid food could be eaten until something had been done towards satisfying our thirst. It was not that one felt, at least I did not feel, a desire to drink; but the long effort of the lungs during the day in a rarefied atmosphere where evaporation is so rapid had deprived the body of moisture to such an extent that it was impossible to swallow, for instance, a ration biscuit. We must first melt snow and have water. But where were the cooking pots? We searched the tents without finding a trace of them. Presumably the porters whom we had expected to find here had taken them down to Camp III in error. As we sat slowly unlacing our boots within the tents, it was impossible to believe in this last misfortune. We waited for a brain-wave; but no way could be devised of melting snow without a vessel. Still supperless, we wriggled into our sleeping-bags. And then something happened in Norton's head. In his visions of all that was succulent and juicy and fit to be swallowed with ease and pleasure there had suddenly appeared an ice-cream. It was this that he now proposed to us; we had the means at hand to make ice-creams, he said. A tin of strawberry jam was opened; frozen Ideal Milk was hacked out of another; these two ingredients were mixed with snow, and it only remained to eat the compound. To my companions this seemed an easy matter; their appetite for strawberry cream ice was hardly nice to watch. I too managed to swallow down a little before the deadly sickliness of the stuff disgusted me. My gratitude to Norton was afterwards cooled by disagreeable sensations. In the last drowsy

* A group of climbers had just reached one of the camps with a fervent "Thank God!"—*Editor.*

moments before complete forgetfulness I was convulsed by shudderings which I was powerless to control; the muscles of my back seemed to be contracted with cramp; and, short of breath, I was repeatedly obliged to raise myself on my elbows and start again that solemn exercise of deep-breathing as though the habit had become indispensable.

Drink

The beneficent superiority with which we now regarded the whole world except Mount Everest no doubt helped us to swallow our luncheon—or was it dinner?—a difficult matter, for our tongues were hanging out after so much exercise of breathing. We had no chance of finding a trickle here as one often may in the blessed Alps; and medical opinion, which knew all about what was good for us, frowned upon the notion of alcoholic stimulant for a climber in distress at high altitude. And so, very naturally, when one of us (Be of good cheer, my friend, I won't give you away!) produced from his pocket a flask of Brandy—each of us took a little nip. I am glad to relate that the result was excellent; it is logically certain therefore that the Brandy contained no alcohol. The non-alcoholic Brandy, then, no doubt by reason of what it lacked, had an important spiritual effect; it gave us just the mental fillip which we required to pull ourselves together for the descent.

Sleep

To the civilized man who gets into bed after the customary routine, tucks himself in, lays his head on the pillow, and presently goes to sleep with no further worry, the dispositions in a climber's tent may seem to be strangely intricate. In the first place, he has to arrange about his boots. He looks forward to the time when he will have to start next morning, if possible with warm feet and in boots not altogether frozen stiff. He may choose to go to bed in his boots, not altogether approving the practice, and resolving that the habit shall not be allowed to grow upon him. If his feet are already warm when he turns in, it may be that he can do no better; his feet will probably keep warm in the sleeping-bag if he wears his bed-socks over his boots, and he will not have to endure the pains of pulling on and wearing frozen boots in the morning. At this camp I adopted a different plan—to wear moccasins instead of boots during the night and keep them on until the last moment before starting. But if one takes his boots off, where is he to keep them warm? Climbing boots are not good to cuddle, and in any case there will be no room for them with two now inside a double sleeping-bag. My boots were happily accommodated in a rucksack and I put them under my head for a pillow. It is not often that one uses the head for warming things, and no one would suspect one of a hot head; nevertheless my boots were kept warm enough and were scarcely frozen in the morning.

It was all-important besides to make ourselves really comfortable, if we were to get to sleep, by making experiments in the disposition of limbs, adjusting the floor if possible and arranging one's pillow at exactly the right level—which may be difficult, as the pillow should be high if one is to breathe easily at a great altitude. I had already found out exactly how to be comfortable before Norton was ready to share the accommodation. I remarked that in our double sleeping-bag I found ample room for myself but not much to spare. Norton's entrance was a grievous disturbance. It was doubtful for some time whether he would be able to enter; considering how long and slim he is, it is astonishing how much room he requires. We were so tightly pressed together that if either was to move a corresponding manœuvre was required of the other. I soon discovered, as the chief item of interest in the place where I lay, a certain boulder obstinately immovable and excruciatingly sharp which came up between my shoulder-blades. How under these circumstances we achieved sleep, and I believe that both of us were sometimes unconscious in a sort of light, intermittent slumber, I cannot attempt to explain. Perhaps the fact that one was often breathless from the exhaustion of discomfort, and was obliged to breathe deeply, helped one to sleep, as deep breathing often will. Perhaps the necessity of lying still because it was so difficult to move was good for us in the end. Norton's case was worse than mine. One of his ears had been severely frost-bitten on the way up; only one side was available to lie on; and yet the blessed sleep we sometimes sigh for in easy beds at home visited him too.

Talk

I often remarked during the Expedition how large a part of a day had been spent by some of us in conversation. Down at the Base Camp we would often sit on, those of us who were no expert photographers, or painters, or naturalists, sit indefinitely not only after dinner, but after each succeeding meal, talking the hours away. When a man has learned to deal firmly with an imperious conscience, he will be neither surprised nor ashamed in such circumstances to enter in his diary, "so many hours talking and listening." It is true that conscience has the right to demand, in the case of such an entry, that the subjects talked of should also be named. But our company was able to draw upon so wide a range of experience that a fair proportion of our subjects were worth talking of. Perhaps in the higher camps there was a tendency to talk, though from less active brains, for the sake of obliterating the sense of discomfort. However, I believe that most men, once they have faced the change from armchairs and spring mattresses, and solid walls and hot baths, and drawers for their clothes and shelves for their books, do not experience discomfort in camp life except in the matter of feeding.

But to return to the subject from which I have naughtily digressed, time passed swiftly enough for Somervell and me at Camp III. We did not keep the ball rolling so rapidly and continuously to and fro as it was wont to roll in the united Mess; but we found plenty to say to one another, more particularly after supper, in the tent. We entered upon a serious discussion of our future prospects on Mount Everest, and were both feeling so brave and hardy after a day's rest that we decided, if necessary, to meet the transport difficulty half-way and do without a tent in any camp we should establish above the North Col, and so reduce the burden to be carried up to Camp IV to three rather light or two rather heavy loads. Our conversation was further stimulated by two little volumes which I had brought up with me, the one Robert Bridges' anthology, *The Spirit of Man*, and the other one-seventh of the complete works of William Shakespeare, including *Hamlet* and *King Lear*. It was interesting to test the choice made in answer to the old question, "What book would you take to a desert island?" though in this case it was a desert glacier, and the situation demanded rather lighter literature than prolonged edification might require on the island. The trouble about lighter literature is that it weighs heavier because more has to be provided. Neither of my books would be to every one's taste in a camp at 21,000 feet; but *The Spirit of Man* read aloud now by one of us and now by the other, suggested matters undreamt of in the philosophy of Mount Everest, and enabled us to spend one evening very agreeably. On another occasion I had the good fortune to open my Shakespeare at the very place where Hamlet addresses the ghost. "Angels and Ministers of Grace defend us," I began, and the theme was so congenial that we stumbled on enthusiastically reading the parts in turn through half the play.

From *The Assault on Mount Everest: 1922.*

JAMES RAMSEY ULLMAN:

The first attempt on Everest had carried to a new altitude record of almost 27,000 feet; but it was still more than 2,000 feet short of the summit, and the challengers were not minded to call it quits without another try. As the exhausted first party stumbled down the snow-slope from Camp IV to the glacier, they were passed by the second party, going up. This was composed of only two climbers, George Finch and Geoffrey Bruce, and, unlike the first group, they were planning to make their try with the aid of oxygen.

CAPT. GEORGE FINCH:

On May 24, Captain Noel, Tejbir,* Geoffrey Bruce, and I, all using oxygen, went up to the North Col (23,000 feet). Bent on a determined attack, we camped there for the night. Morning broke fine and clear though somewhat windy, and at eight o'clock we sent off up the long snow-slopes leading towards the North-east shoulder of Mount Everest, twelve porters carrying oxygen cylinders, provisions for one day, and camping gear. An hour and a half later, Bruce, Tejbir, and I followed, and, in spite of the fact that each bore a load of over 30 lb., which was much more than the average weight carried by the porters, we overtook them at a height of about 24,500 feet. They greeted our arrival with their usual cheery, broad grins. But no longer did they regard oxygen as a foolish man's whim; one and all appreciated the advantages of what they naïvely chose to call "English air." Leaving them to follow, we went

* A Gurkha N.C.O.—*Editor.*

on, hoping to pitch our camp somewhere above 26,000 feet. But shortly after one o'clock the wind freshened up rather offensively, and it began to snow. Our altitude was 25,500 feet, some 500 feet below where we had hoped to camp, but we looked round immediately for a suitable camping site, as the porters had to return to the North Col that day, and persistence in proceeding further would have run them unjustifiably into danger. This I would under no circumstances do, for I felt responsible for these cheerful, smiling, willing men, who looked up to their leader and placed in him the complete trust of little children. As it was, the margin of safety secured by pitching camp where we did instead of at a higher elevation was none too wide; for before the last porter had departed downwards the weather had become very threatening. A cheerful spot in which to find space to pitch a tent it was not; but though I climbed a couple of hundred feet or so further up the ridge, nothing more suitable was to be found. Remembering that a wind is felt more severely on the windward side of a ridge than on the crest, a possible position to the West of the ridge was negatived in favour of one on the very backbone. The leeside was bare of any possible camping place within reasonable distance. Our porters arrived at 2 p.m., and at once all began to level off the little platform where the tent was soon pitched, on the very edge of the tremendous precipices falling away to the East Rongbuk and Main Rongbuk Glaciers, over 4,000 feet below. Within twenty minutes the porters were scurrying back down the broken, rocky ridge towards the snow-slopes leading to the North Col, singing, as they went, snatches of their native hillside ditties. What splendid men! Having seen the last man safely off, I looked to the security of the guy-ropes holding down the tent, and then joined Bruce and Tejbir inside. It was snowing hard. Tiny, minute spicules driven by the wind penetrated everywhere. It was bitterly cold, so we crawled into our sleeping-bags, and, gathering round us

"Tigers."

North Col camp and the northeast ridge.

all available clothing, huddled up together as snugly as was possible.

With the help of solidified spirit we melted snow and cooked a warm meal, which imparted some small measure of comfort to our chilled bodies. A really hot drink was not procurable, for the simple reason that at such an altitude water boils at so low a temperature that one can immerse a hand in it without fear of being scalded. Over a *post-prandium* cigarette,* Bruce and I discussed our prospects of success. Knowing that no man can put forward his best effort unless his confidence is an established fact, the trend of my contribution to the conversation was chiefly, "Of course, we shall get to the top." After sunset, the storm rose to a gale, a term I use deliberately. Terrific gusts tore at our tent with such ferocity that the ground-sheet with its human burden was frequently lifted up off the ground. On these occasions our combined efforts were needed to keep the tent down and prevent its being blown away. Although we had blocked up the few very small openings in the tent to the best of our powers, long before midnight we were all thickly covered in a fine frozen spindrift that somehow or other was blown in upon us, insinuating its way into sleeping-bags and clothing, there to cause acute discomfort. Sleep was out of the question. We dared not relax our vigilance, for ever and again all our strength was needed to hold the tent down and to keep the flaps of the door, stripped of their fastenings by a gust that had caught us unawares, from being torn open. We fought for our lives, realising that once the wind got our little shelter into its ruthless grip, it must inevitably be hurled, with us inside it, down on the East Rongbuk Glacier, thousands of feet below.

And what of my companions in the tent? To me, who had

---

* Some of the climbers could not smoke at all at high altitudes. Others —Finch among them—found tobacco not merely uninjurious but actually an aid to breathing.—*Editor.*

certainly passed his novitiate in the hardships of mountaineering, the situation was more than alarming. About Tejbir I had no concern; he placed complete confidence in his sahibs, and the ready grin never left his face. But it was Bruce's first experience of mountaineering, and how the ordeal would affect him I did not know. I might have spared myself all anxiety. Throughout the whole adventure he bore himself in a manner that would have done credit to the finest of veteran mountaineers, and returned my confidence with a cheerfulness that rang too true to be counterfeit. By one o'clock on the morning of the 26th the gale reached its maximum. The wild flapping of the canvas made a noise like that of machine-gun fire. So deafening was it that we could scarcely hear each other speak. Later, there came interludes of comparative lull, succeeded by bursts of storm more furious than ever. During such lulls we took it in turn to go outside to tighten up slackened guy-ropes, and also succeeded in tying down the tent more firmly with our Alpine rope. It was impossible to work in the open for more than three or four minutes at a stretch, so profound was the exhaustion induced by this brief exposure to the fierce cold wind. But with the Alpine rope taking some of the strain, we enjoyed a sense of security which, though probably only illusory, allowed us all a few sorely needed moments of rest.

Dawn broke bleak and chill; the snow had ceased to fall, but the wind continued with unabated violence. Once more we had to take it in turns to venture without and tighten up the guy-ropes, and to try to build on the windward side of the tent a small wall of stones as an additional protection. The extreme exhaustion and the chill produced in the body as a result of each of these little excursions were sufficient to indicate that, until the gale had spent itself, there could be no hope of either advance or retreat. As the weary morning hours dragged on, we believed we could detect a slackening off in the storm. And I was thankful, for I was beginning quietly to wonder how much longer human beings could stand the strain. We prepared another meal. The dancing flames of the spirit stove caused me anxiety bordering on anguish lest the tent, a frail shelter between life and death, should catch fire. At noon the storm once more regained its strength and rose to unsurpassed fury. A great hole was cut by a stone in one side of the tent, and our situation thus unexpectedly became more desperate than ever.

But we carried on, making the best of our predicament until, at one o'clock, the wind dropped suddenly from a blustering gale to nothing more than a stiff breeze. Now was the opportunity for a retreat to the safety of the North Col camp. But I wanted to hang on and try our climb on the following day. Very cautiously and tentatively I broached my wish to Bruce, fearful lest the trying experience of the last twenty-four hours had undermined his keenness for further adventure. Once again might I have spared myself all anxiety. He jumped at the idea, and when our new plans were communicated to Tejbir, the only effect upon him was to broaden his already expansive grin.

It was a merry little party that gathered round to a scanty evening meal cooked with the last of our fuel. The meal was meagre for the simple reason that we had catered for only one day's short rations, and we were now very much on starvation diet. We had hardly settled down for another night when, about 6 p.m., voices were heard outside. Our unexpected visitors were porters, who, anxious as to our safety, had left the North Col that afternoon when the storm subsided. With them they brought thermos flasks of hot beef-tea and tea provided by the thoughtful Noel. Having accepted these most gratefully, we sent the porters back without loss of time.

That night began critically. We were exhausted by our previous experiences and through lack of sufficient food. Tejbir's grin lost some of its expanse. On the face of Geoffrey Bruce, courageously cheerful as ever, was a strained, drawn expression that I did not like. Provoked, perhaps, by my labours outside the tent, a dead, numbing cold was creeping up my limbs—a thing I had only once before felt and to the seriousness of which I was fully alive. Something had to be done. Like an inspiration came the thought of trying the effect of oxygen. We hauled an apparatus and cylinders into the tent, and, giving it the air of a joke, we took doses all round. Tejbir took his medicine reluctantly, but with relief I saw his face brighten up. The effect on Bruce was visible in his rapid change of expression. A few minutes after the first deep breath, I felt the tingling sensation of returning life and warmth to my limbs. We connected up the apparatus in such a way that we could breathe a small quantity throughout the night. The result was marvellous. We slept well and warmly. Whenever the tube delivering the gas fell out of Bruce's mouth as he slept, I could see him stir uneasily in the uric, greenish light of the moon as it filtered through the canvas. Then half unconsciously replacing the tube, he would fall once more into a peaceful slumber. There is little doubt that it was the use of oxygen which saved our lives during this second night in our high camp.

Before daybreak we were up, and proceeded to make ready for our climb. Putting on our boots was a struggle. Mine I had taken to bed with me, and a quarter of an hour's striving and tugging sufficed to get them on. But Bruce's and Tejbir's were frozen solid, and it took them more than an hour to mould them into shape by holding them over lighted candles. Shortly after six we assembled outside. Some little delay was incurred in arranging the rope and our loads, but at length at 6:30 a.m., soon after the first rays of the sun struck the tent, we shouldered our bundles and set off. What with cameras, thermos bottles, and oxygen apparatus, Bruce and I each carried well over 40 lb.; Tejbir with two extra cylinders of oxygen shouldered a burden of about 50 lb.

Our scheme of attack was to take Tejbir with us as far as the North-east shoulder, there to relieve him of his load and send him back. The weather was clear. The only clouds seemed so far off as to presage no evil, and the breeze, though intensely cold, was bearable. But it soon freshened up, and before we had gone more than a few hundred feet the cold began to have its effect on Tejbir's sturdy constitution, and he showed signs of wavering. Bruce's eloquent flow of Gurumuki, however, managed to boost him up to an altitude of 26,000 feet. There he collapsed entirely, sinking face downwards on to the rocks and crushing beneath him the delicate instruments of his oxygen apparatus. I stormed at him for thus maltreating it, while Bruce exhorted him for the honour of his regiment to struggle on; but it was all in vain. Tejbir had done his best; and he has every right to be proud of the fact that he has climbed to a far greater height than any other native. We pulled him off his apparatus and, relieving him of some cylinders, cheered him up sufficiently to start him with enough oxygen on his way back to the high camp, there to await our return. We had no compunction about letting him go alone, for the ground was easy and he could not lose his way, the tent being in full view below.

After seeing him safely off, and making good progress, we loaded up Tejbir's cylinders, and in view of the easy nature of the climbing, mutually agreed to dispense with the rope, and thus enable ourselves to proceed more rapidly. Climbing not very steep and quite easy rocks, and passing two almost level places affording ample room for some future high camp, we gained an altitude of 26,500 feet. By this time, however, the wind, which had been steadily rising, had acquired such force that I considered it necessary to leave the ridge and continue our ascent by traversing out across the great Northern face of Mount Everest, hoping by so doing to find more shelter from the icy blasts. It was not easy to come to this decision, because I saw that between us and the shoulder the climbing was all plain sailing and presented no outstanding difficulty. Leaving the ridge, we began to work out into space. For the first few yards the going was sufficiently straightforward, but presently the general angle became much steeper, and our trials were accentuated by the fact that the stratification of the rocks was such that they shelved outward and downward, making the securing of adequate footholds difficult. We did not rope, however. I knew that the longer we remained un-roped, the more time we should save—a consideration of vital importance. But as I led out over these steeply sloping, evilly smooth slabs, I carefully watched Bruce to see how he would tackle the formidable task with which he was confronted on this his first mountaineering expedition. He did his work splen-didly and followed steadily and confidently as if he were quite an old hand at the game.

Sometimes the slabs gave place to snow—treacherous, powdery stuff, with a thin, hard, deceptive crust that gave the appearance of compactness. Little reliance could be placed upon it, and it had to be treated with great care. And some-times we found ourselves crossing steep slopes of scree that yielded and shifted downwards with every tread. Very occa-sionally in the midst of our exacting work we were forced to indulge in a brief rest in order to replace an empty cylinder of oxygen by a full one. The empty ones were thrown away, and as each bumped its way over the precipice and the good steel clanged like a church bell at each impact, we laughed aloud at the thought that "There goes another 5 lb. off our backs." Since leaving the ridge we had not made much height although we seemed to be getting so near our goal. Now and then we consulted the aneroid barometer, and its readings en-couraged us on. 27,000 feet; then we gave up traversing and began to climb diagonally upwards toward a point on the lofty North-east ridge, midway between the shoulder and the summit. Soon afterwards an accident put Bruce's oxygen apparatus out of action. He was some 20 feet below me, but struggled gallantly upwards as I went to meet him, and after connecting him on to my apparatus and so renewing his supply of oxygen, we soon traced the trouble and effected a satisfactory repair.

The barometer here recorded a height of 27,300 feet. The highest mountain visible was Chö Uyo, which is just short of 27,000 feet. We were well above it and could look across it into the dense clouds beyond. The great West Peak of Everest, one of the most beautiful sights to be seen from down in the Rongbuk Valley, was hidden, but we knew that our standpoint was nearly 2,000 feet above it. Everest itself was the only mountain top which we could see without turning our gaze downwards. We could look across into clouds which lay at some undefined distance behind the North-east shoulder, a clear indication that we were only a little, if any, below its level. Pumori, an imposing ice-bound pyramid, 23,000 feet high, I sought at first in vain. So far were we above it that it had sunk into an insignificant little ice-hump by the side of the Rongbuk Glacier. Most of the other landmarks were blotted out by masses of ominous, yellow-hued clouds swept from the West in the wake of an angry storm-wind. The point we reached is unmistakable even from afar. We were standing on a little rocky ledge, just inside an inverted V of snow, immediately below the great belt of reddish-yellow rock which cleaves its way almost horizontally through the otherwise greenish-black slabs of the mountain. Though 1700 feet below, we were well within half a mile of the summit, so close, indeed, that we could distinguish individual stones on a little patch of scree lying just underneath the highest point. Ours were truly the tortures of Tantalus; for, weak from hunger and exhausted by that nightmare struggle for life in our high camp, we were in no fit condition to proceed. Indeed, I knew that if we were to persist in climbing on, even if only for another 500 feet, we should not both get back alive.

The decision to retreat once taken, no time was lost, and, fearing lest another accidental interruption in the oxygen supply might lead to a slip on the part of either of us, we roped together. It was midday. At first we returned in our tracks, but later found better going by aiming to strike the ridge between the North-east shoulder and the North Col at a point above where we had left it in the morning. Progress was more rapid, though great caution was still necessary. Shortly after 2 p.m., we struck the ridge and there reduced our burdens to a minimum by dumping four oxygen cylinders. The place will be easily recognised by future explorers; those four cylinders are perched against a rock at the head of the one and only large snow-filled couloir running right up from the head of the East Rongbuk Glacier to the ridge. The clear weather was gone. We plunged down the easy, broken rocks through thick mists driven past us from the West by a violent wind. For one small mercy we were thankful—no snow fell. We reached our high camp in barely half an hour, and such are the vagaries of Everest's moods that in this short time the wind had practically dropped. Tejbir lay snugly wrapped up in all three sleeping-bags, sleeping the deep sleep of exhaustion. Hearing the voices of the porters on their way up to bring down our kit, we woke him up, telling him to await their arrival and to go down with them. Bruce and I then proceeded on our way, met the ascending porters and passed on, greatly cheered by their bright welcomes and encouraging smiles. But the long descent, coming as it did on the top of a hard's day's work, soon began to find out our weakness. We were deplorably tired, and could no longer move ahead with our accustomed vigour. Knees did not always bend and unbend as required. At times they gave way altogether and forced us, staggering, to sit down. But eventually we reached the broken snows of the North Col, and arrived in camp there at 4 p.m.

A craving for food, to the lack of which our weakness was mainly due, was all that animated us. Hot tea and a tin of spaghetti were soon forthcoming, and even this little nourishment refreshed us and renewed our strength to such an extent that three-quarters of an hour later we were ready to set off for Camp III. An invaluable addition to our little party was Captain Noel, the indefatigable photographer of the Expedition, who had already spent four days and three nights on the North Col. He formed our rearguard and nursed us safely down the steep snow and ice slopes on to the almost level basin of the glacier below. Before 5:30 p.m., only forty minutes after leaving the col, we reached Camp III. Since midday, from our highest point we had descended over 6,000 feet; but we were quite finished.

From *The Assault on Mount Everest: 1922.*

JAMES RAMSEY ULLMAN:

One more attempt the expedition of 1922 was to make. And it was doomed to be the most short-lived and disastrous one that has ever been made against the king of mountains.

The main base, at which the whole party gathered after the Finch-Bruce attempt, resembled a field hospital more than a mountaineers' camp, and of the high climbers only Mallory and Somervell were fit for further work. Also, dark banks of monsoon clouds had appeared to the south, and snow was falling in deep drifts on the upper slopes of the mountain. Resolved on a last try, however, Mallory and Somervell again pushed up the glaciers and, with Crawford, Wakefield, and a squad of porters helping, began their preparations for a third ascent.

GEORGE LEIGH-MALLORY:

But the North Col had first to be reached. With so much new snow to contend with we should hardly get there in one day. If we were to make the most of our chance in the interval of fair weather, we should lose no time in carrying up the loads for some part of the distance. It was decided therefore to begin this work on the following day, June 7.

In the ascent to the North Col after the recent snowfall we considered that an avalanche was to be feared only in one place, the steep final slope below the shelf. There we could afford to run no risk; we must test the snow and be certain that it was safe before we could cross this slope. Probably we should be obliged to leave our loads below it, having gained, as a result of our day's work, the great advantage of a track. An avalanche might also come down, we thought, on the first steep slope where the ascent began. Here it could do us no harm, and the behaviour of the snow on this slope would be a test of its condition.

The party, Somervell, Crawford, and I, with fourteen porters (Wakefield was to be supply officer at Camp III), set out at 8 a.m. In spite of the hard frost of the previous night, the crust was far from bearing our weight; we sank up to our knees in almost every step, and two hours were taken in traversing the snowfield. At 10.15 a.m., Somervell, I, a porter, and Crawford, roped up in that order, began to work up the steep ice-slope, now covered with snow. It was clear that the three of us without loads must take the lead in turns stamping out the track for our porters. These men, after their immense efforts on the first and second attempts, had all volunteered to "go high," as they said, once more, and everything must be done to ease the terrible work of carrying the loads over the soft snow. No trace was found of our previous tracks, and we were soon arguing as to where exactly they might be as we slanted across the slope. It was remarkable that the snow adhered so well to the ice that we were able to get up without cutting steps. Everything was done by trenching the snow to induce it to come down if it would; every test gave a satisfactory result. Once this crucial place was passed, we plodded on without hesitation. If the snow would not come down where we had formerly encountered steep bare ice, a fortiori, above, on the gentler slopes, we had nothing to fear. The thought of an avalanche was dismissed from our minds.

It was necessarily slow work forging our way through the deep snow, but the party was going extraordinarily well, and the porters were evidently determined to get on. Somervell gave us a long lead, and Crawford next, in spite of the handicap of shorter legs, struggled upwards in some of the worst snow we met until I relieved him. I found the effort at each step so great that no method of breathing I had formerly employed was adequate; it was necessary to pause after each lifting movement for a whole series of breaths, rapid at first and gradually slower, before the weight was transferred again to the other foot. About 1.30 p.m. I halted, and the porters, following on three separate ropes, soon came up with the leading party. We should have been glad to stay where we were for a long rest. But the hour was already late, and as Somervell was ready to take the lead again, we decided to push on. We were now about 400 feet below a conspicuous block of ice and 600 feet below Camp IV, still on the gentle slopes of the corridor. Somervell had advanced only 100 feet, rather up the slope than across it, and the last party of porters had barely begun to move up in the steps. The scene was peculiarly bright and windless, and as we rarely spoke, nothing was to be heard but the laboured panting of our lungs.

This stillness was suddenly disturbed. We were startled by an ominous sound, sharp, arresting, violent, and yet somehow soft like an explosion of untamped gunpowder. I had never before on a mountainside heard such a sound; but all of us, I imagine, knew instinctively what it meant, as though we had been accustomed to hear it every day of our lives. In a moment I observed the surface of the snow broken and puckered where it had been even for a few yards to the right of me. I took two steps convulsively in this direction with some quick thought of getting nearer to the edge of the danger that threatened us. And then I began to move slowly downwards, inevitably carried on the whole moving surface by a force I was utterly powerless to resist. Somehow I managed to turn out from the slope so as to avoid being pushed headlong and backwards down it. For a second or two I seemed hardly to be in danger as I went quietly sliding down with the snow. Then the rope at my waist tightened and held me back. A wave of snow came over me and I was buried. I supposed that the matter was settled. However, I called to mind experiences related by other parties; and it had been suggested that the best chance of escape in this situation lay in swimming. I thrust out my arms above my head and actually went through some sort of motions of swimming on my back. Beneath the surface of the snow, with nothing to inform the senses of the world outside it, I had no impression of speed after the first acceleration—I struggled in the tumbling snow, unconscious of everything else—until, perhaps, only a few seconds later, I knew the pace was easing up. I felt an increasing pressure about my body. I wondered how tightly I should be squeezed, and then the avalanche came to rest.

My arms were free; my legs were near the surface. After a brief struggle, I was standing again, surprised and breathless, in the motionless snow. But the rope was tight at my waist; the porter tied on next me, I supposed, must be deeply buried. To my further surprise, he quickly emerged, unharmed as myself. Somervell and Crawford, too, though they had been above me by the rope's length, were now quite close, and soon extricated themselves. We subsequently made out that their experiences had been very similar to mine. But where were the rest? Looking down over the foam of snow, we saw one group of porters some little distance, perhaps 150 feet, below us. Presumably, the others must be buried somewhere between us and them, and though no sign of these missing men appeared, we at once prepared to find and dig them out. The porters we saw still stood their ground instead of coming up to help. We soon made out that they were the party who had been immediately behind us, and they were pointing below them. They had travelled further than us in the avalanche, presumably because they were nearer the centre, where it was moving more rapidly. The other two parties, one of four and one of five men roped together, must have been carried even further. We could still hope that they were safe. But as we hurried down we soon saw that beneath the place where the four porters were standing was a formidable drop; it was only too plain that the missing men had been swept over it.

We had no difficulty in finding a way round this obstacle; in a very short time we were standing under its shadow. The ice-cliff was from 40 to 60 feet high in different places; the crevasse at its foot was more or less filled up with avalanche snow. Our fears were soon confirmed. One man was quickly uncovered and found to be still breathing; before long we were certain that he would live. Another whom we dug out near him had been killed by the fall. He and his party appeared to have struck the hard lower lip of the crevasse, and were lying under the snow on or near the edge of it. The four porters who had escaped soon pulled themselves together after the first shock of the accident, and now worked here with Crawford and did everything they could to extricate the other bodies, while Somervell and I went down into the crevasse. A loop of rope which we pulled up convinced us that the other party must be here. It was slow work loosening the snow with the pick or adze of an ice-axe and shovelling it with the hands. But we were able to follow the rope to the bodies. One was dug up lifeless; another was found upside down, and when we uncovered his face Somervell thought he was still breathing. We had the greatest difficulty in extricating this man, so tightly was the snow packed about his limbs; his load, four oxygen cylinders on a steel frame, had to be cut from his back, and eventually he was dragged out. Though buried for about forty minutes, he had survived the fall and the suffocation, and suffered no serious harm. Of the two others in this party of four, we found only one. We had at length to give up a hopeless search with the certain knowledge that the first of them to be swept over the cliff, and the most deeply buried, must long ago be dead. Of the other five, all bodies were recovered, but only one was alive. The two who had so marvellously escaped were able to walk down to Camp III, and were almost perfectly well next day. The other seven were killed.

This tragic calamity was naturally the end of the third attempt to climb Mount Everest. The surviving porters who had lost their friends or brothers behaved with dignity, making no noisy parade of the grief they felt. We asked them whether they wished to go up and bring down the bodies for orderly burial. They preferred to leave them where they were. For my part, I was glad of this decision. What better burial could they have than to lie in the snow where they fell? In their honour a large cairn was built at Camp III.

A few words must be added with regard to this accident. No one will imagine that we had pushed on recklessly disregarding the new conditions of fresh snow. Three members of the Alpine Club, with experience of judging snow for themselves, chiefly, of course, in the Alps, had all supposed that the party was safe. They had imagined that on those gentle slopes the snow would not move. In what way had they been deceived? The fact that the avalanche snow came to rest on the slope where they were proves that their calculation was not so very far wrong. But the snow cannot all have been of the quality that adhered so well to the steep ice-slope lower down. Where the avalanche started, not from the line of their steps, but about 100 feet higher, it was shaded to some extent by a broken wall of ice. There, perhaps, it had both drifted more deeply and remained more free and powdery, and the weight of this snow was probably sufficient to push the other down the slope once its surface had been disturbed. More experience, more knowledge might perhaps have warned us not to go there. One never can know enough about snow. But looking up the corridor again after the event, I wondered how I ever could be certain not to be deceived by appearances so innocent.

The regret of all members of the Expedition for the loss of our seven porters will have been elsewhere expressed. It is my part only to add this: the work of carrying up our camps on Mount Everest is beyond the range of a simple contract measured in terms of money; the porters had come to have a share in our enterprise, and these men died in an act of voluntary service freely rendered and faithfully performed.

From *The Assault on Mount Everest: 1922.*

4

Second Assault

The Expedition of 1924

He is the pioneer who climbs,
Who dares to climb,
Although he fall
A thousand times;
Who dares to crawl
On bloody hands and knees
Along its stony ecstasies
Up to the utmost snows;
Nor knows
He stands on these . . .
Or knowing, does not care,
Save to climb on from there!

Leonora Speyer: From Of Mountains

JAMES RAMSEY ULLMAN:

The 1922 expedition ended in disaster, but a scant two years later, in the early spring of 1924, a third party was already trekking in toward the mountain, across the high, wild plateaus of Tibet. And before it returned it was destined to write one of the most famous chapters in the history of mountaineering.

Several of the old climbers were back for another try: the indefatigable Mallory, of course; Norton, Somervell, and Geoffrey Bruce; Noel with his cameras. General Bruce had again been appointed leader, but he fell ill on the trip in and had to return to India, while Norton took over as first-in-command. Newcomers included N. E. Odell, a geologist; E. O. Shebbeare, of the Indian Forest Service, as transport officer; Major R. W. G. Hingston, as physician; two experienced mountaineers named Beetham and Hazard, and Andrew Irvine, a young undergraduate from Oxford. There were also, of course, a few Gurkha N.C.O.s, the indispensable Sherpas—many of them veterans from 1922—and three-hundred-odd Tibetan porters for work at the lower camps.

On April twenty-ninth base camp was again established near the Rongbuk Monastery, and climbers and helpers began the laborious work of packing their supplies up the glaciers. The struggles and problems of the days that followed are graphically described by Mallory in the section that follows.

GEORGE LEIGH-MALLORY:

May 3. Irvine, Odell, Hazard and self to Camp I. Half the porters lagged badly. Having added a good deal of stuff on their own account to what we had given them to carry they had big loads.

May 4. I decided to leave five loads not urgently required at Camp I and have five men to carry all the porters' blankets, etc. The result was good and the men must have gone well. Irvine and I had gone ahead and reached Camp II at about 12.30; we had hardly finished a leisurely tiffin when the first porters arrived. Camp II looked extraordinarily uninviting, although already inhabited by an N.C.O. and two others in charge of the stores (150 loads or so), which had already been carried up by Tibetans. A low irregular wall surrounded a rough compound, which I was informed was the place for the Sahibs' tents, and another already covered by the fly of a Whymper tent was the home of an N.C.O. The Sahibs' compound was soon put sufficiently in order; two Whymper tents were pitched there for the four of us, while a wonderful brown tent of Noel's was pitched for him. No tents were provided here for porters: the intention was to build comfortable huts or "sangars," as we call them, using the Whymper flys for roofs, but no sangars had yet been built, and accommodation for twenty-three men is not so easily provided in this way. However, I soon saw that the ground would allow us to economize walls, and Irvine and I with three or four men began building an oblong sangar, the breadth only about 7 feet; other men joined in after resting. It is an extraordinary thing to watch the conversion of men from listlessness to some spirit of enterprise; a very little thing will turn the scale: on this occasion the moving of a huge stone to form one corner started the men's interest, and later we sang! And so these rather tired children were persuaded to do something for their comfort; without persuasion they would have done nothing to make life tolerable.

May 4 to 5. An appalling night, very cold, considerable snow-fall and a violent wind.

May 5. Result: signs of life in camp very late. The first audible one in camps up to and including II is the blowing of yak-dung fire with Tibetan bellows.

The men were an extraordinarily long time getting their food this morning. The N.C.O. seemed unable to get a move on, and generally speaking an Oriental inertia was in the air. It was with difficulty in fact that the men could be got out of their tents, and then we had further difficulty about loads; one man, a regular old soldier, having possessed himself of a conveniently light load, refused to take a heavier one I wanted taken instead. I had to make a great show of threatening him with my fist in his face before he would comply, and so with much difficulty about it and about what should be left behind in the way of coolie rations and blankets and cooking-pots, and the degree of illness of those reported sick, we didn't get fairly away until 11 a.m.

Now, making a new track is always a long affair compared to following an old one, and on this occasion snow had fallen in the night. The glacier which had looked innocent enough the evening before was far from innocent now. The wind had blown the higher surfaces clear. The days, I suppose, had been too clear for melting and these surfaces were hard, smooth, rounded ice, almost as hard as glass and with never a trace of roughness, and between the projecting lumps lay the new powdery snow. The result of the conditions was much expenditure of labour either in making steps in the snow or cutting them in ice, and we reached a place known as "The Trough," a broken trough in the ice, 50 feet deep and about one-third of the way up, knowing we should have all that we could do to reach Camp III. We followed along in the trough some way, a lovely warm place, and then came out of it into the open glacier where the wind was blowing up the snow maliciously. The wind luckily was at our backs until we rounded the corner of the North Peak, and then we caught it blowing straight at us from the North Col. As the porters were now nearly exhausted and feeling the altitude badly our progress was a bitter experience. I was acting as lone horse, finding the best way, and consequently arrived first in camp. It was a queer sensation, reviving memories of that scene with the dud oxygen cylinders piled against the cairn which was built to commemorate the seven porters killed two years ago. The whole place had changed less than I could have believed possible, seeing that the glacier is everywhere beneath the stones. My boots were frozen hard on my feet, and I knew we could do nothing now to make a comfortable camp. I showed the porters where to pitch their tents at 6.30 p.m., got hold of a rucksack containing four Unna cookers, dished out three and Meta * for their cooking to the porters and one to our own cook; then we pitched our own two Meade tents with doors facing about a yard apart for sociability.

The porters seemed to me very much done up, and considering how cold it was even at 6 p.m. I was a good deal depressed by the situation. Personally I got warm easily enough. Our wonderful Kami produced some sort of a hot meal, and I lay comfortably in my sleeping-bag. The one thing I could think of for our porters was the high-altitude sleeping-sacks (intended for Camp IV and upwards), now at Camp II, which I had not ordered to come on next day with the second party of porters (two parties A and B each of twenty had been formed for these purposes, and B were a day behind us). The only plan was to make an early start next morning and get to Camp II in time to forestall the departure of B party. I remember making this resolve in the middle of the night and getting up

* Methylated fuel.—*Editor.*

to pull my boots inside the tent from under the door. I put them inside the outer covering of my flea-bag and near the middle of my body—but of course they remained frozen hard and I had a tussle to get them on in the morning. Luckily the sun strikes our tents early—6.30 a.m. or a little later at Camp III, and I was able to get off about 7. I left directions that half the men, or as many less as possible, should come one-quarter of the way down and meet the men coming up so as to get the most important load to Camp III.

I guessed that B party, after a cold night, would not start before 9 a.m., and as I was anxious if possible to find a better way over the glacier I wasted some time in investigations and made an unsatisfactory new route, so that it was after 8.30 when I emerged from the trough, and a little farther on I saw B party coming up. It was too late to turn them back. I found some of them had resolved they would not be able to get to Camp III and go back to Camp II the same day and consequently increased their loads with blankets, etc., determining to sleep at Camp III. This was the last thing I wanted. My chief idea at the moment was to get useful work out of B party without risking their *moral* or condition as I saw we were risking that of A. So after dispatching a note to Noel at II I conducted B party slowly up the glacier. After making a convenient dump and sending down B party I got back to Camp III early in the afternoon, somewhat done and going very slowly from want of food at the last. In camp nothing doing. All porters said to be sick and none fit to carry a load. Irvine and Odell volunteered to go down to the dump and get one or two things specially wanted, e.g. Primus stoves, which was done. The sun had left the camp some time before they returned. A little wall-building was done this day, notably round the N.C.O.'s tent, otherwise nothing to improve matters. The temperature at 5 p.m. (we hadn't thermometers the previous night) was observed to be 2° F.—30° of frost an hour before sunset; under these conditions it is only during the sunny, windless hours that anything to speak of can be done; this day there were such hours, but I gather that sahibs as well as porters were suffering from altitude lassitude.

May 7. The night had been very cold—[minus] 21½°, i.e. 53° of frost. Personally I slept beautifully warmly and yet was not well in the morning. Odell and Irvine also seemed distinctly unfit. I decided to send Hazard down with some of A party to meet at the dump and bring up some of B party (it had been arranged that some of this party should come up again). Investigation again showed that no porters were fit to carry loads; several were too unwell to be kept up at III. They had to be more or less pulled from their tents. An hour and a half must have been taken in getting their meals of tsampa, which they must clearly have before going down; and much time too in digging out the sicker men who tried to hide away in their tents—one of them, who was absolutely without a spark of life to help himself, had swollen feet and we had to pull on his boots without his socks; he was almost incapable of walking; I supported him with my arm for some distance and then told off a porter to do that; eventually roped in three parties in charge of the N.C.O. I sent them off by themselves from the dump, where shortly afterwards I met Hazard. Four men of B had gone on to Camp III, but not to sleep. Three others whom we now proceeded to rope up and help with their loads alone consented to stay there. A second day therefore passed with only seven more loads got to Camp III, and nothing done to establish the camp in a more comfortable manner, unless it counted that this third night each of the six men would have a high-altitude sleeping-sack; and meanwhile the *moral* of A party had gone to blazes. It was clear to me that the *moral* of porters must be established if possible at once by bringing B party up and giving them a day's rest to make camp.

May 8. I made another early start and reached Camp II at 9 a.m., and here met Norton and Somervell. By some mental aberration I had thought they would only reach Camp II on this day—they had proceeded according to programme and come to Camp II on the 7th. We discussed plans largely while I ate breakfast, in the mild, sheltered, sunny alfresco of Camp II (by comparison). Norton agreed with my ideas and dispatched all remaining B party to Camp III with Somervell, to pick up their loads at the dump and carry them on. A had been filled up the previous night with hot food and were now lying in the sun looking more like men; the only question was whether in future to establish the correct standard and make them carry all the way to Camp III and back as was always done in 1922. I was strongly opposed to this idea; the best way of re-establishing their *moral*, I thought, would be to give them a job well within their powers and, if they improved as I hoped, they might well carry loads the three-quarter journey to the dump on three successive days—while B could ferry the last quarter once or twice on the two of the days when they would not be engaged in making camp. This was agreed to more particularly by Geoffrey Bruce, who really runs the porters altogether and who had now come up from Camp I.

A day of great relief this with the responsibility shared or handed over; and much lying in the sun and untroubled sleep at Camp II.

May 9. I intended going ahead of the party to see how things were moving at Camp III, for this day the camp was to be made wonderful. Seven men with special loads, fresh heroes from the Base, were to go through to Camp III; the A men to return from the dump to Camp II. As it turned out I escorted the first batch who were going through to Camp III. The conditions when we emerged from the trough were anything but pleasant; under a grey sky a violent wind was blowing up the snow; at moments the black dots below me on the glacier, all except the nearest, were completely lost to view. The men were much inclined to put down their loads before reaching the dump and a good deal of driving had to be done. Eventually after waiting some time at the dump I joined Norton and Geoff, and we escorted the last three loads for Camp III the last bit of the way. On such a day I did not expect Camp III to be more congenial than it had been. However, it was something to be greeted by the cheery noise of the Roarer Cooker: the R.C. is one of the great Inventions of the Expedition; we have two in point of fact, one with a vertical, and one with a horizontal flame—a sort of super-Primus stove. Irvine and Odell had evidently been doing some useful work. It has been a triumph getting the R.C. to Camp III—it is an extravagant load weighing over 40 lb. and it now proved to be even more extravagant of fuel than had been anticipated; moreover, its burning was somewhat intermittent, and as the cook, even after instruction, was still both frightened and incompetent when this formidable stove was not functioning quite sweetly and well, a sahib had often to be called in to help. Nevertheless the R.C. succeeded in cooking food for the troops, and however costly in paraffin oil that meal may have been it made the one great difference between Camp III as A party experienced it and Camp III now.

Otherwise on this day, set apart for the edification and beatification of this camp, the single thing that had been done was the erection of one Meade tent to accommodate two more sahibs (only two more because Hazard came down this day). And no blame to anyone; B party was much as A party had been—in a state of Oriental inertia; it is unfair, perhaps, to our porters to class them with Orientals in general, but they have this Oriental quality that after a certain stage of physical discomfort or mental depression has been reached they simply curl up. Our porters were just curled up inside their tents. And it must be admitted that the sahibs were most of the time in their tents—no other place being tolerable. Personally I felt that the task of going round tents and seeing how the men were getting on and giving orders about the arrangements of the camp now naturally fell to Geoffrey Bruce, whose "pigeon" it is to deal with the porters. And so presently in my old place, with Somervell now as a companion instead of Hazard, I made myself comfortable, i.e. I took off my boots and knickers, put on my footless stockings, knitted for me by my wife for the last Expedition and covering the whole of my legs, a pair of grey flannel bags and two pairs of warm socks, besides my cloth-sided shoes, and certain garments too for warming the upper parts, a comparatively simple matter. The final resort in these conditions of course is to put one's legs into a sleeping-sack. Howard and I lay warmly enough and presently I proposed a game of picquette, and we played cards for some time until Norton and Geoff. came to pay us a visit and discuss the situation. Someone a little later tied back the flaps of the two tents facing each other so that after Norton and Geoff. had retired to their tent the other four of us were inhabiting, as it were, one room, and hopefully talked of the genius of Kami and the Roarer Cooker and supposed that a hot evening meal might sometime come our way. Meanwhile I produced *The Spirit of Man* and began reading one thing and another. Howard reminded me that I was reproducing on the same spot a scene which had occurred two years ago when he and I lay in a tent together. We all agreed that Kubla Khan was a good sort of poem. Irvine was rather poetry shy, but seemed to be favourably impressed by the Epitaph to Gray's Elegy. Odell was much inclined to be interested and liked the last lines of Prometheus Unbound. Somervell, who knows quite a lot of English literature, had never read a poem of Emily Brontë's, and was happily introduced.—And suddenly hot soup arrived.

The following night was one of the most disagreeable I remember. The wind came in tremendous gusts and, in spite of precautions to keep it out, the fresh snow drifted in; if one's head were not under the bedclothes one's face was cooled by the fine cold powder, and in the morning I found 2 inches of snow all along my side of the tent. It was impossible to guess how much snow had fallen during the night when one first looked out. The only certain thing was the vile appearance of things at present. In a calm interval one could take stock of a camp now covered in snow—and then would come the violent wind and all would be covered in the spindrift. Presently Norton and Geoff. came into our tent for a powwow. Geoff., speaking from the porters' point of view, was in favour of beating a retreat. We were all agreed that we must not risk destroying the *moral* of the porters, and also that for two or three days no progress could be made towards the North Col. But it seemed to me that, in the normal course of events, the weather should now re-establish itself and might even be sufficiently calm to get something done that afternoon, and that for the porters the best thing of all would be to weather the storm up at Camp III. In any case it would be early enough to decide for a retreat next day. These arguments commended themselves to Norton and so it was agreed. Meanwhile one of the most serious features of the situation was the consumption of fuel. A box of meta, and none could say how much paraffin (not much, however), had been burnt at Camp II; here at Camp III no water had yet appeared, and snow must be melted for every one at every meal—a box of meta had to be consumed here too, and Primus stoves had been used before the Roarer made its appearance yesterday. Goodness knows how much oil it used. It was clear that the first economy must be in the number of sahibs (6) at Camp III. We planned that Somervell, Norton and Odell should have the first whack at the North Col, and Irvine and I finish the good work next day—Irvine and I therefore must go down first. On the way down Irvine suffered very much and I somewhat from the complaint known as glacier lassitude—a mysterious complaint, but I am pretty certain in his case that the sun and the dazzling light reflected from the new snow had something to do with the trouble.

A peaceful time at Camp II with Beetham and Noel.

May 11. The weather hazy and unsettled looking. I dispatched fifteen loads up to the dump and arranged for the evacuation of two sick men, of whom one had badly frostbitten feet, apparently a Lepcha, unfit for this game, and the other was Sanglu, Kellas's old servant, who had been attached to Noel this Expedition and last, a most valuable man, who seemed exceedingly ill with bronchitis. The parties had been gone half an hour before we were aroused by a shout and learned that a porter had broken his leg on the glacier. We quickly gathered ourselves into a competent help party, and had barely started out when a man turned up with a note from Norton to tell me, as I half expected, that he had decided to evacuate Camp III for the present and retire all ranks to the Base Camp. The wounded man turned out to be nearer at hand than, and not so badly wounded (a bone broken in the region of the knee) as I feared.

This same evening Beetham, Noel, Irvine and I were back at the Base Camp, the rest coming in next day.

Well, that is the bare story of the reverse so far as it goes. I'm convinced that Norton had been perfectly right. We pushed things far enough. Everything depends on the porters and we must contrive to bring them to the starting point, i.e. Camp III, at the top of their form. I expect we were working all the time in '22 with a smaller margin than we knew—it certainly amazed me that the whole bandobast, so far as porters were concerned, worked so smoothly. Anyway this time the conditions at Camp III were much more severe, and not only were temperatures lower but the wind was more continuous and more violent. I expect that these porters will do as well in the end as last time's. Personally I felt that I was going through a real hard time in a way I never did in '22. Meanwhile our retreat has meant a big waste of time. We have waited down here for the weather—at last it looks more settled and we are on the point of starting up again. But the day for the summit is put off from the 17th to the 28th, and the great question is, Will the monsoon give time?

May 27. It has been a bad time altogether. I look back on tremendous effort and exhaustion and dismal looking out of a tent door into a world of snow and vanishing hopes—and yet, and yet, and yet there have been a good many things to set on the other side. The party has played up wonderfully. The first visit to the North Col was a triumph for the old gang. Norton and I did the job, and the cutting of course was all my part— so far as one can enjoy climbing above Camp III I enjoyed the conquest of the ice wall and crack, the crux of the route, and the making steps too in the steep final 200 feet. Odell did very useful work leading the way on from the camp to the Col; I was practically bust to the world and couldn't have led that half-hour though I still had enough mind to direct him. We made a very bad business of the descent. It suddenly occurred to me that we ought to see what the old way down was like. Norton and I were ahead unroped and Odell behind in charge of a porter who had carried up a light load. We got only ground where a practised man can just get along without crampon (which we hadn't with us), chipping occasional steps in very hard snow or ice. I was all right ahead, but Norton had a nasty slip and then the porter, whose knot didn't hold, so that he went down some way and was badly shaken. Meanwhile I below, finding the best way down, had walked into an obvious crevasse; by some miscalculation I had thought I had prodded the snow with which it was choked and where I hoped we could walk instead of cutting steps at the side of it—all the result of mere exhaustion, no doubt. But the snow gave way and in I went with the snow tumbling all round me, down, luckily, only about 10 feet before I fetched up half blind and breathless to find myself most precariously supported only by my ice axe somehow caught across the crevasse and still held in my right hand—and below was a very unpleasant black hole. I had some nasty moments before I got comfortably wedged and began to yell for help up through the round hole I had come through where the blue sky showed—this because I was afraid my operations to extricate myself would bring down a lot more snow and perhaps precipitate me into the bargain. However, I soon grew tired of shouting—they hadn't seen me from above—and bringing the snow down a little at a time I made a hole out towards the side (the crevasse ran down a slope) after some climbing, and extricated myself—but was then on the wrong side of the crevasse, so that eventually I had to cut across a nasty slope of very hard ice and farther down some mixed unpleasant snow before I was out of the wood. The others were down by a better line ten minutes before me. That cutting against time at the end after such a day just about brought me to my limit. . . .

My one personal trouble has been a cough. It started a day or two before leaving the Base Camp but I thought nothing of it. In the high camp it has been the devil. Even after the day's exercise I have described I couldn't sleep, but was distressed with bursts of coughing fit to tear one's guts—and a headache and misery altogether, besides which of course it has a very bad effect on one's going on the mountain. Somervell also had a cough, which started a little later than mine, and he has not been at his physical best. . . .

Norton has been quite right to bring us down for rest. It is no use sending men up the mountain unfit. The physique of the whole party has gone down sadly. The only chance now is to get fit and go for a simpler, quicker plan. The only plump fit man is Geoffrey Bruce. Norton has made me responsible for choosing the parties of attack, himself first choosing me into the first party if I like. But I'm quite doubtful if I shall be fit enough. But again I wonder if the monsoon will give us a chance. I don't want to get caught, but our three-day scheme from the Chang La will give the monsoon a good chance. We shall be going up again the day after to-morrow. Six days to the top from this camp!

From *The Fight for Everest: 1924.*

JAMES RAMSEY ULLMAN:

The North Col having been reached by the advance climbers, the next task was to get the porters up en masse for the establishment of Camp IV. This was accomplished in fairly short order, but presently snow and bitter cold set in again, leaving one climber—Hazard—and twelve porters marooned on the crest. For two days there was no communication between them and the rest of the expedition at Camp III. Then, on the third morning, those below stared up to see "rows of little black dots like flies on a whitewashed wall slowly moving downward. . . ."

LT. COL. E. F. NORTON:

We spent an anxious two hours waiting for the arrival of Hazard's party; some instinct must have warned us that all was not well. At 5 p.m. he arrived, accompanied by only eight of his twelve men. It appeared that he had gone first across the traverse to test the condition of the fresh surface snow, which rendered it a very dangerous passage; eight men had followed him, one crossing at a time, but the last four had turned back either because they were sick—the remaining porters said that two of them were suffering from frostbite—or, more probably

George Leigh-Mallory.

E. F. Norton.

T. Howard Somervell.

A. C. Irvine.

E. O. Shebbeare.

Everesters.

because one of them had started a patch of the surface snow slipping and they had been afraid to come on. Certain marks on the steepest part of the traverse next day gave colour to this explanation.

The situation had suddenly taken a very serious turn. The snow was falling persistently and—an ominous sign—had begun to take the form of soft feathery flakes, such as we had been accustomed to associate with nothing but monsoon conditions. The four men were alone at Camp IV, a prey to the superstitious terrors to which those of their race are always prone on the big snow mountains. Two of them were reported frostbitten, and we now learnt for the first time that, during their ascent two days before, a load of assorted food had been lost over an ice cliff. They were thus restricted to a diet of barley-meal, unless they had the initiative (and the tin-opener) to use the small amount of sahib's food already in the camp. It was quite evident that they must be rescued, and that no later than next day; for the frostbite question alone made it imperative to avoid even one more day's delay.

It was equally obvious that it was at present out of the question to continue our attempts on the mountain; the whole party at Camp III was already in a bad way. Mallory and Somervell were both suffering from very bad high-altitude throats. Odell had had hardly any sleep for several nights; Irvine had diarrhœa, and Hazard had just had a very trying three days. The porters were for the most part quite unfit, morally and physically, for further efforts at present.

Both above and below the North Col there was sufficient fresh snow to put any attempt to climb the mountain out of the question for the present, while we were all more or less convinced that this was really the beginning of the monsoon.

Sitting huddled in our dining-tent by the light of a candle lantern, we made our plans for next day. Mallory and I had had a longer period of rest at Camp III than any of the others, and as a party of at least three was required to bring down the four men, it was decided that Somervell should accompany us; we three had climbed together in 1922, and we knew we could go well as a party. Bruce, with Hazard and Irvine, was to evacuate Camp III, leaving only Odell and Noel (the latter having arrived from Camp II) with half a dozen porters to wait for our return in case there should be casualties to carry down the glacier.

It was a gloomy little conference; we could not but recognize that to turn our backs once more on the mountain at this date might well mean the abandonment of all hope of success for the year. We were about to send three of the four climbers detailed for the first attempt on what must be a severe test of endurance, and this would still further diminish our chances of success if a change in the weather permitted resumption of the attack. But at the time these seemed but minor considerations; the only thing that mattered was to get the men down alive. Personally my one fixed determination had all along been that we must on no account have any casualties among our porters this year, and here we were, faced with the very real possibility of losing four men; for it must be admitted that our chances of rescuing the marooned porters did not appear rosy at this time. We were all distinctly the worse for wear; both Mallory and Somervell had very bad coughs and sore throats, which hampered them badly in climbing; the condition of the North Col slopes must make climbing exceedingly slow and laborious, and there was the danger of avalanche. As we lay in our tent that night and listened to the soft pattering of the snow on its walls, I now know that neither Mallory nor I would have taken a bet of two to one against a successful issue to our undertaking next day, though at the time we kept such pessimistic views to ourselves. About midnight the snow stopped falling and the moon came out.

By 7.30 next morning we were off. Though the sun had been up two hours, the temperature was still only 2° Fahrenheit.

Of the climb which followed I remember only certain phases distinctly; the rest was just treadmill—with the snow anything from a foot to waist deep. As usual we were at our worst when we first started, and we looked so like a party of hospital convalescents that my hopes sank to zero. Mallory, who on these occasions lived on his nervous energy, kept urging us on: I remember his chiding us sharply for some momentary delay and later apologizing for his impatience. I wore crampons, and owing to the constriction of their straps, I suffered all day from cold feet. At the foot of the chimney I had to take off my boots while Somervell rubbed my feet, but I never properly restored the circulation that day.

The three of us did the wall and chimney in fifty minutes. Arrived at the top we could see one of the marooned porters, one Phu, standing on the edge of the shelf, and I repeatedly hailed him to find out what was the condition of the four. I had the greatest difficulty in getting an answer out of him, and it was only when we arrived at the foot of the final traverse that the following conversation took place: "Hi, Phu! Are you all fit to walk?" This had to be repeated several times. At last came the answering query, "Up or down?" (so little apparently did he realize the seriousness of their situation). "Down, you fool." Whereupon he disappeared, and almost at once reappeared with the remaining three. They said that one, Namgya, had all the fingers of both hands badly frostbitten, and that another, Uchung, had some toes slightly affected, but that all were fit to come down. This was a relief, for though I had brought one of our "one-man carrier" frames to be prepared for the worst, I very much doubt if we could have got a man down on it—certainly we could not have done so before dark.

Up to the final traverse the condition of the surface snow had proved less dangerous than we had anticipated, but it was obvious that the traverse was to be the crux of the climb. Here Somervell insisted on going across, while Mallory and I prepared to belay the 200 feet of rope that we had brought with us, driving both our ice axes into the snow up to their heads as a holdfast, round which we passed the rope, paying it out yard by yard as Somervell slowly and laboriously made his way diagonally upwards and across; he punched big safe steps and continually stopped to cough and choke in the most painful manner. After one or two of these fits of coughing he leant his head on his forearm in an attitude of exhaustion, and so steep was the slope that the mental picture I have of him as he did this shows him standing almost upright in his steps with his elbow resting on the snow level with his shoulder.

Some five or ten yards short of where the crest of the slope formed the edge of the shelf on which the four men were waiting, Somervell reached the end of the rope; the full 200 feet were out, and by eye we judged it a near thing whether, in the event of his slipping, the length of the rope was not too great to stop him before he disappeared over the lip of the ice cliffs below. It was now 4 p.m. Time was all too short if we were to get down in daylight, and a brief shouted consultation decided us that the men must chance the unbridged ten yards and join Somervell unroped as best they could. Each man as he reached Somervell was to be passed across the taut rope in turn to where Mallory and I, securely anchored by my old friend the big serac, represented safety.

The first two reached him safely. One of them was across with us and the second just starting when, with my heart in my mouth, I saw the remaining two, who had stupidly started from the edge of the shelf together, suddenly flying down the slope. A big patch of fresh snow surface had given way and the men were going down on their backs, feet first, in an almost upright position. For one paralysing second I foresaw the apparently inevitable tragedy, with the two figures shooting into space over the edge of the blue ice cliff, 200 feet below; the next they pulled up after not more than 10 yards, and we breathed again. The accumulated snow under their feet had been bound by the cold of the early morning and the hot sun which followed to a holding consistency. Somervell, as cool as a cucumber, shouted to me, "Tell them to sit still," and still as mice they sat, shivering at the horrid prospect immediately beneath their eyes, while quite calmly Somervell passed the second man across to us, chaffing the wretched pair the while—so that one of them actually gave an involuntary bark of laughter.

Somervell then untied the rope from his waist, drove his ice axe in up to its head in the soft snow, passed the rope round it and strained it so as to make every foot he could, while Mallory and I held our end at extreme arm's length. Holding his own end in the same way he then let himself down to the extreme length of the rope and of his own arm, while with the other hand he grasped, one after the other, the two porters by the scruff of the neck and pulled them back to the anchor of his axe. Somehow they got across to us, for their nerve had gone and they slid and slipped, ruining the steps all the way across, and only saved themselves from repeating their previous performance by the rope handrail. Finally Somervell followed, after again tying the rope round his waist; and it was a fine object lesson in mountain craft to see him, balanced and erect, crossing the ruined track without a slip or mistake.

At 4.30 we started down; the slopes were already in chill shadow and it was evident that we were in for a race with darkness. Mallory led with one porter on a rope, then followed Somervell shepherding two; and I brought up the rear with Namgya and his frostbitten hands. Many times during the descent, but particularly in the chimney, I blessed my crampons, for Namgya's hands were useless and more than once I had to hold his full weight; but he put up a gallant showing until, at dusk, we reached the glacier and safety, where he rather broke down. Poor lad! He must have suffered a lot in those two and a half hours.

About 7.30 p.m., as we were leaving the glacier for the moraine three-quarters of a mile from home, some figures loomed up out of the darkness ahead, and we found Noel and Odell waiting for us with hot soup in a liquid-air flask—almost as memorable a drink as the never-to-be-forgotten coffee and brandy which greeted us in nearly the same place after another trying descent two years before. I think a laconic entry in my diary is the most sincere tribute I can pay to Noel and Odell, for it was written at the time: "Both awfully good to us here and, later, in camp." Noel had a peculiar genius for coming out strong on times like this, and I look back with gratitude to more than one occasion on which the shelter of his specially designed tent or some of his own private delicacies comforted me marvellously after a hard day.

Mallory's cough and the condition of my feet (which never really warmed up till next morning) precluded our enjoying, that night, the sleep we had earned, and we lay awake exchanging a murmured word from time to time. But our feelings were somewhat different from what they were when we had lain in the same tent the night before listening to the rustle of the falling snow and counting our chances for the morrow. Next morning we thankfully turned our backs on Camp III and, escorting a miserable little convoy of the halt, the lame and the blind, reached Camp II in due course in the teeth of a north-east wind, and with the snow falling again. The following day, May 26, Somervell and I reached Camp I.

From *The Fight for Everest: 1924.*

JAMES RAMSEY ULLMAN:

There were Everesters whose names were Mallory, Norton, Somervell, Bruce. But there were others whose names were

Lobsang, Llakpa Chédé, Angchetin, Semchumbi. They were not the men who dreamt the Everest dream. They were not the ones who planned and led and made the decisions and wrote the books. But they were as integral and indispensable a part of every expedition as the white men who employed them.

For the routine transport from India in to the base of the mountain almost any kind of coolie labor would do; but the load-carrying on the peak itself was a different matter altogether, and only a handful of Orientals have ever been found who were willing and able to do the job. Best of all, as we have seen, were the sturdy Sherpas, of Nepal. Moody, unpredictable and, by Western standards, childlike and irresponsible, they were occasionally, true enough, trials and problems to their employers. But, beyond all comparison, their good qualities outweighed their bad. Their labors at immense altitudes could probably not have been matched by any other breed of men; with negligibly few exceptions they faced hardship, danger and even death with cheerfulness and courage; and the best of them had a truly marvelous way of coming through when the need was greatest.

Everest climbers have been in disagreement with one another on many aspects of their expeditions. Not, however, on the Sherpas. And the tribute by Captain Noel, which follows, is typical of the esteem and affection in which all the "sahibs" held them.

Capt. John Noel:

It was a marvel to see our Sherpas work. Probably nobody but the Sherpa could have done what they did. All their lives these men have lived in the highest mountains, accustomed from childhood to altitude and to the carrying of heavy loads. They inherit the cheerful spirit of the Nepalese plus the acclimatization to a rarefied atmosphere of the Tibetans, since the Sherpa race is an intermixture of Nepalese and Tibetan blood. Their villages lie in Nepal, on the borders of Tibet on the south side of the Himalaya.

Sherpas are fighting people; and no little trouble arose from their "scraps" with the Tibetans, whom they look down on and treat rather roughly. They fight among themselves too. I remember one awful fight between two of our men. They battered each other unmercifully with fists and stones and bars of wood. Both were in hospital under our doctor; but next morning we actually saw them doing up each other's bandages with the greatest care and mutual pity. They had exhausted their steam; the fight was over and their happy natures were restored.

At sixteen thousand feet they could carry loads of fifty to sixty pounds in weight. They carried twenty to twenty-five pounds weight to a height of twenty-five thousand feet where white men could hardly progress even when unburdened. These supermen of our porters were nicknamed the "Tigers." There is almost no limit to the powers of these men in weight-carrying on mountains; and should they ever become animated by a sporting desire to reach the top of the mountain, they could undoubtedly do it more easily than any white man. When they first saw our unsightly and awkward oxygen tanks, they laughed heartily and said, "the air in our country, Sir, is quite good. Why then do you bring bottled air from England?" But later, when, at grips with the mountain, all were at the end of their tether, we used to give the men the gas to revive them. When they tasted it, they realized how wonderful it was and how it stilled the heaving of the heart. Then often they would come to us and say, "Sir, I—little sick to-day—please, Sir—I want a little 'English air.'"

The men who succeeded best on the mountain, it was interesting to note, were of the small, supple, trim type. These did better than the big men.

One must remember that they were not in a true sense picked men. They were recruited from men seeking work in Darjeeling, and the life of the bazaar and the town must inevitably have a deteriorating influence on the spirit and physique of mountain dwellers. As a general principle, it would be better to recruit the porters on any future occasion from the heart of their own country. This could be done with the good help of the Ruler of Nepal by permitting some one to go to Solakumbu, or else by sending a native representative to inform the people of the objects of the expedition and tell them that men were wanted. They could then come to Darjeeling specially to join the expedition.

We noticed on the whole, exceptions apart, that the veterans of the former expedition were not so successful as the fresh men. Their morale was not so good. They had become "old soldiers" and, knowing the ropes, some of them shifted their work on to the new men. Our common human nature! Always the stumbling block that stands in the way of achievement! But on the whole the entire corps worked splendidly; and one cannot praise their spirit too much, particularly when one realizes what losses and hardships they suffered and how at the end of the 1922 Expedition seven of them met a terrible death in the great disaster on the Ice Cliff. A proof of their spirit is that survivors who had even had relatives among the killed volunteered again for the 1924 Expedition.

Bruce introduced a spirit of competition among the men. He promoted the "stars" into troop leaders with promise of honors and extra pay. So the corps became a trained team, which is the goal to be aimed at. They followed with the keenest interest the progress of the various climbs, and competed to be included in the parties to go highest. All, with the exception of the few "old soldiers," vied with each other to carry the heaviest loads. It was never necessary to tell any man—"to-day you will carry this," and to another "you will carry that." Each man selected the heaviest he could bear. They felt that the eyes of the world were upon them; and they knew that they would win glory when they returned to their homes in Darjeeling. They would all get good chits—mementos from the leader of the expedition —and perhaps medals which they could cherish all their lives. It was gratifying that when they did return to Darjeeling, the residents received them with pride and hospitality, and made them feel that they had done great work. Who could say that these men were not real sportsmen?

From *The Story of Everest*.

JAMES RAMSEY ULLMAN:

After the harrowing experience of the porters' rescue, a few days' rest at lower altitudes was absolutely necessary, and for the second time the climbers found themselves driven back to the base camp. Their situation could scarcely have been more discouraging. They had planned to be on the northeast ridge by the middle of May, and it was now almost June and no man had yet set foot on the mountain proper. In another ten days, at most, the monsoon would blow in and all hope of success would be gone. They must strike hard and strike fast, or go down again to defeat.

Their plan called for an assault in continuous waves, each climbing party consisting of two men, each attempt to begin on the day after the preceding one. The base of operations was to be Camp IV on the North Col. Camp V was to be set up on the ridge, near the site of the 1922 bivouac, and a sixth camp higher yet—as near to the summit as the porters could possibly take it. The climbers believed that the establishing of Camp VI was the key to the ascent; for the experiences of the previous expedition had convinced them that the top could be reached only if the final "dash" were reduced to not more than 2,000 vertical feet. In the first fine weather they had experienced in weeks the band of determined men struggled back up the glaciers.

Mallory and Geoffrey Bruce were chosen for the first try. With Odell, Irvine, and nine porters they reached the North Col safely, spent the night there, and the next morning struck out up the ridge, accompanied by eight of the "Tigers." Odell, Irvine, and one helper remained on the col in support. The climbers made good progress the first day and set up Camp V at 25,300 feet. A night of zero cold and shrieking wind, however, was too much for the porters, and the next morning no amount of persuasion would induce them to go higher. Seething with frustration, Mallory and Bruce were forced to descend with them.

Meanwhile Norton and Somervell, who formed the second climbing team, began working their way up the mountain, one day behind the others.

LT. COL. E. F. NORTON:

At 3 p.m. on June 1, Somervell and I with our six porters reached Camp IV, where Odell and Irvine took charge of us, allotted us tents and cooked and served us our meals, for they were now installed in their new role as "supporters." And a thankless job this was, for almost the whole day was taken up with performing alternately the menial duties of cook, waiter, or scullion; going out to escort returning parties of porters or climbers across the crevasses and seracs leading to the North Col, or, not infrequently, descending to Camp III for more stores, while more fortunate climbers passed through and disappeared in succession up the mountain. Yet, thankless though the task may have been, Odell and Irvine gave such an exhibition of how it should be done that those of us who once passed through their hands are now spoilt for life; never again shall we enjoy such support as we were given by the "old firm." In a year when, to a conspicuous degree, all played for the side, none did so more conscientiously or with less thought of self than these two.

The morning of June 2 broke fine, and by 6.30 Somervell and I were off with our little party of six porters. The reader will understand that Mallory and Bruce were to have established Camp V overnight; this morning they should have been heading up the North Ridge for Camp VI, carrying with them the tent and sleeping-bags in which they had slept the night before. Our loads, therefore, must comprise one 10-lb. tent, two sleeping-bags, food and "meta" (solid spirit) for ourselves for a possible three nights and for the porters for one; above the North Col porters' loads were always cut down to a maximum of 20 lb. a man, preferably a little under that weight. I cannot remember the exact details of the loads our men carried, but I know they were laden so near the limit that Somervell and I had to carry (as we had done the day before) a light rucksack apiece, with compass, electric torch, a few spare woollen garments, a change of socks, etc., for our own personal use.

Our route crossed the actual Col just below the western lip and, as we emerged from the snow hummocks to traverse it, we suddenly found ourselves in shadow and exposed to the full force of the west wind—from which we were completely sheltered both at Camp IV and in the intervening section; that was a bad moment, its memory is still fresh. The wind, even at this early hour, took our breath away like a plunge into the icy waters of a mountain lake, and in a minute or two our well-protected hands lost all sensation as they grasped the frozen rocks to steady us.

Some little way above the Col we emerged into sunlight again, and though we got the full benefit of the wind all the way up the ridge, we never again experienced anything quite so blighting as those few minutes in the shady funnel of the Col. Nevertheless the wind was all day a serious matter. Though it seemed to cut clean through our windproof clothes, it yet had so solid a push to it that the laden porters often staggered in their steps.

I should here explain that our kit was specially designed to exclude the wind. Personally I wore thick woollen vest and drawers, a thick flannel shirt and two sweaters under a lightish knickerbocker suit of windproof gaberdine the knickers of which were lined with light flannel, a pair of soft elastic Kashmir putties and a pair of boots of felt bound and soled with leather and lightly nailed with the usual Alpine nails. Over all I wore a very light pyjama suit of Messrs. Burberry's "Shackleton" windproof gaberdine. On my hands I wore a pair of long fingerless woollen mits inside a similar pair made of gaberdine; though when step-cutting necessitated a sensitive hold on the axe-haft, I sometimes substituted a pair of silk mits for the inner woollen pair. On my head I wore a fur-lined leather motorcycling helmet, and my eyes and nose were protected by a pair of goggles of Crookes's glass, which were sewn into a leather mask that came well over the nose and covered any part of my face which was not naturally protected by my beard. A huge woollen muffler completed my costume. Somervell was dressed in much the same style, and the porters were equally well equipped—each in a light green canvas windproof suit over a variety of woollen and leather garments. We got used to one another's appearance in time, but every now and then I was struck afresh with the absurdly "gollywog" appearance of the party.

We followed our old route of 1922—the blunt ridge known as the North Arête. For the first 1,500 feet or more the edge of a big snow-bed forms the crest of the ridge, representing the very top of that great mass of hanging ice which clothes the whole of the eastern slopes and cliffs of the North Col. Ascending, we stuck to the rocks just clear of this snow-bed; descending, it is possible to glissade the whole length of it down to the

Col. The rocks are quite easy, but steep enough to be very hard work at those heights. About half-way up this day's climb was the spot where two years before I had, while taking a short rest, placed between my feet my rucksack, containing a few woollen comforts for the night, and something starting it off, it slipped from my grasp, and in a second was leaping and bounding like a great football with the evident intention of stopping nowhere short of the main Rongbuk Glacier below. This gives a fair picture of the general angle of the climb.

Somewhere about this same spot we heard something above and, looking up, were not a little disconcerted to see one Dorjay Pasang, descending to meet us. He was Mallory's and Bruce's leading porter, their first pick and one of the men on whom our highest hopes centred. We had hardly heard his tale of woe and read a note he brought from Mallory when we saw above Mallory, Bruce, and three more porters descending in his tracks.

The wind was too cold for a long conversation, and their story was distressingly simple. On the preceding day they had met a very bitter wind all the way up the arête on which we now stood—so bitter that it had quite taken the heart out of their porters. They had pitched two tents at Camp V at a little over 25,000 feet and spent the night, but next morning nothing —not even Bruce's command of the language and well-known influence over these men—would induce any of the porters to go higher, and the end of it was they had to return. Incidentally, Bruce had had to help the last two or three porters into camp the night before, carrying their loads for them for a short distance, and it was quite evident to us that these excessive exertions had affected him in some way—a surmise which was later confirmed by the discovery that he had strained his heart. So he himself was in no fit state to go on, though none who know him will doubt that he would have done so could the porters have been induced to accompany him. Now there is a moral attached to this story. My diary (written at Camp IV) for the day when this fatal wind was encountered mentions the fact that the weather was "quite perfect"; the porters who failed were the pick of the "Tigers," presumably among the best men we had. Yet these picked men, under the one Sahib of all our party who knew best how to lead the Sherpa porter and on a day which at Camp IV appeared "quite perfect," were clean knocked out by wind and couldn't be induced to advance beyond 25,200 feet. How evident it becomes that it will never be possible to ensure success on any given day at these extreme altitudes!

As Camp V had been left all standing with tents and bedding destined to go higher that morning, Somervell and I were able to detach two of the porters who had accompanied us so far, to return with the descending party, and we now continued with four men, the three whose names I have already given and one Lobsang Tashi, a simple good-natured giant from the eastern borders of Tibet. We reached Camp V without incident about 1 p.m. We had no difficulty in finding the camp from Mallory's description and from certain strips of coloured cloth which each party carried to serve as sign-posts and which had been put up at the point where we were to leave the ridge. The two tents were pitched one above the other on crumbling platforms built on the steep slope just over the edge, and on the east or sheltered side of the North Arête.

The afternoon was spent as every afternoon must always be spent under these conditions. On arrival one crawls into the tent, so completely exhausted that for perhaps three-quarters of an hour one just lies in a sleeping-bag and rests. Then duty begins to call, one member of the party with groans and pantings and frequent rests crawls out of his bag, out of the tent and a few yards to a neighbouring patch of snow, where he fills two big aluminum pots with snow, what time his companion with more panting and groans sits up in bed, lights the meta burner and opens some tins and bags of food—say a stick of pemmican, some tea, sugar and condensed milk, a tin of sardines or bully beef and a box of biscuits.

Presently both are again ensconced in their sleeping-bags side by side, with the meta cooker doing its indifferent best to produce half a pot of warm water from each piled pot of powdery snow. It doesn't sound a very formidable proceeding, and it might appear that I have rather overdrawn the panting and groans; but I have carried out this routine on three or four occasions, and I can honestly say that I know nothing—not even the exertion of steep climbing at these heights—which is so utterly exhausting or which calls for more determination than this hateful duty of high-altitude cooking. The process has to be repeated two or three times as, in addition to the preparation of the evening meal, a thermos flask or two must be filled with water for to-morrow's breakfast and the cooking pots must be washed up. Perhaps the most hateful part of the process is that some of the resultant mess must be eaten, and this itself is only achieved by will power: there is but little desire to eat —sometimes indeed a sense of nausea at the bare idea—though of drink one cannot have enough.

When we had done our duty, I visited the tent where the four porters were packed like sardines, to persuade them to do theirs. For some time I could elicit nothing but grunts, but I succeeded at last in infusing some life into the comatose, unwilling figures, and it then appeared that some stones had fallen from our tent platform and, landing on the porters' tent, had cut Lobsang Tashi's head—a slight affair despite a good showing of blood—and Semchumbi's knee. The latter was a much more serious matter—a nasty gash right across the knee-cap.

With one look at the panorama of glacier and mountain spread out below—a world composed of three elements only, rock, snow and ice, the mountain-tops now gilded by the declining sun and Camp III just discernible in the cold shadow of the North Peak under our feet—we turned in for the night, with gloomy forebodings for the morrow; for there was nothing whatever in the attitude of our porters to-night to encourage us to hope that we should next day succeed any better than Mallory and Bruce.

My diary records that we spent a "fair night"; only some 200 feet below we had seen the collapsed forms of two tents in which two years before Mallory, Somervell, Morshead and I had spent a truly miserable night, scarcely any of us getting any sleep. The difference was largely accounted for by improvements in our equipment and in the organization of our camp, and it is by this progressive raising of the standard of comfort high on the mountain that we shall some day reach the top.

On the morning of June 3 we were up at 5 a.m., and while Somervell busied himself with preparations for breakfast I climbed down to the porters' tent with some misgivings as to what their condition would prove to be. My fears were justified, and for some time groans were the only answer to my questions. But having at last, as I thought, inspired the men sufficiently to induce them to cook and eat a meal, I returned and had breakfast. I then again tackled them, for they seemed incapable of making any sort of a move without much stimulating, and it was at once evident that Lobsang Tashi was finished and useless for any higher climbing. His head wound was nothing, but he complained of sickness, and it was evident that his heart was not in the task of going any higher. Semchumbi was genuinely lame, his knee was much swollen, and he looked an unlikely starter, despite the fact that he showed a good deal more spirit than the other wounded man.

Llakpa Chédé I judged fit and willing to go higher provided that any of the others would, and so I concentrated most of my persuasive powers on Narbu Yishé. I talked for a long time to these men, pointing out the honour and glory that they would achieve if they would but carry their loads another 2,000 feet —thus passing by 1,500 feet the highest point to which loads had ever been carried.

I remember saying, "If you put us up a camp at 27,000 feet and we reach the top, your names shall appear in letters of gold in the book that will be written to describe the achievement." To make a very long story short I succeeded in inducing the three—Narbu Yishé, Llakpa Chédé and Semchumbi—lame as he was—to come on, and we actually started from camp at 9 a.m.—four hours after we had got up. Truly it is not easy to make an early start on Mount Everest! Lobsang Tashi was sent down alone to Camp IV; as soon as his face was turned in the right direction he showed considerable alacrity, and we had the satisfaction of seeing him reach that camp in safety an hour or two later.

Of our ascent of the ridge there is little to tell; it was a repetition of the climb of the day before and was over ground familiar to Somervell and myself, as we had traversed exactly the same route when making for our highest point two years before. Narbu Yishé and Llakpa Chédé went splendidly when once they were started. Somervell was feeling his throat very badly and had constantly to stop and cough, so he took on himself the task of shepherding Semchumbi, who, to do him justice, performed a very fine feat indeed in climbing for four and a half hours with a 20 lb. load, and, though inevitably slow and a drag on the whole party, he remained cheerful and willing and did his very best. The weather continued fine and the wind was markedly less severe than on the day before.

Some time after midday we recognized and passed the highest point that Mallory, Somervell and I had reached in 1922. As I have said before, one's sensations are dulled at these altitudes, but I remember a momentary uplift at the thought that we were actually going to camp higher than the highest point ever reached without oxygen. With a clear day ahead of us, and given favourable conditions, what might we not achieve!

About 1.30 it became evident that it would be impossible to urge the gallant Semchumbi much farther, so I selected a site for our tent, a narrow cleft in the rocks facing north and affording the suggestion—it was little more—of some shelter from the north-west wind. Here I set the two leading porters to scrape and pile the loose stones forming the floor of the cleft into the usual platform for a tent. I can safely say that in two excursions up and down the whole length of the North Arête of Mount Everest I have never seen a single spot affording the 6-foot square level area on which a tent could be pitched without having to build a platform. As Somervell helped and encouraged Semchumbi up the last steep pitch, I went off for three-quarters of an hour to reconnoitre the beginning of the next day's climb.

About 2.30 we sent the three porters down. They had nearly 4,000 feet to descend, for we have since estimated the height of Camp VI at about 26,800 feet, and one of them was lame: so there was not too much time for them to reach Camp IV by daylight. I gave the men a note to be shown to the Sahib in charge of each camp to say that they had done splendidly, and were to be fed on the fat of the land and passed comfortably to the Base Camp and a well-earned rest.

We afterwards learnt that on this day, Odell and Hazard, the latter of whom had reached Camp IV the day before, climbed to Camp V, returning to Camp IV the same night. Odell was after fossils, and actually found the first ever collected on Mount Everest, and Hazard accompanied him for air and exercise. This little stroll is a curious commentary on the fact that two years before the scientists were debating whether human beings could exist without oxygen at 25,000 feet.

Somervell and I spent the afternoon as on the day before, with the exception that we had now no porters to stimulate, and this was fortunate, for as you near 27,000 feet you have no great surplus of determination. My diary for the day finishes with the surprising entry: "Spent the best night since I left Camp I"; yet it was true in my case, and Somervell was at least fairly comfortable if he didn't sleep quite so well as I did. As one of our doubts had always been whether it would be possible to sleep, or even rest well, at 27,000 feet, this is an interesting point. Besides my boots I took to bed with me in my eiderdown sleeping-bag two thermos flasks filled with warm tea; towards morning I found that one of these had got rid of its cork, and its contents—no longer warm—had emptied into my bed.

Once more our hopes of an early start were shattered; snow had to be fetched and melted to provide the essential drink for breakfast. If—as I have before described—vitality is low in the early hours at Camp III at 21,000 feet, it can be guessed how near the limit 6 a.m. found us at 27,000. Yet somehow the job was done and we were off at 6.40.

Perhaps an hour beyond camp we encountered the bottom edge of the great 1,000-foot-deep band of yellow sandstone that crosses the whole north face of Everest from shoulder to shoulder, and is so conspicuous a feature of the mountain as seen from the north. This afforded easy going as we traversed it diagonally, for it was made up of a series of broad ledges running parallel to its general direction and sufficiently broken up to afford easy access, one to the next.

The day was fine and nearly windless—a perfect day for our task—yet it was bitterly cold, and I remember shivering so violently as I sat in the sun during one of our numerous halts, dressed in all the clothes I have described, that I suspected the approach of malaria and took my pulse. I was surprised to find it only about sixty-four, which is some twenty above my normally very slow pulse. I was not wearing snow goggles except when actually on snow—a very small proportion of the day's climb—as I had found that the rims of my goggles somewhat interfered with a clear view of my steps. At a height of about 27,500 feet I began to experience some trouble with my eyes; I was seeing double, and in a difficult step was sometimes in doubt where to put my feet. I thought that this might be a premonitory symptom of snow-blindness, but Somervell assured me that this could not be the case, and he was undoubtedly right, for I have since been told that it was a symptom of lack of control and due to the insufficiency of oxygen in the air I was breathing.

Our pace was wretched. My ambition was to do twenty consecutive paces uphill without a pause to rest and pant elbow on bent knee; yet I never remember achieving it—thirteen was nearer the mark. The process of breathing in the intensely cold dry air, which caught the back of the larynx, had a disastrous effect on poor Somervell's already very bad sore throat and he had constantly to stop and cough. Every five or ten minutes we had to sit down for a minute or two, and we must have looked a sorry couple.

The view from this great height was disappointing. From 25,000 feet the wild tangle of snowy peaks and winding glaciers, each with its parallel lines of moraine like cart tracks on a snowy road, was imposing to a degree. But we were now high above the highest summit in sight, and everything below us was so flattened out that much of the beauty of outline was lost. To the north, over the great plateau of Tibet, the eye travelled over range upon range of minor hills until all sense of distance was lost, only to be sharply regained on picking up a row of snow-peaks just appearing over the horizon like tiny teeth. The day was a remarkably clear one in a country of the clearest atmosphere in the world, and the imagination was fired by the sight of these infinitely distant peaks tucked away over the curve of the horizon.

Towards noon we found ourselves just below the top edge

of the band of sandstone and nearing the big couloir or gully which runs vertically down the mountain and cuts off the base of the final pyramid from the great northern shoulder. The line we had followed was one roughly parallel to and perhaps 500 to 600 feet below the crest of the North-east Arête; this was the line Somervell and I had always favoured in preference to the actual crest, which Mallory advocated.

At midday Somervell succumbed to his throat trouble. He declared that he was only delaying me, and urged me to go on alone and reach the top. I left him sitting under a rock just below the topmost edge of the sandstone band and went on. I followed the actual top edge of the band, which led at a very slightly uphill angle into and across the big couloir; but to reach the latter I had to turn the ends of two pronounced buttresses which ran down the face of the mountain, one of which was a prolongation of a feature on the skyline ridge which we called the second step, and which looked so formidable an obstacle where it crossed the ridge that we had chosen the lower route rather than try and surmount it at its highest point. From about the place where I met with these buttresses the going became a great deal worse; the slope was very steep below me, the foothold ledges narrowed to a few inches in width, and as I approached the shelter of the big couloir there was a lot of powdery snow which concealed the precarious footholds. The whole face of the mountain was composed of slabs like the tiles on a roof, and all sloped at much the same angle as tiles. I had twice to retrace my steps and follow a different band of strata; the couloir itself was filled with powdery snow into which I sank to the knee or even to the waist, and which was yet not of a consistency to support me in the event of a slip. Beyond the couloir the going got steadily worse; I found myself stepping from tile to tile, as it were, each tile sloping smoothly and steeply downwards; I began to feel that I was too much dependent on the mere friction of a boot nail on the slabs. It was not exactly difficult going, but it was a dangerous place for a single unroped climber, as one slip would have sent me in all probability to the bottom of the mountain. The strain of climbing so carefully was beginning to tell and I was getting exhausted. In addition my eye trouble was getting worse and was by now a severe handicap. I had perhaps 200 feet more of this nasty going to surmount before I emerged on to the north face of the final pyramid and, I believe, safety and an easy route to the summit. It was now 1 p.m., and a brief calculation showed that I had no chance of climbing the remaining 800 or 900 feet if I was to return in safety.

At a point subsequently fixed by theodolite as 28,126 feet I turned back and retraced my steps to rejoin Somervell. In an hour I had gained but little—probably under 100 feet in height, and in distance perhaps 300 yards—on the position where we had separated. Surveying is an exact science, and I must not quarrel with Hazard for fixing our highest point 24 feet below the height of Kinchinjunga, the third highest mountain in the world.

I feel that I ought to record the bitter feeling of disappointment which I should have experienced on having to acknowledge defeat with the summit so close; yet I cannot conscientiously say that I felt it much at the time. Twice now I have had thus to turn back on a favourable day when success had appeared possible, yet on neither occasion did I feel the sensations appropriate to the moment. This I think is a psychological effect of great altitudes; the better qualities of ambition and will to conquer seem dulled to nothing, and one turns downhill with but little feelings other than relief that the strain and effort of climbing are finished.

I was near the end of my powers, and had for some time been going too slowly to hope to reach the summit. Whether the height I had reached was nearing the limit of human endurance without the artificial aid of oxygen, or whether my earlier exertions and hardships in the month of May accounted for my exhaustion, I cannot, of course, say, but I incline to the latter opinion; and I still believe that there is nothing in the atmospheric conditions even between 28,000 and 29,000 feet to prevent a fresh and fit party from reaching the top of Mount Everest without oxygen.

One small incident will serve to show that I must have been very much below my proper form at this time, and that my nerve had been shaken by the last two hours of climbing alone on steep and slippery going. As I approached Somervell I had to cross a patch of snow lying thinly over some sloping rocks. It was neither steep nor difficult, and not to be compared to the ground I had just left, yet suddenly I felt that I could not face it without help, and I shouted to Somervell to come and throw me the end of the rope. Here again I remember the difficulty I had in making my voice carry perhaps 100 yards. Somervell gave me the required aid, and I could see the surprise he felt at my needing it in such a place.

Then came the descent. Soon after we started down, at about 2 p.m., Somervell's axe slipped from his numb fingers and went cart-wheeling down the slopes below. This must have been somewhere about the point where an hour or two before he had taken his highest photograph; and it is a proof of the deceptive picture of the true angle of the mountain conveyed by these photographs that it does not give the impression that a dropped axe would go any distance without coming to rest, yet his never looked like stopping, and disappeared from our view still going strong.

We retraced our steps of the morning; we made very poor going, descending at a very much slower pace than we had made two years before when we turned back from our highest point some 1,000 feet lower.

We looked in at our tent at Camp VI, finding it without difficulty, collected one or two of our belongings and a section of tent pole as a substitute for Somervell's axe, collapsed and weighted the tent with stones, and started down the interminable North Arête. Sunset found us level with Camp V, which we left below us on the right without departing from the blunt crest of the Arête. We were unroped, for here the going was both safe and easy. Arrived on the big snow-bed I glissaded for some little distance before I realized that Somervell had stopped behind, and I had to wait quite half an hour for him to catch up. I concluded that he had stopped to sketch or photograph the effect of the sunset glow on the great panorama of peaks surrounding us—a proof that I had by no means realized his condition; actually he had been stopped by a more than usually severe fit of coughing which had ended by very nearly choking him, and he was probably only saved by coughing up the obstructing matter along with a lot of blood. When he rejoined me, coming very slowly down the rocks, as he could not trust himself to glissade on the snow, it was already dark and I lit up my electric torch.

As we neared the Col I began to shout to Camp IV, for it was one of our rules that any party of porters or climbers descending from the mountain be met at the Col and escorted and roped over the intricate route into camp by one or more of the supporters, who knew the way by heart. At last I made myself heard, and an answering shout informed us that our escort was coming and was bringing an oxygen apparatus and cylinder. But there was something we wanted far more than oxygen, for we were parched and famished with thirst. I remember shouting again and again, "We don't want the d——d oxygen; we want drink." My own throat and voice were in none too good a case, and my feeble wail seemed to be swallowed up in the dim white expanse below glimmering in the starlight.

A hundred feet or more above the Col, Mallory and Odell met us, and told us that Irvine was in camp hard at work preparing our dinner. Somervell had a go at the oxygen, but seemed to get little benefit from it, and I tried with the same result. But we were perfectly fit to get along without it, and perhaps another three-quarters of an hour saw us arrive in camp. Mallory and Odell were kindness itself, and they kept congratulating us on having reached what we estimated as a height of 28,000 feet, though we ourselves felt nothing but disappointment at our failure. We reached Camp IV at 9.30 p.m., and what a different welcome it gave us to that we had received at the same place two years before on our arrival at eleven at night in an empty and deserted camp! Young Irvine had both tea and soup ready for us, and we had something to eat; but our appetites were meagre, and herein lies one of the difficulties of high climbing: one eats from a sense of duty, and it is impossible to force oneself to take enough food even to begin to make good the day's wastage of tissue.

As Mallory and I lay in our tent, he explained that he had decided that if we two failed to reach the summit, he was determined to make one more attempt, this time with oxygen, and how he had been down to Camp III with Bruce and collected sufficient porters to enable the attempt to be staged.* I entirely agreed with his decision, and was full of admiration for the indomitable spirit of the man, determined, in spite of his already excessive exertions, not to admit defeat while any chance remained, and I must admit that—such was his will power and

* It may be asked how it came that sufficient porters were now available for an attempt with oxygen, seeing that we had decided against an oxygen attempt at Camp I on the grounds of inadequate transport.

Mallory and Irvine decided to use practically no oxygen up to Camp VI; two or three porters who had returned from Camp V after the abortive attempt, were employed again; the continued fine weather had so heartened the porters that two extra volunteers over and above the fifteen "tigers" were found; and, lastly, Camp VI having been established with tents and bedding by Somervell and me, nearly every available porter could now be used for carrying oxygen cylinders.

It was to Bruce's energy (despite his strained heart) that the successful organization of the transport for this attempt must be credited.

nervous energy—he still seemed entirely adequate to the task. I differed with him in his decision to take Irvine as his companion—for two reasons: firstly, that Irvine was now suffering from the prevalent throat trouble, though certainly not as badly as Somervell had been before the start of our climb; secondly, that he was not the experienced climber that Odell was, while Odell was obviously fit and strong, and, acclimatizing very slowly as he had done, was now beginning to show unmistakably that we had in him a climber of unequalled endurance and toughness. Mallory's reasons for his choice were that though Odell and Irvine were both thoroughly *au fait* with every detail of the oxygen apparatus, yet the latter had a peculiar genius for mechanical expedients, and had taken the lead in devising means to obviate its numerous shortcomings; and he insisted that those who were to use the apparatus must have faith in its efficacy. Odell, having used it with Bruce on the day of their abortive attempt to reach Camp IV without apparently benefiting from it, certainly had not this confidence.

But it was obviously no time for me to interfere with the composition of the party, and when I found that Mallory had completed his plans I made no attempt to do so.

Some time after eleven o'clock that night, as I was dozing off to sleep, I was suddenly wakened by sharp pain in my eyes, and found that I had been smitten with a severe attack of snow blindness. In the morning I found myself completely blind, and I remained in this condition for the next sixty hours, suffering a good deal of pain.

June 5 was spent in the usual preparations for Mallory and Irvine's climb, on which they were to start next day. I was only able to help by periodically coming to the door of my tent and talking to the porters, for, poor though was my knowledge of Nepalese, there was no one else at Camp IV who could do so even as effectively as I; Mallory had learnt a sufficient smattering of Hindustani to communicate with these men to a certain extent, but it was evident that his party might have considerable trouble in getting their porters on from Camp V to Camp VI (though we hoped that their reluctance would be reduced to some extent by the fact that the carry had now been once successfully accomplished), and I had to do my best to stimulate the porters in advance for this crucial moment. That afternoon Somervell descended to Camp III and thence next day went on down to the Base Camp, and Hazard arrived from Camp III to take Irvine's place, with Odell as supporter at Camp IV.

On June 6 at 7.30 a.m. we said good-bye to Mallory and Irvine, little guessing that we should see them no more. My last impression of my friends was a handshake and a word of blessing, for it was only in my imagination that I could see the little party winding its way amid the snow humps and ice crevasses leading to the Col—the two climbers, never to return, accompanied by four or five porters.

About 10.30 a.m. Hingston arrived from Camp III with two porters, to see what could be done for my eyes, of which Somervell had told him. Hingston is nothing if not efficient; he had already proved himself a remarkable goer on the glacier as far as Camp III, and we were scarcely surprised when he arrived in Camp IV with the matter-of-fact ease of an experienced mountaineer. Yet with a view to what followed it is worthy of note that he had never previously climbed a mountain in the Alpine sense.

An examination of my eyes showed that nothing could be done to restore my sight at the moment, though there was little question that they would recover in a day or two; but I was anxious not to remain a useless encumbrance on the supporters at Camp IV and, Hingston volunteering to escort me with his two porters, I decided to go down, blind as I was, to Camp III.

Hazard offered to accompany us as far as the top of the ice chimney to rope me from above down this steepest portion of the route, including the chimney itself and the wall below it. Accordingly, about 11 a.m. we started the descent. The two porters, Nima Tundrup and Chutin, were both strong and steady climbers, and between them and Hingston—the last doing all the really responsible work—my every footstep was guided and my feet placed for me the whole way down, while Hazard held me with a rope down each steep section in succession. It was indeed a remarkable performance on the part of Hingston: he gave me the impression of having the steadiness and confidence of an Alpine guide. I was shod with crampons, and thanks to them and to the help of my companions I never had an anxious moment, though it was necessarily a most laborious and tedious process. To make a long story short we reached the glacier without incident and hence sent one porter on to fetch six men, with the one-man carrier, from Camp III to meet me where our route took to the moraine; for on its rough boulders I could never have made any progress at all.

These six men took it in turns to carry me, and did so over the most appalling going—boulders, ice, and frozen scree—without a single false step until, about 5 p.m., we reached Camp III; there I was welcomed by Bruce and Noel with that extraordinary solicitude and kindness which I have come to recognize as the one great reward that awaits the unsuccessful Everest climber.

Next morning I was beginning to see a little, and in two more days was completely recovered. Bruce, Noel, Hingston and I decided to remain at Camp III until the fate of Mallory and Irvine's attempt was decided. During the next four days we were to pass through every successive stage of suspense and anxiety from high hope to hopelessness, and the memory of them is such that Camp III must remain to all of us the most hateful place in the world.

From *The Fight for Everest: 1924.*

JAMES RAMSEY ULLMAN:

Everest was George Mallory's mountain, more than any other man's. He had pioneered the way to it and blazed the trail to its heights; his flaming spirit had been the principal driving force behind each attack; the conquest of the summit was the great dream of his life. His companions, watching him during these early June days of 1924, realized that he was preparing for his mightiest effort, and it seems fitting to pause briefly at this point and hear, through their words, what manner of man he was.

CAPT. JOHN NOEL:

Mallory was no ordinary man. Raeburn, the veteran climber, before he was afflicted with the illness which unfortunately finished his climbing days, said that for sheer dash there was no one to touch this young climber. He applied himself to the task, which might have appalled most other men by its danger and magnitude, with indomitable energy and will. When he found his mistake over the missing of the East Rongbuk approach to Everest, he got his caravan of exhausted porters and his companions over the Lakpa-La in soft snow, nearly tearing their hearts out, and then encouraged them on still further even to surmount the greater obstacle of the terrible Ice Cliff.

With his physical strength he had a vivid imagination and a great heart. He seemed to live in a realm remote from everyday life. It could be seen that he had great imagination and ideals. He was stubborn to a degree; and his ideas were, perhaps, lacking in flexibility; but yet in another sense this same rigidity contributed to the strength of that determination which caused him to push through with dauntless energy any enterprise he might take up. In camp on the later expeditions, we often used to tease him in fun for his "advanced views." Some of these views on political and social questions were indeed advanced. (You see even in the camps on Everest, as in every remote corner of the world, men are wont to talk on politics forever.) He was lofty as the peaks he loved.

He was always young at heart and fond of a game. In America, after his sensational climbs in 1922, a photographer caught him climbing a fire escape at a New York skyscraper hotel, but not in the manner the builders intended. He was going up underneath the steps hand over hand, sometimes upside down!

But yet he always preserved a certain aloofness. If he had lived, after conquering the heights which were his ambitions, no doubt he would with his intellect and energy have accomplished fine things. Above all, he was a mountaineer. By that I do not mean so much a climber of crags, but a man who lives among mountains and loves them. On Everest he seemed to have centered all his ambition and energy.

How this mountain obsessed him! He threw his whole body and soul into the fight against her. He seemed always as if he were measuring and calculating. Yet I always felt in my own acquaintance with him that some strange fatalism overshadowed his ambition. I could notice that he was always trying to convince himself that he could beat the mountain but at the same time he seemed to show a consciousness somehow or other that the mountain held the mastery.

"The chances of a given party to reach the summit in a given time are fifty to one against." That was the expression, now become historic in the story of Everest, which he used on the occasion of the first public lecture he gave in London after his return in 1921.

How the "personality", I might say, of this mountain had impressed itself upon Mallory can be traced in things he said from time to time. For instance, in 1924, when he started up the Rongbuk Glacier for the last time, to make his biggest effort—the effort from which he never returned—he said, "We expect no mercy from Everest.— But yet it will be well for her that she deign to take notice of the little group that approaches stealthily over her glaciers again, and that she shall observe among the scattered remnants she has thrice put to flight still a power to string her very nose tip."

From *The Story of Everest.*

T. HOWARD SOMERVELL:

I usually shared a tent with Mallory, in whom I felt that I had found a kindred spirit. Sometimes we played card games for two, such as picquet, but more often we read selections from the *Spirit of Man*, by Robert Bridges, or bits of modern poetry, each reading aloud to the other passages of which we were particularly fond. We discussed climbs in the Alps and planned expeditions for the future. We made, among other things, a detailed plan for the first complete ascent of the Péteret ridge of Mont Blanc. Alas! the sad accident of 1924 put a stop to all the plans that Mallory and I had made of conquests of the Alps.

But during this and the subsequent Everest Expeditions, George Mallory was the man whom I always felt that I knew the best, and I have seldom had a better or more intimate friend. When one shares a tent for days on end throughout the better part of six months with a man, one gets an insight into his character such as is vouchsafed to few other men. These many days of companionship with a man whose outlook on life was lofty and choice, human and loving, and in a measure divine, still remain for me a priceless memory. I forget the details of George Mallory's views on most of the many subjects we discussed, but in general he took always the big and liberal view. He was really concerned with social evils, and

The northeast ridge and shoulder. The summit of Everest
to the right in background.

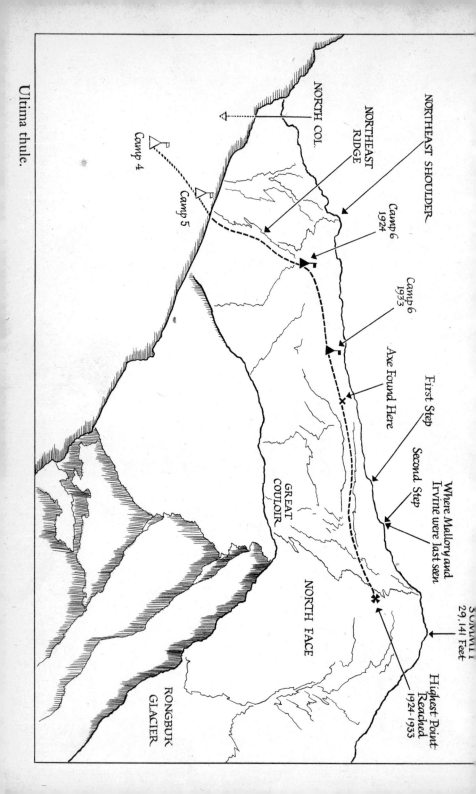

Ultima thule.

Norton at 28,000 feet. This photograph, taken by Somervell,
is the highest ever made on the earth's surface.

recognized that they could only be satisfactorily solved by the changing and ennobling of individual character. He hated anything that savoured of hypocrisy or humbug, but cherished all that is really good and sound. His was a great soul, and I pray that some of its greatness may live on in the souls of his friends.

From *After Everest.*

LT. COL. E. F. NORTON:

Mallory's was no common personality. Physically he always seemed to me the beau ideal of the mountaineer; he was very good looking, and I have always thought that his boyish face —for he looked absurdly young for his thirty-seven years— was the outward and visible sign of a wonderful constitution. His graceful figure was the last word in wiry activity and he walked with a tireless swing which made him a man with whom few could live uphill; he was almost better downhill, for his years of mountain training had added balance and studied poise to his natural turn of speed.

But it was the spirit of the man that made him the great mountaineer he was: a fire burnt in him and caused his willing spirit to rise superior to the weakness of the flesh; he lived on his nerves, and throughout two campaigns on Mount Everest (I never climbed with him elsewhere) it was almost impossible to make out whether he was a tired man or not, for he responded instantly to every call that was made on him, and while the call lasted his would remain the dominant spirit in any enterprise. The conquest of the mountain became an obsession with him, and for weeks and months he devoted his whole time and energy to it, incessantly working at plans and details of organization; and when it came to business he expended on it every ounce of his unrivalled physical energy.

Such was Mallory the mountaineer; but there was another and quite different Mallory, whom we knew in the mess tent and at times when there was no call for action. This aspect of him was curiously at variance with the other; it showed us a nature æsthetic and gentle combined with a keen and cultured intelligence; though here too a flash of the same impatience with which he urged on our flagging footsteps on the mountain would sometimes break out in our arguments and discussions; for his views were always clear-cut and decided and his nature masterful. We used to dub him a "high brow" and in fancy I can hear Longstaff chaffing him in 1922: "Mallory, you know the one good thing the Bolsheviks have done in Russia? They've obliterated the Intelligentsia."

His death robs us of a right loyal friend, a knight "sans peur et sans reproche" amongst mountaineers and the greatest antagonist that Everest has had—or is like to have.

From The Fight for Everest: 1924.

R. L. G. Irving: *

Till he was eighteen George Mallory had been on nothing higher than the Malvern Hills. Then he was asked to join a small party in the Alps, and he came back with 'the great door of the mountains' opened wide before him. You may see in that mere chance of the 'Providence that shapes our ends'; in his case it is difficult to believe it was anything but the latter, for in climbing he found the perfect way of fulfilment for what his body and his soul desired.

The smooth oval face with its extraordinary likeness to a Botticelli madonna was very different from the rough, rugged type we often associate with great mountaineers. It was not till you saw him at work on steep rocks or ice, the perfect

---

* Irving, though not an Everest climber, was—and is today—one of the most distinguished of the older generation of English mountaineers and mountain-writers. A close personal friend of Mallory's, it had been he who first introduced him to climbing when he was a master and Mallory a student at Winchester School.—*Editor.*

balance and the completely natural grace of upward movement, that you knew his body to be the perfect servant of his
mind; and that mind was, above all else, a climbing mind. He
was always striving after the higher, bigger things, the great
truths to whose sources mountains pointed him. And so there
was in him a continuous and rapid development of mind after
the age at which education in the narrower sense is often regarded as complete. It is in mental grasp and breadth of outlook
rather than in climbing technique that the Mallory of Everest
differs from the youth who discovered the Slab Route on
Lliwedd in recovering a pipe.

One feels, as one reads his letters from Tibet and his chapters on the Reconnaissance, that Everest is revealing itself to
a man as fitted to understand its majesty as to accept its challenge. Everest in 1921 is a thing of mystery and romance. In
1922 and still more in 1924 it appears as the familiar, mind-
obsessing goal at the end of the two miles of breathless, wind-
swept, pitiless, and almost hateful ridge that joins it to the
North Col. I believe the abandonment of the enterprise after
1922 would have been no disappointment to Mallory. For him
snow mountains were not simply opponents to be overcome;
they were things that feed the springs of reverence and affection, making a man go with a lighter step and a more grateful
heart along the road of life. But being asked to go, such a man
could not refuse. And his fitness on the third expedition was
amazing. His letters, always the most critical of his physical
condition, are proof of it.

The story of his last climb is known to every reader of the
Journal. Soon after midday on 8th June, just below the steep
final step of the North Ridge, he was seen with Irvine 'going
strong for the top.' That is the last glimpse we have of George
Mallory. The progress of the great climb was being watched
through the Press by thousands who never before watched and
will never again watch any other climb. And we who knew him

saw the same modest, idealistic George obeying the call made upon his physical and spiritual vitality by the sight of any up-soaring ridge and wall of rock or snow, whether in Britain or the Alps or the Himalaya. Only, in the Everest expeditions, there was an element of duty, increasing in force with each succeeding attempt, imparting for him a special nobility and sternness to the greatest mountaineering adventure of his life.

Did he and Irvine reach the summit? It is probable that we shall never know. And what wonderful justice there would be in the decree of Fate that the honour of the first ascent should never be awarded to any but the man who explored the approaches to the mountain and found the only route, who saved his three companions on the return from the magnificent attempt in 1922, and who came back in 1924 to give his life to accomplish what he had set out to do. With better fortune in the matter of weather, with a less cumbrous means of carrying oxygen, Everest may be climbed, shall we say, a second time? How little it matters, after all, whether those last few hundred feet are still untrodden! It was George Mallory himself who wrote of the successful ending of a great climb: 'Have we vanquished an enemy? None but ourselves. Have we gained success? That word means nothing here. . . . To struggle and to understand, never this last without the other; such is the law.' Let us leave him to his rest on Everest, this Galahad of mountaineering, pure of heart, high of purpose. 'To struggle and to understand. . . .' Has he won that goal seeing now face to face, knowing even as we are known? We may believe it if we cannot prove.

From *The Alpine Journal*, vol. 36, 1924.

JAMES RAMSEY ULLMAN:

Now, back to the mountain. . . .

On the night of June fifth, five climbers slept in the huddle of tents on the North Col: the snowblind Norton on his way down, Mallory and Irvine on their way up, and Odell and Hazard acting as support for both parties. It is Odell's account of the hours and days which followed that forms the culminating chapter in the story of the expedition of 1924.

N. E. ODELL:

I think most of the party, with perhaps the exception of the unfortunate Norton, slept well that night, though Irvine admitted his sorely sun-scorched face had caused him distinct discomfort at times. Hazard and I were up early the morning of the 6th, and soon had frizzling and crackling over the Primus stove a choice fry of sardines, to be served up in Mallory and Irvine's tent with biscuits and ample hot tea, or chocolate. On the announcement of this breakfast they seemed pleased enough, but I must admit that either owing to the excitement or restlessness to be off they hardly did justice to the repast, or flattered the cooks! At 8.40 they were ready to start, and I hurriedly "snapped" them as they were loading up with the oxygen apparatus. Their personal loads consisted of the modified apparatus with two cylinders only and a few other small items such as wraps and a food ration for the day, amounting to not more than perhaps 25 lb. This may sound to many a very heavy load to carry at such altitudes, and in actual fact it is, but it is an easy load compared with the total of 40 lb. or more that the original breathing apparatus as well as the items of extra clothing, etc., that must be carried, amounted to. The eight porters, who accompanied them from Camp IV, carried provisions, bedding, and additional oxygen cylinders, but of course no breathing apparatus for their own use. It always amazed us how little on the whole our Sherpas were affected by moderate loads, though as a matter of fact at these altitudes we contrived to give them no more than 20 to 25 lb. to carry.

The party moved off in silence as we bid them adieu, and they were soon lost to view amidst the broken ice-masses that concealed from view the actual saddle of the North Col and the lower part of the North Ridge of the mountain.

Though a brilliant morning, my diary records it as very cloudy in the afternoon and even snowing a little in the evening. It was at 9.45 that morning that Hingston arrived and conducted Norton in his sightless condition down to Camp III, Hazard going down as far as the rope ladder and then returning to me on the North Col. I occupied myself meanwhile with various camp duties and observations. That evening, soon after 5 o'clock, four of Mallory's porters returned from Camp V, where his party was spending the night, and brought me a note saying, "There is no wind here, and things look hopeful."

On the 7th Mallory's party was to go on up to Camp VI, and I that same day with Nema, who was the only porter of the two available at the North Col, followed up in support to Camp V. This method of support, a stage as it were behind, was rendered necessary by the limited accommodation at these two high camps, consequent upon the inadequate number of porters available to carry up sufficient tentage, etc. I had expected on my way up to Camp V to find a spare oxygen-breathing set that had been left there earlier, but discovered that Irvine the previous day had taken the mouthpiece from it for a spare, and so rendered it useless to me. However, I carried it on up to Camp V in case another mouthpiece were available there; but this was not so, though it did not bother me, since I found I was able to get along as well without its aid, and better without the bulky inconvenience of the whole apparatus. Not long after my arrival Mallory and Irvine's four remaining porters returned from Camp VI, their advent having been heralded by stones falling unpleasantly near the tent, that had been unwittingly displaced by them during their descent of the steep slopes above. The exposure of Camp V in this respect had been borne in on me during my first visit with Hazard, when Norton and Somervell's returning porters had likewise unknowingly bombarded our frail tents with stones and struck a porter of ours, though fortunately with no severe results. Mallory's porters brought me the following message:

"Dear Odell,—

"We're awfully sorry to have left things in such a mess— our Unna Cooker rolled down the slope at the last moment. Be sure of getting back to IV to-morrow in time to evacuate before dark, as I hope to. In the tent I must have left a compass—for the Lord's sake rescue it: we are without. To here on 90 atmospheres * for the two days—so we'll probably go on two cylinders—but it's a beastly load for climbing. Perfect weather for the job!

Yours ever,

"G. Mallory."

Nema, my porter, was obviously much affected by mountain sickness, which made it very unlikely that he would be able to go higher next day, and consequently I decided to send him down that evening with the other four returning men. It is wonderful how soon that strange malady, so often described as "mountain sickness," seems to disappear not only with the descent, but when the decision to descend has been made: at any rate I have noticed it time and again with these native porters, if not with other climbers! When no further effort is to be called for, the psychological effect is such that a fresh stimulus to normality is given, and sickness and other effects disappear. And as the little party started down Nema seemed as active and fit as the rest of them. However, I was not loath to let him go, as I knew by so doing I should be freer on the morrow to wander about over the North Face and make a more

---

* This refers to the pressure, and consequent amount of oxygen they had been using. For full supply, the pressure stood at 120 atmospheres.

thorough geological examination of it on my way up to Camp VI. After a short search within the tent I duly found Mallory's missing prismatic compass. That evening as I looked out from the little rock ledge on which my tent was situated, the weather seemed most promising, and I knew with what hopeful feelings and exultant cheer Mallory and Irvine would take their last look around before closing themselves in their tiny tent at VI that night. My outlook, situated though I was 2,000 feet lower down the mountain-side than they, was nevertheless commanding and impressive in the extreme, and the fact that I was quite alone certainly enhanced the impressiveness of the scene. To the westward was a savagely wild jumble of peaks towering above the upper Rongbuk Glacier and its many affluents, culminating in the mighty Cho-uyo (26,730 feet) and Gyachung Kang (25,910 feet), bathed in pinks and yellows of the most exquisite tints. Right opposite were the gaunt cliffs of Everest's North Peak, their banded structure pregnant with the more special and esoteric interest of their past primeval history, and in this respect not detracting by its impression from the vision of such as can behold with more than single eye. This massive pyramid of rock, the one near thing on God's earth, seemed only to lend greater distance to the wide horizon which it intercepted, and its dark bulk the more exaggerate the brilliant opalescence of the far northern horizon of Central Tibet, above which the sharp-cut crests of distant peaks thrust their purple fangs, one in particular rising supreme among them. To the eastward, floating in thin air, 100 miles away, the snowy top of Kanchenjunga appeared, and nearer, the beautifully varied outline of the Gyankar Range, that guards the tortuous passages of the Arun in its headlong plunge towards the lowlands of Nepal. It has been my good fortune to climb many peaks alone and witness sunset from not a few, but this was the crowning experience of them all, an ineffable transcendent experience that can never fade from memory.

A meal of "Force" and a little jam varied with macaroni and tomatoes completed my supper, and then by dint of two sleeping-bags and the adoption of a position to avoid the larger stones of the floor, I stretched myself diagonally across the tiny tent in an endeavour to obtain what sleep I might pending a visit from the notorious Sukpas, or even the watchdogs of Chomolungma! For all I know none put in an appearance, and even the wind did not attain its usual boisterous degree, or threaten to start the somewhat precarious built-up platform on which the tent was perched on a glissade down the mountain-side. I kept reasonably warm and consequently had a fair amount of sleep. I was up at 6, but the great efforts necessitated and energy absorbed at these altitudes, by the various little obligations of breakfast and putting on one's boots, etc., prevented my starting off before eight o'clock. Carrying a rucksack with provisions in case of shortage at Camp VI, I made my solitary way up the steep slope of snow and rock behind Camp V and so reached the crest of the main North Ridge. The earlier morning had been clear and not unduly cold, but now rolling banks of mist commenced to form and sweep from the westward across the great face of the mountain. But it was fortunate that the wind did not increase. There were indications though that this mist might be chiefly confined to the lower half of the mountain, as on looking up one could see a certain luminosity that might mean comparatively clear conditions about its upper half. This appearance so impressed me that I had no qualms for Mallory and Irvine's progress upward from Camp VI, and I hoped by this time that they would be well on their way up the final pyramid of the summit. The wind being light, they should have made good progress and unhampered by their intended route along the crest of the north-east shoulder.

At about 26,000 feet I climbed a little crag which could possibly have been circumvented, but which I decided to tackle direct, more perhaps as a test of my condition than for any other reason. There was scarcely 100 feet of it, and as I reached the top there was a sudden clearing of the atmosphere above me and I saw the whole summit ridge and final peak of Everest unveiled. I noticed far away on a snow slope leading up to what seemed to me to be the last step but one from the base of the final pyramid, a tiny object moving and approaching the rock step. A second object followed, and then the first climbed to the top of the step. As I stood intently watching this dramatic appearance, the scene became enveloped in cloud once more, and I could not actually be certain that I saw the second figure join the first. It was of course none other than Mallory and Irvine, and I was surprised above all to see them so late as this, namely 12.50, at a point which, if the "second rock step," they should have reached according to Mallory's schedule by 8 a.m. at latest, and if the "first rock step" proportionately earlier. The "second rock step" is seen prominently in photographs of the North Face from the Base Camp, where it appears a short distance from the base of the final pyramid down the snowy first part of the crest of the North-east Arête. The lower "first rock step" is about an equivalent distance again to the left. Owing to the small portion of the summit ridge uncovered I could not be precisely certain at which of these two "steps" they were, as in profile and from below they are very similar, but at the time I took it for the upper "second step." However, I am a little doubtful now whether the latter would not be hidden by the projecting nearer ground from my position below on the face. I could see that they were moving expeditiously as if endeavouring to make up for lost time. True, they were moving one at a time over what was apparently but moderately difficult ground, but one cannot definitely conclude from this that they were roped together—a not unimportant consideration in any estimate of what may have eventually befallen them. I had seen that there was a considerable quantity of new snow covering some of the upper rocks near the summit ridge, and this may well have caused delay in the ascent. Burdened as they undoubtedly would be with the oxygen apparatus, these snow-covered débris-sprinkled slabs may have given much trouble. The oxygen apparatus itself may have needed repair or readjustment either before or after they left Camp VI, and so have delayed them. Though rather unlikely, it is just conceivable that the zone of mist and clouds I had experienced below may have extended up to their level and so have somewhat impeded their progress. Any or all of these factors may have hindered them and prevented their getting higher in the time.

I continued my way up to Camp VI, and on arrival there about two o'clock snow commenced to fall and the wind increased. I placed my load of fresh provisions, etc., inside the tiny tent and decided to take shelter for a while. Within were a rather mixed assortment of spare clothes, scraps of food, their two sleeping-bags, oxygen cylinders, and parts of apparatus; outside were more parts of the latter and of the duralumin carriers. It might be supposed that these were undoubted signs of reconstructional work and probable difficulties with the oxygen outfit. But, knowing Irvine's propensities, I had at the time not the slightest qualms on that score. Nothing would have amused him more—as it ever had, though with such good results—than to have spent the previous evening on a job of work of some kind or other in connection with the oxygen apparatus, or to have invented some problem to be solved even if it never really had turned up! He loved to dwell amongst, nay, revelled in, pieces of apparatus and a litter of tools, and was never happier than when up against some mechanical difficulty! And here to 27,000 feet he had been faithful to himself and carried his usual traits, though his workshop for the purpose would be decidedly limited, and could not have run to much more than a spanner and possibly a pair of pliers! But it was wonderful what he could do with these. I found they had left no note, which left me ignorant as to the time they had actually started out, or what might have intervened to cause delay. The snow continued, and after a while I began to wonder whether the weather and conditions higher up would have necessitated the party commencing their return.

Camp VI was in a rather concealed position on a ledge and backed by a small crag, and in the prevailing conditions it seemed likely they would experience considerable difficulty in finding it. So I went out along the mountain-side in the direction of the summit and having scrambled up about 200 feet, and whistled and jodelled meanwhile in case they should happen to be within hearing, I then took shelter for a while behind a rock from the driving sleet. One could not see more than a few yards ahead so thick was the atmosphere, and in an endeavour to forget the cold I examined the rocks around me in case some new point of geological significance could be found. But in the flurry of snow and the biting wind even my accustomed ardour for this pursuit began to wane, and within an hour I decided to turn back, realizing that even if Mallory and Irvine were returning they could hardly yet be within call, and less so under the existing conditions. As I reached Camp VI, the squall, which had lasted not more than two hours, blew over, and before long the whole north face became bathed in sunshine, and the freshly fallen snow speedily evaporated, there being no intermediate melting phase as takes place at lower altitudes. The upper crags became visible, but I could see no signs of the party. I waited for a time, and then I remembered that Mallory had particularly requested me in his last note to return to the North Col as he specially wished to reach there, and presumably if possible evacuate it and reach Camp III that same night, in case the monsoon should suddenly break. But besides this the single small tent at Camp VI was only just large enough for two, and if I remained and they returned, one of us would have had to sleep outside in the open—a hazardous expedient in such an exposed position.

I placed Mallory's retrieved compass that I had brought up from Camp V in a conspicuous place in the corner of the tent by the door, and after partaking of a little food and leaving ample provisions against their return, I closed up the tent. Leaving Camp VI therefore about 4.30, I made my way down by the extreme crest of the North Ridge, halting now and again to glance up and scan the upper rocks for some signs of the party, who should by now, it seemed to me, be well on their downward tracks. But I looked in vain: I could, at that great distance and against such a broken background, little hope to pick them out, except by some good chance they should be crossing one of the infrequent patches of snow, as had happened that morning, or be silhouetted on the crest of the Northeast Arête, if they should be making their way back by that of their ascent, as seemed most likely. I was abreast of Camp V at 6.15, but there being no reason to turn aside to visit it, situated as it was a hundred yards or so off the main ridge eastward along the face, I hurried downwards. It was interesting to find, as I had earlier, that descending at high altitudes is little more fatiguing than at any other moderate altitudes, and of course in complete contrast to the extraordinarily exhausting reverse of it, and it seemed that a party that has not completely shot its bolt and run itself to a standstill, so to speak, on the ascent, and in any attempt on the summit, should find itself unexpectedly able to make fast time downward and escape being benighted. And as I shall mention later, the unnecessity of oxygen for the properly acclimatized climber seems never more evident than in this capability of quick descent. I was able to speed up my headlong descent upon the North Col by taking to the crest of the snow cornice to the leeward of the North Ridge, and finding the snow between 24,800 and 23,500 feet hard and conveniently steep, it was possible to indulge in a fast standing glissade that brought me to Camp IV by 6.45 p.m. It was rather surprising and withal useful to know that this distance between Camps IV and V, which upwards necessitated at any time between three to four hours of arduous toil, could be covered in barely thirty-five minutes descending by means of a glissade; but it was a glissade that involved care and judgment to avoid the Scylla of the rocks on the one hand, and the Charybdis of the cornice edge on the other!

Hazard welcomed me at Camp IV, and right glad was I of his wonderful brew of hot soup made from a mixture of at least six varieties of Maggi. Fortunately I am not habitually cursed with thirst on a mountain, but I was rather surprised to find how little Everest with its excessive dryness affected me in that way. However, whatever necessary moisture had been evaporated from my constitution during the last two days was now speedily replaced from the amazing quantities of soup and tea put in front of me by Hazard. And what a two days had it been—days replete with a gamut of impressions that neither the effect of high altitude, whatever this might be, nor the grim events of the two days that were to follow could efface from one's memory! A period of intensive experiences, alike romantic, æsthetic, and scientific in interest, these each in their various appeals enabling one to forget even the extremity of upward toil inherently involved, and ever at intervals carrying one's thoughts with expectancy to that resolute pair who might at any instant appear returning with news of final conquest. They would be late, for were they not behind their scheduled time when last seen! And hence they would succeed in reaching Camp VI only, or Camp V possibly, before darkness. The evening was a clear one, and we watched till late that night for some signs of Mallory and Irvine's return, or even an indication by flare of distress. The feeble glow that after sunset pervaded the great dark mountain face above us was later lost in filtered moonlight reflected from high summits of the West Rongbuk. We hoped that this would aid them if perchance some incident had precluded their return as yet to Camp V or VI.

Next morning we scrutinized through field-glasses the tiny tents of those camps far up above us, thinking they must be at one or other, and would not as yet have started down. But no movement at all could be seen, and at noon I decided to go up in search. Before leaving, Hazard and I drew up a code of signals so that we could communicate to some extent in case of necessity: this was by a fixed arrangement of sleeping-bags placed against the snow for day signals, and as far as I was concerned Hazard was to look out for them at stated times at either of the upper camps. Answering signals from him were also arranged. For use after dark we arranged a code of simple flash signals, which included, of course, in case of need, the International Alpine Distress Signal. We had by this time three porters at the North Col Camp, and two of these I managed after some difficulty to persuade to come with me. We started off at 12.15, and on our way up the North Ridge we encountered that bitter cross-wind from the west that almost always prevails, and which had really been the means of rendering abortive Mallory and Bruce's earlier attempt. I found my two Sherpas repeatedly faltering, and it was with difficulty that one in particular could be persuaded to proceed. We reached Camp V, however, where the night was to be spent, in the fairly good time of three and a quarter hours. I hardly expected, I must admit, to find that Mallory and Irvine had returned here, for if they had, some movement must have been seen from below.

And now one's sole hopes rested on Camp VI, though in the absence of any signal from here earlier in the day, the prospects could not but be black. And time would not allow, even if I could have induced my men to continue in the conditions, of our proceeding on to Camp VI that evening. We made ourselves as comfortable at V as the boisterous wind would permit, but gusts sweeping over the North Ridge would now and again threaten to uproot our small tents bodily from the slender security of the ledges on which they rested, and carry them and us down the mountain-side. Fleeting glimpses of stormy sunset could at intervals be seen through the flying scud, and as the night closed in on us the wind and the cold increased. The porters in their tent below mine were disinclined for much food, and were soon curled up in their sleeping-bags, and I went down and added a stone or two to the guys for the security of their tent. I did likewise to mine and then repaired inside, and fitted up for use next day the oxygen apparatus that had lain idle here since I brought it from the ridge two days previously: having with me another mouthpiece, it was now ready for use. I managed to cook a little macaroni and tomatoes on the Meta stove, and that with tea and "Force" comprised my meal. The cold was intense that night and aggravated by the high wind, and one remained chilled and unable to sleep—even inside two sleeping-bags and with all one's clothes on.

By morning the wind was as strong and bitter as ever, and on looking in at the porters' tent, I found them both heavy and disinclined to stir. I tried to rouse them, but both seemed to be suffering from extreme lassitude or nausea. After partaking of a little food myself I indicated that we must make a start, but they only made signs of being sick and wishing to descend. The cold and stormy night and lack of sleep had hardly been conducive to their well-being, and to proceed under these conditions was more than they could face. I told them, therefore, to return without delay to Camp IV, and seeing them well on their way downwards, I then set off for Camp VI. This time with an artificial oxygen supply available I hoped to make good time on my upward climb. But the boisterous and bitter wind, blowing as ever from the west athwart the ridge, was trying in the extreme, and I could only make slow progress. Now and then

I had to take shelter behind rocks, or crouch low in some recess to restore warmth. Within an hour or so of Camp VI, I came to the conclusion that I was deriving but little benefit from the oxygen, which I had been taking only in moderate quantities from the single cylinder that I carried. I gave myself larger quantities and longer inspirations of it, but the effect seemed almost negligible: perhaps it just allayed a trifle the tire in one's legs. I wondered at the claims of others regarding its advantages, and could only conclude that I was fortunate in having acclimatized myself more thoroughly to the air of these altitudes and to its small percentage of available oxygen. I switched the oxygen off and experienced none of those feelings of collapse and panting that one had been led to believe ought to result. I decided to proceed with the apparatus on my back, but without the objectionable rubber mouthpiece between my lips, and depend on direct breathing from the atmosphere. I seemed to get on quite as well, though I must admit the hard breathing at these altitudes would surprise even a long-distance runner.

On reaching the tent at Camp VI, I found everything as I had left it: the tent had obviously not been touched since I was there two days previously: one pole had, however, given way in the wind, though the anchorages had prevented a complete collapse. I dumped the oxygen apparatus and immediately went off along the probable route Mallory and Irvine had taken, to make what search I could in the limited time available. This upper part of Everest must be indeed the remotest and least hospitable spot on earth, but at no time more emphatically and impressively so than when a darkened atmosphere hides its features and a gale races over its cruel face. And how and when more cruel could it ever seem than when balking one's every step to find one's friends? After struggling on for nearly a couple of hours looking in vain for some indication or clue, I realized that the chances of finding the missing ones were indeed small on such a vast expanse of crags and broken slabs, and that for any more extensive search towards the final pyramid a further party would have to be organized. At the same time I considered, and still do consider, that wherever misfortune befell them some traces of them would be discovered on or near the ridge of the North-east Arête: I saw them on that ridge on the morning of their ascent, and presumably they would descend by it. But in the time available under the prevailing conditions, I found it impossible to extend my search.

Only too reluctantly I made my way back to Camp VI, and took shelter for a while from the wind, which showed signs of relenting its force. Seizing the opportunity of this lull, with a great effort I dragged the two sleeping-bags from the tent and up the precipitous rocks behind to a steep snow-patch plastered on a bluff of rocks above. It was the only one in the vicinity to utilize for the purpose of signalling down to Hazard at the North Col Camp the results of my search. It needed all my efforts to cut steps out over the steep snow slope and then fix the sleeping-bags in position, so boisterous was the wind. Placed in the form of a T, my signal with the sleeping-bags conveyed the news that no trace of the missing party could be found. Fortunately the signal was seen 4,000 feet below at the North Col, though Hazard's answering signal, owing to the bad light, I could not make out. I returned to the tent, and took from within Mallory's compass that I had brought up at his request two days previously. That and the oxygen set of Irvine's design alone seemed worth while to retrieve. Then, closing up the tent and leaving its other contents as my friends had left them, I glanced up at the mighty summit above me, which ever and anon deigned to reveal its cloud-wreathed features. It seemed to look down with cold indifference on me, mere puny man, and howl derision in wind-gusts at my petition to yield up its secret—this mystery of my friends. What right had we to venture thus far into the holy presence of the Supreme Goddess, or, much more, sling at her our blasphemous challenges to "string her very nose-tip"? If it were indeed the sacred ground of Chomo-lungma—Goddess Mother of the Mountain Snows, had we violated it—was I now violating it? Had we approached her with due reverence and singleness of heart and purpose? And yet as I gazed again another mood appeared to creep over her haunting features. There seemed to be something alluring in that towering presence. I was almost fascinated. I realized that no mere mountaineer alone could but be fascinated, that he who approaches close must ever be led on, and oblivious of all obstacles seek to reach that most sacred and highest place of all. It seemed that my friends must have been thus enchanted also: for why else should they tarry? In an effort to suppress my feelings, I turned my gaze downwards to the North Col far below, and I remembered that other of my companions would be anxiously awaiting my return, eager to hear what tidings I carried. How then could I justify my wish, in face of such anxiety, to remain here the night, and prolong my search next day? And what hope, if I did, of finding them yet alive?

Alone and in meditation I slowly commenced my long descent. But it was no place for silent contemplation, for buffeted by storm-blasts that seemed to pierce one through, it needed all one's attention and calculation to negotiate safely the exposed slabs of the ridge and prevent a slip on their débris-sprinkled surfaces. Hampered as I was with the unwieldy oxygen outfit, which I had no need to use but wished to recover, these slabs were in places, under these conditions, decidedly awkward. I quickened my pace on the easier ground farther down, but at times found it necessary to seek protection from the biting gale in the lee of rocks and reassure myself that no symptoms of frostbite were imminent. Hazard had seen me coming, and sent his own remaining Sherpa to welcome me at the foot of the ridge. Arrived at the North Col Camp I was pleased to find a note from Norton and to discover that I had anticipated his wishes that I should return and not prolong my search on the mountain, seeing that the monsoon seemed likely to break at any moment. Next day Hazard, the porter and myself, leaving the tents standing and loading ourselves up with all we can save, evacuated the North Col Camp, and went down in good weather, and in quick time, by the "avalanche route" to Camp III, where we found the rest of the party gone, save Hingston and Shebbeare who were about to evacuate it. After a rest and good meal here, we proceeded on down the changed and wasted glacier to Camp II, where we spent the night, and the following day rejoined the main party at the Base Camp, to revel in the joys of opening spring, so long withheld and now let loose on us in all their glory of flower and insect life, as we plunged forth from our erstwhile Arctic environment.

I have already mentioned the possible reasons why Mallory and Irvine were so late in reaching the point at which they were last seen, which if the "second rock step," as referred to earlier, would be an altitude of about 28,230 feet, as determined by theodolite from the Base Camp by Hazard; if the "first rock step," then not more than 28,000 feet. And in the latter event, we must assuredly and deservedly attribute the *known* altitude record, the greatest mountain height definitely attained by man, to Norton, who reached not less than 28,100 feet. I propose, therefore, very briefly just to speculate on the probable causes of their failure to return. From the "second step" they had about 800 feet of altitude to surmount, and say 1,600 feet of ground to cover, to reach the top, and if no particularly difficult obstacle presented itself on the final pyramid they should have got to the top at about 3 to 3.30. Before, however, he left Camp VI Mallory had sent a note to Noel at Camp III saying he hoped to reach the foot of the final pyramid (about 28,300 feet odd) by 8 a.m. So on this schedule they would be perhaps five or six hours late in reaching the top, and hence they would find it almost impossible to get down to Camp VI before night-fall, allowing five or six hours for the return. But at the same time it must be remembered there was a moon, though it rose rather late, and that evening it was fine and the mountain clear of mist as far as could be seen. In spite of this they may have missed their way and failed to find Camp VI, and in their over-wrought condition sought shelter till daylight—a danger that Mallory, experienced mountaineer that he was, would be only too well aware of, but find himself powerless to resist. Sleep at that altitude and in that degree of cold would almost cer-tainly prove fatal. Norton, I know, finds it difficult to reconcile this explanation with the fact that no light was seen on the mountain after dark, and I am well aware it is a potent argu-ment against it. But to me it is by no means conclusive since anything might have happened, in the way of damage or loss of their lantern or flash-light, to have prevented their showing a light. And the same applies to the magnesium flares which we supposed that they carried. In the tent at Camp VI I found one or two of the latter, which indicates the possibility of their having forgotten them the morning of their departure.

The other likely possibility, that many will not unnaturally subscribe to, is that they met their death by falling. This im-plies that they were roped together, a suggestion that I have mentioned earlier need not necessarily be inferred from their observed movements when last seen. It is at the same time just possible that though unroped they may have been climbing, on the ascent or descent, on some steepish pitch in close order, and the one above fallen on the lower and knocked him off. But it is difficult for any who knew the skill and experience of George Mallory on all kinds and conditions of mountain ground to believe that he fell, and where the difficulties to him would be so insignificant. Of Sandy Irvine it can be said that although less experienced than Mallory, he had shown himself to be a natural adept and able to move safely and easily on rock and ice. He could follow, if not lead, anywhere. Such had been my experience of him in Spitzbergen, Norway, and on our own home mountains. They were, of course, hampered by the oxygen apparatus—a very severe load for climbing with, as Mallory had mentioned in his last note to me. But could such a pair fall, and where technically the climbing appeared so easy? Experts nevertheless have done so, under stress of circumstances or exhaustion. Following what we called the "ridge route," i.e. by the crest of the North-east Arête, there seemed to be only two places which might in any way cause them trouble. The first was the "second step," already referred to more than once. This seemed steep, though negotiable at any rate on its north side. And if it were this step, as I thought at the time it was, that I saw the first figure (presumably Mallory) actually surmount within the five minutes of my last glimpse of them, then we had been deceived as to its difficulties, as at the distance we might well be.

The only other part of the ascent that might have presented any difficulty, and probably not more than awkwardness, is the very foot of the final pyramid, where the slabs steepen before the relatively easy-looking ridge to the final summit can be attained. Norton at his highest point was close below this section, and he has expressed the opinion that these slabs, sprinkled with snow, might constitute a considerable source of danger in the case of a slip. But with all due deference to Norton's actual view of this place, from what can be seen of the local detail both in Somervell's photograph taken at 28,000 feet and in Noel's wonderful telephotograph of the final pyramid taken from above Camp III, the difficulties here look decidedly as if they could be circumvented by a nearly horizontal traverse to the right to the actual foot of the ridge of the final pyramid. In any case to a leader of Mallory's experience and skill such moderate difficulties, as these would present, cannot long have detained him, much less defeated him, and during the descent such places as the above, and the probable consequences of a slip thereon, would be so impressed upon him, as well of course as on Irvine, that the greatest care and attention would be exercised.

Again, it has been suggested that the oxygen apparatus may have failed and thereby rendered them powerless to return. I cannot accept the validity of this argument, for from my own personal experience, to be deprived of oxygen—at any rate when one has not been using it freely—does not prevent one from continuing and least of all getting down from the mountain. On my second journey up to Camp VI, as related earlier, when I was using oxygen, I switched it off at about 26,000 feet and continued on, and returned, without it. Mallory in his last note to me said they were using little oxygen, and that they hoped to take only two cylinders each, instead of the full load of three each, from Camp VI. But even if later they were using much oxygen, they had both during the previous weeks spent adequate time at extreme altitudes, namely 21,000 feet and over, to become sufficiently acclimatized and not liable to collapse in the event of the oxygen failing.

Hence I incline to the view first expressed that they met their death by being benighted. I know that Mallory had stated he would take no risks in any attempt on the final peak; but in action the desire to overcome, the craving for the victory that had become for him, as Norton has put it, an obsession, may have been too strong for him. The knowledge of his own proved powers of endurance, and those of his companion, may have urged him to make a bold bid for the summit. Irvine I know was willing, nay, determined, to expend his last ounce of energy, to "go all out," as he put it, in an utmost effort to reach the top: for had not his whole training in another hardy pursuit been to inculcate the faculty of supreme final effort? And who of us that has wrestled with some Alpine giant in the teeth of a gale, or in a race with the darkness, could hold back when such a victory, such a triumph of human endeavour, was within our grasp?

The question remains, "Has Mount Everest been climbed?" It must be left unanswered, for there is no direct evidence. But bearing in mind all the circumstances that I have set out above, and considering their position when last seen, I think myself there is a strong probability that Mallory and Irvine succeeded.

From *The Fight for Everest: 1924.*

JAMES RAMSEY ULLMAN:

The question remains unanswered—but not unasked. In the years since their disappearance many men have speculated on the fate of Mallory and Irvine, and speculation will continue as long as high adventure has the power to stir the human imagination.

Among those who have concerned themselves deeply with the mystery is R. L. G. Irving, Mallory's old teacher, climbing-mentor, and friend. And it is interesting, and perhaps significant, to note that his opinions differ in many respects from those of Odell.

R. L. G. IRVING:

Let us try, then, to join the two climbers at the top of the First Step. A stretch of ridge at a comparatively easy angle invited them to go on and get to grips with the Second Step. They must have seen clearly what a terrific obstacle it was, but you cannot really judge the prospects of overcoming a tower like this upon a ridge till you are at its foot, and can see the slopes that fall on either side of it.

Here the question of turning back must have presented itself. The scales were heavily weighted against prudence. For the third time Mallory had been chosen to do battle with Everest. From him more than from any one a supreme effort might be expected, and this was the last chance he might ever have of grappling with those last defences of the mountain. Irvine, whose climbing experience was negligible compared with his own, could only be a keen supporter of any decision he might make; he could not, as Odell might have done, question the possibility of passing the grim sheer edge of the Second Step that now challenged them. And we know from Irvine himself how desperately keen he was 'to have a shot at the summit.'

And so, having climbed the First Step and seen what was ahead of them, we may suppose that they went on till they came to the foot of the Second Step, where it rose above their heads. It is hard for me to believe that Mallory left that defiant rise in the ridge without making a supreme effort to surmount it. I am thankful that no search was made for the two climbers at the foot of the precipices that fall for thousands of feet on either side of the ridge, but I think such visits might have told us on which side they tried to turn the Second Step and fell. For it is almost certain that they fell. Some sort of light would have been seen by the watchers at the camps if they had been benighted; moreover, there was a moon, and these two were not men to stay and freeze to death.

Is not this Second Step beyond the powers of any climber who has passed through the strain of the previous weeks at such a height? Irvine could do next to nothing to secure his leader, whether he were trying to scale the sheer rocks of the north-west face or to cut a way along the ice that is plastered on the south-east face. Of the two I think the latter might offer greater possibilities of success. If we imagine the extraordinary effort needed to turn this obstacle on either side, and ask ourselves whether any man drawing gasping breaths of oxygen through a tube with the deadly weight of the cylinders at his back could do it, the obvious answer is probably the right one.

That is conjecture; it is not fact. It may be that that seemingly impossible Second Step was passed, and that disaster happened on the final pyramid, even perhaps in a descent from the summit when it would have been night. I am not curious to know more.

From *Ten Great Mountains*.

5

Siege

The Expeditions of the 'Thirties

. . . Fight on, my merry men all;
I am a little hurt, but I am not slain;
I will lay me down for to bleed a while,
Then I'll rise and fight with you again.
The Ballad of Johnnie Armstrong

James Ramsey Ullman:

For nine years after the 1924 assault no climbers approached Everest. Tibet again closed its gates firmly to white men, and it was not until 1933 that permission was once more granted for an expedition to try its luck.

By this time most of the veterans of the previous attempts were too old for another ordeal on the mountain, and the enterprise was passed on to a younger generation of climbers.* The new leader was Hugh Ruttledge, a mountaineer of wide experience in the Alps and Himalayas, and the expedition he led out from Darjeeling in the early spring of 1933 was the largest and most elaborate that had yet been assembled. Outstanding among its fourteen English members were Frank S. Smythe, Eric Shipton, Wyn Harris, L. R. Wager, J. L. Longland, T. A. Brocklebank, C. E. Greene, and E. Birnie—most of them still in their twenties and early thirties, but ranking among the finest mountaineers of their time. Smythe and Shipton, in particular, during the decade preceding the Second World War, compiled what are beyond doubt the two finest records of any living climbers.

Setting out from Darjeeling earlier than any of its predecessors, the expedition made good time in the long journey across Tibet and by the middle of April was established, like a small army, in the shadow of its goal.

* The only two holdovers from the earlier expeditions were E. O. Shebbeare and C. G. Crawford, and neither was expected to participate in the highest climbing.

ERIC SHIPTON:

The work of carrying loads up from the Base Camp began on April 19th and on May 2nd we established and occupied Camp III in the upper basin of the East Rongbuk glacier at a height of 21,000 feet. We were now in full view of the North Col. At last we were confronted with a real mountaineering proposition which would require some concentration of energy and skill. The prospect was a good one. Pleasant and intensely interesting though the journey had been, most of us I imagine had been keyed up by the anticipation of the toughest climbing of our lives. So far it had all been make-believe, and it was difficult to avoid the question, "When are we going to be called upon to do a job of work; when will we have something really to bite on?"

The eastern slopes of the North Col are composed of steep broken glacier and rise about 1,500 feet from the level ice below to the crest of the Col. As the glacier is moving slowly downwards the slopes present a different appearance from year to year. Our task then was to find a way up them, to make a ladder of large safe steps and to fix ropes to serve as hand rails over all the difficult sections, so that it would be possible for laden porters to pass up and down with ease and safety.

We started the work almost at once. It was about an hour's walk from Camp II to the foot of the steep slopes below the Col. The ice of the upper basin had been swept clear of snow by the wind. It was rather like walking on an ice-skating rink and required some little practice to avoid sitting down heavily. But fortunately the slopes above were composed of hard snow, for it would have been a tremendously laborious task to cut steps all the way up in hard ice, and also very difficult to fix the ropes. As it was it was very hard work. Even at that height any physical exertion left one gasping for breath. We took

turns of about twenty minutes each at cutting the steps. Even
that seemed an eternity and it was a great relief to be told that
the time was up. We climbed about a third of the way up to
the Col on the first day.

There followed days of storm and wind which rendered
work impossible. Below, we had experienced fairly severe conditions, but Camp II was much more exposed to the weather,
which deteriorated a good deal during the fortnight after our
arrival there. I gathered from the Sherpas who had been with
the 1924 Expedition that the conditions were very similar to
those experienced in that year. But we had an additional item
of equipment, which added enormously to our comfort and
rendered us impervious to the buffeting of the wind. This was
a large, double skinned, dome-shaped tent of a type that had
been used by Watkins in the Arctic. It had a circular floor
about 15 feet in diameter, and was built round a bamboo frame,
the outer skin fitting over the frame while the inner skin hung
from it, so that there was an air space about a foot wide between the two. It was difficult to erect, but once up it was as
snug as a well built log hut.

As soon as there was a lull in the wind, we resumed work
on the slopes below the Col. We found that the steps we had
already cut had been swept away, and that not a trace of them
remained. So as to take advantage of brief periods of fine
weather, we put a camp (IIIA) at the foot of the slopes. This
was a bleak and comfortless spot, and even more exposed to
the wind than Camp III, which was situated on rocks close
under the cliffs of the North Peak. The new camp was pitched
on hard, smooth ice on which it was difficult to anchor the
tents. One night, during a particularly violent storm, one of
them broke loose from its moorings causing a certain amount
of excitement. But the new position was a great help, and from
it we were able to make progress. But our advance was very
slow, and as we set out day after day I began to wonder if we

should ever reach the Col. The most difficult part was about half way up. This consisted of an ice wall about 20 feet high, topped by a very steep ice slope. We had a lot of fun getting up it, and succeeded largely owing to a fine lead by Smythe. We hung a rope ladder down it for subsequent use.

At last, by the 15th of May, the road of steps and fixed ropes was complete, and we established Camp IV on an ice ledge, some 20 feet wide, about 200 feet below the crest of the Col. The ledge was formed by the lower lip of a great crevasse, the upper lip of which, 40 feet above, almost overhung the ledge. The camp was well sheltered and quite comfortable, the only disadvantage being the danger of small snow avalanches falling from above.

For the next four days the storm was continuous, and we could do nothing but lie in our sleeping-bags. Nor was any communication possible with the camps below. But on the evening of the 19th, the wind dropped and Smythe and I climbed up the last 200 feet. Apart from the ice wall this was by far the steepest part of the North Col slopes. When we reached the narrow crest of the Col we were met by a most glorious view to the west, over range after range of giant peaks, draped by dark cloud banners, wild and shattered by the gale. The mighty scene was partly lit by an angry red glow, and rose from a misty shadow-lake of deep indigo that often appears among high mountains in the evening after a storm.

The next day Wyn Harris, Birnie and Boustead started up with ten porters, intending to reach 25,500 feet to choose a site for Camp V. But they were forced to retreat from 24,500 owing to the wind. Actually there was some difference of opinion about the wisdom of this decision, and a hot-tempered argument raged most of the succeeding night, by the end of which the subject under debate had become rather confused. Nerves were already frayed, and we were all liable to lose our tempers at the slightest provocation, and to take our silly griev-

Mallory's last note.

The mists close in.

ances sorely to heart. This seems to be a common manifestation of the effects of life at high altitudes. In our case it was undoubtedly aggravated by the rough handling we had received from the weather, and by having been forced to spend so much of our time during the past month cooped up in a tent with too little to do and too much to anticipate. Being unable to speak above a whisper, I found it difficult to quarrel successfully with anyone, and it would have been too exhausting to attempt to pull my opponent's beard. Had I been psycho-analysed at the time, I would no doubt have been found to be suffering from some fierce repressions.

We were very comfortable at Camp IV. Cooking and breathing soon produced a pleasant fug in the tents: we had large double eiderdown sleeping-bags, and our snow beds were soon made to conform with the shapes of our bodies. The crevasse provided a convenient latrine, though it required a strong effort of will to emerge from the tent. It was only at the upper camps that the cold compelled us to use a bed-pan in the form of a biscuit box. So long as we did not have to do anything, the time passed pleasantly enough. Lethargy of mind and body was the chief trial. Once one got going it was not so bad, but the prospect of toil was hateful. At the higher camps, of course, this lethargy increased tenfold.

Eating, however, was the serious problem, and one which, to my mind, did not receive nearly enough attention. This was entirely the fault of the individual, for we had more than enough food, and its quality and variety could not have been better. The trouble is that at such an altitude the appetite is jaded, and unless a man forces himself to eat regular and sufficient meals he does not consume anything like enough to maintain his strength. Melting a saucepan full of snow for water and bringing it to the boil took so long that people tended to delude themselves that they had eaten a hearty meal. Over and over again I saw men starting for a long and exhausting day's work on the mountain with only a cup of cocoa and a biscuit or two inside them; the cold and the wind discouraged eating during the climb, and they were generally too tired to eat anything much when they returned. This state of affairs contributed largely towards the rapid physical deterioration of the party. There was endless talk about rations, and certainly these were carefully and efficiently planned beforehand; but in actual practice we ate whatever we wanted and whenever we felt inclined. Sweets were the easiest kind of food to swallow, but it is doubtful if haphazard sweet-eating is as beneficial as the taking of regular substantial meals, which it certainly discourages. In most cold climates people develop a craving for fat, which has a higher calorific value than any other food. Unfortunately at high altitudes fat of any kind is particularly repugnant.

On the 21st of May, Smythe and I climbed some 1,500 feet above the North Col for exercise. We both felt extremely fit, and without undue effort we maintained an average speed of 1,000 feet an hour, which would not have been a bad performance had we been at sea-level. Individuals differ very widely in their physical reactions to the effects of high altitudes, some vomit a great deal, some suffer from blinding headaches, some cannot sleep, while others can hardly keep awake, some gasp and pant even when at rest. I used not to suffer much from any of these maladies; my particular trouble was physical lethargy which grew progressively more intense the longer I remained at a high altitude. For example, in 1933, I made three climbs up the north-east spur above the North Col. On the first occasion, after six nights at Camp IV (about 23,000 feet), I felt very strong, and as though I could go on indefinitely; the second time, after eight nights at Camp IV, I was weaker, though I still went fairly well; on the third occasion, after two nights spent at Camp V (25,700 feet) and twelve at Camp IV, I only reached Camp V, for my second sojourn there, after a very hard struggle. Smythe and I reacted to the effects of altitude in very much the same manner, though in 1933 he deteriorated considerably less quickly than I did. For men with no previous Himalayan experience, and considering that they had spent a whole fortnight laid up at the Base Camp while the rest of us were working slowly up the glacier, Wager and Wyn Harris acclimatised remarkably quickly. Longland was slow in adjusting himself, which made his subsequent performance all the more remarkable. Crawford and Brocklebank were at their best when it was too late for further attempts on the mountain, and thus were robbed of the chance of going higher, though they spent weeks of monotonous but vital work keeping the North Col route open.

Weather conditions now appeared to have reached that state of comparative quiet that we had expected just before the arrival of the monsoon. Wireless messages received at the Base Camp spoke of an exceptionally early monsoon in Ceylon and its rapid spread over India. This news was confirmed by the appearance of great banks of cloud from the south which, however, were still far below us. Obviously the critical moment had arrived. On the 22nd of May, Birnie, Boustead, Greene, and Wyn Harris, with twenty porters carrying 12 lbs. each, established Camp V at 25,700 feet. The plan was for these four climbers and eight of the porters to stop the night at Camp V and to carry Camp VI as high as possible on the following day; Birnie and Boustead would then return to Camp V with the porters, while Wyn Harris and Greene would stop at Camp VI and attempt to climb the mountain by the "ridge route." Meanwhile Smythe and I would follow up to Camp V on the 23rd, take the place of the first party at Camp VI on the 24th, and make our attempt on the summit on the 25th, choosing our route in the light of the experiences of the first pair. Greene unfortunately strained his heart during the climb to Camp V, and his place was taken by Wager who had accompanied the party for exercise.

It was hard to believe that the time for the supreme test had arrived. Waiting at the North Col on the 22nd of May, I felt as I imagine an athlete must feel just before the boat-race, Marathon or boxing contest for which he has been training for months. It was difficult to keep one's mind from the nagging questions, "Will the weather hold long enough to give us a decent chance?" "How will I react to the extreme exhaustion that must inevitably accompany the final effort?" "What is the climbing really like on that upper part?" "For all our previous optimism, is it, in fact, possible to climb to or even to live at 29,000 feet?" Three more days, seventy-two hours!

From *Upon That Mountain.*

JAMES RAMSEY ULLMAN:

Everest has slight respect for either men's hopes or their arithmetic, and considerably more than seventy-two hours were to elapse before Shipton and Smythe had their go at the summit. Camp V was established, according to schedule, at 25,700 feet, but gales and blizzards soon forced the climbers to evacuate it, and it was not until six days later, on May twenty-eighth, that it could be reoccupied. Harris and Wager again formed the lead climbing-team, with Birnie, Longland, and twelve freshly selected porters in support.

This time the weather held fair, and on the twenty-ninth Harris, Wager, Longland, and eight porters pushed on up the mountain and succeeded in pitching Camp VI at the amazing height of 27,400 feet—a full six hundred feet higher than the final camp of 1924 and less than three hundred below the summit ridge. From here on it was up to Harris and Wager, and Longland, with the porters in tow, prepared to descend. It is not hard to imagine his feelings of "so-near-yet-so-far" as he turned his back to the summit. His would not be the prize and the glory if Everest were conquered; but there was a job to be done, and he was the one who must do it.

There is exultation in mountaineering, but also drudgery; achievement, but also sacrifice. And such exploits as Longland's descent with the porters (here told by Hugh Ruttledge, the 1933 expedition leader) are as integral and important a part of the Everest saga as the spotlighted ventures of the summit challengers.

HUGH RUTTLEDGE:

Longland took one look at the summit which now seemed so close (perhaps 1,600 feet higher and half a mile away), wished the climbers good luck, and led off along the break in the yellow band, horizontally eastwards. Long ago, when we decided to try to place Camp VI higher than before and away along the north face, a rule had been made that porters making the carry must not be allowed to return unescorted. The rule was now doubly vindicated. Left to themselves, the men would have charged off down the steep slopes by which they had ascended. Fatigue inevitably promotes carelessness, and undermines balance. One or more would probably have slipped and fallen to their death on the glacier thousands of feet below. The morale of the rest would have gone to pieces immediately—such is the almost certain effect of an accident—with only one result, total collapse. Longland knew the danger, and did the right thing. It was imperative to lose no time in finding the north ridge. Once on that, direction-finding would be far easier than on the great indeterminate slabs of the face. He worked his way along to a point where it seemed possible to traverse downwards across scree slopes to the ridge. The ground was steep, and delay occurred in helping the men.

The traverse was made just in time. As the last man cautiously moved over on to the ridge, a furious storm of wind and snow came roaring over from the west. A moment before all had been quiet and peaceful. In a few seconds Nature seemed to go mad. The far horizons vanished as the voice of the wind rose to a scream and the snow tore past in blinding sheets. The effect upon tired men may be imagined. Their world disappeared, their goggles iced up till they had to be discarded, whereupon their eyelashes froze together, making it very difficult to see at all. They were literally fighting for their lives.

Well for them that they had a great leader and a great mountaineer at their head. Longland never faltered though, to use his own words, "visibility suddenly narrowed to a snow-swept circle of some twenty yards, and—I was taking a party of porters down a ridge which I had never been on before, but which I knew to be ill-defined and easy to lose, particularly in such conditions." He kept his men in close order, and they staggered downwards, leaning sideways against the wind to keep their balance and peering through the storm for a glimpse of the North Peak and the ridge, but seeing nothing beyond the rocks just ahead. Every few minutes they halted to count their numbers, lest someone should be lost or left behind. The men were responding magnificently to example, and not one fell out.

Suddenly, below a little cliff, they came upon a spot of green, Norton's Camp VI of 1924, where Mallory and Irvine spent their last night of life and where Odell came in his great effort to find them. The tent was no longer usable after nine years of exposure, yet it looked surprisingly new. The men, much cheered by this discovery, rummaged about and found a folding candle-lantern and a lever-torch. The latter worked at the first touch. Then they hurried on downwards, for to remain still in these conditions meant death. The storm continued relentlessly.

About 200 feet lower down a terrible thought occurred to Longland. He remembered that in one of the 1924 photographs

of Mount Everest as seen from the Base Camp, the position of
that year's Camp VI was marked by an arrow pointing, not to
the main north ridge, but to a subsidiary ridge farther to the
east. Could it be that he was leading his party straight for the
appalling ice-slopes above the East Rongbuk glacier, instead of
down the main ridge to Camps V and IV, and safety? It was a
dreadful moment, and the worst of it was that he could see no
landmark through the flying snow. But he kept his head and
watched for the appearance of a great snow couloir, which he
knew must be on the left if he were on the wrong ridge. The
anxious descent continued slowly, down little snow-covered
cliffs and icy screes, reassured to some extent by the invisibility
of the couloir. But it was a painful passage. Some of the more
exhausted porters were beginning to sit down, unable to face
any longer the torture of the wind. They had to be urged to
their feet and encouraged to keep on down that doubtful, perhaps fatal ridge, the problem of which the leader had to keep
to himself. At last, over a little edge, and not a hundred feet
below, appeared a green tent. It was Camp V. Longland had
brought his party safe through a test which even Mount Everest
could hardly make more severe. He had not enjoyed one care-
free moment for two hours.

Birnie, Smythe and Shipton were ready with the hot drinks
now so sorely needed. Two exhausted porters, including poor
Kipa, were put to bed at once. The rest moved off slowly
downwards at about 3.45 p.m. Longland followed, after endeavouring, in vain, to persuade Birnie to take a rest down at
Camp IVa, and caught up the last and most tired of them just
below Finch's camp of 1922. To quote his own words once
more, "persuading this man downwards was sufficient task to
keep one's mind off one's own condition, and it was not until
the little rise leading to Camp IVa, which we reached just before dark, that I realised how near my own limit I had gone."

Those simple words convey, better than anything I can write, the feelings of a man who had spent himself to the utmost for his gallant companions.

From *Attack on Everest.*

JAMES RAMSEY ULLMAN:

The first 1933 summit attempt, now launched by Harris and Wager, was a remarkable feat, particularly in view of the fact that it was accomplished by two young men with no previous Himalayan experience. Their assignment was not only to climb, but to reconnoiter, in an effort to determine whether Mallory's "ridge route" or Norton's "traverse" offered the better possibilities of success. And in the course of their day's climbing they covered more ground on the upper slopes of Everest than any other men before or since.

In the following section, Ruttledge, who was directing the activities of the expedition from Camp III, tells the story of their splendid but unsuccessful try.

HUGH RUTTLEDGE:

Meanwhile, some 7,000 feet above us, Wyn Harris and Wager were making their great effort. The account which I am about to give is taken from notes which I recorded immediately upon their arrival down at Camp III, knowing that even the most accurate observer's memory for detail fades rapidly after a climb to high altitudes, and from narratives subsequently written by both men.

They had a somewhat disturbed night at Camp VI, after a light meal of Brand's essence of chicken, tinned loganberries, biscuit and condensed milk. Both men's appetites were poor, they were thirsty, and slept badly. Wager had the lower berth, so to speak, for the floor of the tent sloped downwards, and his companion kept slipping down upon him. Wyn Harris managed to sleep for about four hours. He was up at 4.30 on the 30th. A ten-mile-an-hour wind was blowing, and the cold was not excessive, considering the altitude. But the Thermos flask, prepared the night before, had not been able to keep its contents warm, and they were obliged to spend an hour heating water (obtained, of course, from snow), over a "Tommy cooker." After a very poor meal, during which they thawed out their frozen boots over another "Tommy cooker," they put on their windproofs, and emerged slowly and stiffly from their tent at 5.40 a.m. All movement is terribly slowed down when your oxygen supply from the air has been reduced to one third of normal.

The sun had not yet reached them, and they suffered much from cold during the first hour while traversing diagonally upwards towards the north-east ridge. Wager noticed that excessive panting resulted in rapid loss of body heat. Both felt the beginnings of frost-bite; and the moment the sun appeared, nearly an hour after they had left Camp VI, Wager sat down to remove his boots and rub his feet. Soon after this, about 60 feet below the crest of the ridge and 250 yards east of the first step, Wyn Harris, who was leading, found the ice-axe about which there has been so much controversy. It was lying free on smooth, brown "boiler-plate" slabs, inclined at an easy angle but steepening considerably just below. It was in perfect condition, looking quite new. On the polished steel head was stamped the name of the maker—Willisch of Täsch, in the Zermatt valley. I will state in a later part of the chapter the conclusions at which we have arrived from careful consideration of this discovery.*

The climbers left the axe lying where they found it, and proceeded upwards to the foot of the first step, which is actually

* See page 241.—*Editor.*

composed of two large towers on the ridge. It will be remembered that their first object was to reconnoitre the second step, now about two hundred yards away; to climb it if they could; and to ascend thence along the ridge itself and up the final pyramid to the summit. If the step could not be climbed, they would go by Norton's 1924 route, keeping more or less along the top of the yellow band, two or three hundred feet below the crest of the ridge, cross the great couloir, and attack the slabs on its western wall, thus effecting a lodgement on the north face of the pyramid.

It was now 7 a.m. Their first thought was to turn the first step and climb straight up on to the ridge. But they soon saw that the ridge was difficult, and that it would be easier to traverse along the top of the yellow band. They could not, from their view-point, see that the cliffs directly below the second step were impregnable to direct assault; the step itself was obviously so. They therefore moved off horizontally westwards, over snow-covered slabs, keeping roughly to the line where the yellow band adjoins the bottom of the dark-grey limestone precipice forming the continuation of the first step. The going was not very difficult here, and they were still unroped. Arrived under the second step, they at once saw that, not only was the second step itself impossible from this side, but they could not even reach the foot of it. Above them rose the dark-grey precipice, smooth and holdless. From a distance the second step had seemed to be split by an oblique gully cutting down through it in a north-easterly direction. At close quarters even this could not be traced. But about 200 yards farther along appeared a gully of fair promise. It seemed to cut through both the dark bands which form the first and second steps. If it could be climbed, the second step would be turned and the ridge reached at a point beyond which there seemed to be a straightforward way to the summit. The traverse was accordingly continued along ground that now became more difficult, and the bottom of the gully was reached at about 10 a.m.

More than four hours had thus been spent in a detailed survey of this portion of the north face. Knowing the men as I do, I feel very certain that their adverse opinion of the second step and its approaches carries great weight. They would not turn aside from a climb within the limits of the possible.

The gully was a delusion, a mere shallow scoop in the smooth walls. Moreover it did not even continue to the ridge. The party roped up here. In general, the rock was of a uniform, treacherous smoothness; in detail, a few knobby excrescences could be found which, with less snow about, would afford a tolerably good foothold. For the hands there was nothing. Wyn Harris made an attempt to lead up the shallow scoop, but was brought to a standstill almost at once.

Two ways had now been prospected of which high hopes had been entertained through distant reconnaissance. It seemed that Norton was right, and that the ridge route was impracticable. About 150 yards farther along, round a corner, was the great snow couloir descending from the eastern foot of the final pyramid. The roped party climbed cautiously along immediately under the precipice, and were delayed by some very difficult going over snow-covered, sloping slabs near the corner. A single slip here would have been absolutely fatal. Actually they would have done better to traverse along a better ledge, some fifty to a hundred feet below, where the angle eased off. It was decided that they should give each other mutual support over any difficulties in the neighborhood of the couloir, and that, if easier ground was discovered beyond, Wyn Harris, who was feeling the stronger of the two, should go on alone.

In the couloir a very awkward fifty feet of powder snow had to be crossed. The snow gave no support to the feet, cascading down at a touch, and the greatest care was necessary to prevent a slip. On the left, a few feet away, the rocks overhung. The couloir itself ran precipitously downwards to the main Rongbuk glacier, 10,000 feet below. It was a sensational crossing.

The rocks forming the western wall were even steeper than those just left behind, and they had more snow on them, being more protected on this side from the wind. It seemed just possible to find a way round the base of a flat buttress and then up between minor buttresses. The party crept slowly and carefully along for about 150 feet beyond the couloir, traversing slightly upward till they reached a point some fifty feet above the top of the yellow band, on the edge of a small gully where the snow was particularly deep and soft. Wyn Harris attempted to cross it, though knowing full well that Wager, precariously balanced on a slab affording no belays, could not possibly hold him should the snow slip away. It showed every sign of doing so. Suddenly came the realisation that the limit of reasonable climbing had been reached, if not passed. Wyn Harris retreated to the lesser evil of the slab, and the position was reviewed.

It was now 12.30 p.m. The height already reached was presumably over 28,100 feet, for, from Norton's description, he had reached approximately the same place. There remained, therefore, about 1,000 feet to the summit. The going above did not look absolutely impossible, but in the present conditions of snow on the slabs it would be difficult and very dangerous. Even worse was the prospect of a continued traverse across the little gully and the slabs to a biggish subsidiary couloir, which runs down to meet the main couloir about 200 feet below. In good conditions, with the rocks dry and free from snow, this might well be the best way to reach the easier slabs of the final pyramid above the black bands of the first and second steps. To go on in the existing conditions was to court disaster. The most optimistic estimate could not allot much less than four hours for completion of the climb. This would overstep the time-limit of safety, for the returning climbers must reach

Camp V, at least, before dark. Camp VI, where Smythe and Shipton should by now have arrived, only held two men. Wager thought he might be able to continue upwards for another hour. Except in the last necessity, a man should not be left alone, either to wait or to climb, on ground like this. Lastly, both climbers had an uncomfortable feeling that they had not been able to explore fully the possibilities of the second step. If they could only prove, beyond cavil, that that route was wholly out of the question, Smythe and Shipton could go for Norton's traverse with undivided minds, and could probably reach the couloir in three hours from Camp VI. This would give them a far better chance for the summit.

The word was given for retreat. Neither man liked the thought of repeating the terrific traverse they had made on the ascent. They found a way downwards to a series of ledges between fifty and a hundred feet lower, and had less difficulty in crossing the great couloir and the slabs on both sides of it. This involved a slight diagonal ascent towards the foot of the first step, whence they intended to climb on to the ridge and have a final look at the second step. But they were very near exhaustion point, and the climb to the ridge between the steps proved to be beyond them. They continued slowly towards Camp VI; and while Wyn Harris retrieved the axe left there in the morning (abandoning his own in its place), Wager by a last effort dragged himself up to the ridge east of the first step. He is the only climber who has looked down the stupendous, ice-clad south-east face of the mountain. The ridge here he found to be extremely narrow and indented. By analogy it would be the same between the first and second steps, and he had already seen a tower some twenty-five feet high on that portion, which would present an added difficulty. It was a fair inference that the second step was too well guarded from every side, apart from its own smooth precipice.

From *Attack on Everest.*

James Ramsey Ullman:

Harris and Wager reached Camp VI at about 4 p.m. and there found Smythe and Shipton, who, according to plan, had been working their way up the mountain a day behind them. After a brief rest and discussion of routes the first two continued their descent, and the second team of climbers was left alone in the bivouac in the oncoming darkness.

Frank S. Smythe:

No words can give any idea of our wretched existence in the little tent at a height of twenty-seven thousand four hundred feet. The cooking arrangements were inadequate, and the solid methylated fuel took an hour or longer to melt a saucepan of snow and then failed completely to raise it to the boil, though at that height it is almost possible to plunge the hands in boiling water, owing to the low temperature at which a liquid boils. It was only with difficulty that we could force food down our sore throats, and so lethargic were we that every movement, even the simplest action, cost us an enormous effort. It was all we could do, for instance, to pull off our wind jackets, and once in our sleeping-bags it was next to impossible to extricate ourselves, as every movement, however small, made us gasp and gasp for breath. It was a horrible night. The floor of the tent was steeply inclined and I spent the night rolling on top of Shipton, whilst Shipton spent the night in being rolled on by me.

We had hoped to attempt the summit next morning, but when the day dawned there came yet another of those terrible blizzards that rage on Mount Everest. We spent the day lying in our sleeping-bags, wondering whether the monsoon had broken, and knowing full well that if it had our chances of retreating safely were very small. There is no doubt that this enforced stay at Camp Six resulted in a considerable deterioration of our strength, for at that altitude acclimatization is soon superseded by deterioration, and it is doubtful whether a man could live for more than four or five days at the outside without some artificial aid in the form of oxygen.

The second night was no more comfortable than the first, and next morning, to our dismay, the wind was still blowing hard. Greatly to our relief, however, it suddenly dropped soon after sunrise, and we decided to make our attempt on the summit.

In our hearts we knew that we had no chance of success. For one thing, too much snow had fallen during the blizzard, and though in places it had been blown away from the rocks, in other and more sheltered places it was piled deeply, concealing ledges, handholds, and footholds. Furthermore, Shipton was not feeling at all well; he had eaten scarcely anything and was complaining of pains in his stomach.

Anyone seeing us leave Camp Six would have said: 'There go two crocks who ought to be in hospital.' Very slowly and with frequent halts for breath we made our way upwards and across the slabs of the Yellow Band. The weather was now perfect, but we were quite unable to appreciate our extraordinary position, but afterwards we remembered the glories of the scene near the summit of the world's highest mountain: the overlapping slabs of yellow rock, extending like a gigantic roof before us, the final pyramid, etched sharply against a blue-black sky, from which writhed and swirled a plume of mist like steam from a volcano; the thousands of mountains far below us, great mountains, yet dwarfed by the highest of all, and afar off the golden plains of Tibet, tranquil and serene in the morning sunlight.

Very slowly we progressed. We were almost underneath the First Step in the north-east ridge, when Shipton told me that he felt himself quite unable to go on, and that if he did he would become exhausted. He told me to carry on by myself, and said that he would follow, if possible. It was wretched luck for him, and after assuring myself that he was able to return safely to Camp Six, I continued. At the time it did not strike me as strange that I should make a solitary attempt on the summit of Mount Everest. It seemed quite a natural thing to be doing. There was nothing brave or bold about it. We had come to Everest in order to climb it, and, if possible, it had to be climbed.

There was no question as to the route to be followed. I had to traverse almost horizontally along the top of the Yellow Band, cross the great gully, which cleaves into the north face of the mountain, then climb a steep buttress for about four hundred feet on to the rocks of the final pyramid.

It was not difficult climbing to begin with, though a slip would have been visited by instant destruction. The hardest work was cutting across two beds of frozen snow. At a lower altitude this would have cost me but little energy, but at twenty-eight thousand feet it was all I could do to muster the strength and will-power to cut steps with my ice-axe. Presently, I approached the great gully. It would be difficult to imagine a more impressive place. On three sides rose dungeon-like walls, great overhanging crags that menaced all direct approach to the summit of Everest, and higher still was the summit itself, an abrupt pyramid of yellow-coloured rock ending in a shining point of snow with the usual white plume of mist streaming endlessly from it. It was only a thousand feet higher than the point on which I stood, yet it seemed a thousand miles away, separated from me by an impassable gulf of difficulty and fatigue.

To begin with, as I clambered along the Yellow Band, I found myself going better than I had expected, and there came to me a sudden feeling of optimism and hope that I should reach the summit, but presently, as I approached the great gully, this faded away and was replaced by despair. The steep four hundred feet of rocks that I had to climb on the far side of the gully were impassable owing to the freshly-fallen snow that everywhere covered them. There was no doubt about this, yet I felt I must not give up until I had tried all I could, and I continued on with hope gone, yet determined to climb as high as possible.

A convenient series of ledges led me along the top of the Yellow Band until I approached the great gully. The ledge I was following gradually narrowed, until it was only an inch or so broad. At its narrowest point it passed a steep corner where vertical or overhanging rocks tend to push the climber outwards. I found myself spread-eagled like a man crucified on the corner. It needed only one step to pass it, for immediately beyond it the ledge broadened again, but I funked that step. My balance was too delicate; I felt that at any moment I should topple off backwards. I retreated and considered the situation. It was an easy enough place and to pass it required only a little confidence. With a companion, I am sure I could have done it, but I was alone, and there is a world of difference between climbing alone and climbing with a companion. I apostrophized myself as a coward and tried again, but with no more success. I could not summon up the courage to take that one needful step round the corner.

Fortunately there was an alternative, but it meant a descent of twenty feet, and at twenty-eight thousand feet a mountaineer is loath to lose even that small amount of hard-won height. However, there was nothing for it but to climb down to another ledge, which led without difficulty into the gully, and this I was able to do by getting into a sitting position and supporting myself by the palms of my hands.

Once on the ledge I had seen I breathed a sigh of relief, for it was broad and for the first time since leaving Shipton I was able to stand in comfort. Before me was the great gully. At that point it was filled with snow, which to my surprise was wind-blown and hard. To cross it meant further step-cutting. The angle was steep, about fifty degrees, and step-cutting was ter-ribly laborious. After every few strokes of my ice-axe I had to halt and gasp and gasp for breath, feeling as though I had just completed a 'quarter.' About twenty steps had to be made, and at length I found myself on the far side of the gully. The slope there was steeper than any I had previously climbed, and immediately I saw it I knew that the summit was inaccessible that day. For snow covered the rocks to a depth of two or three feet; every shelving ledge was laden with it. And it was snow of the worst quality; not wind-blown and hard like the snow in the gully, but soft and powdery, having the consistency of flour, or castor sugar, so that although my feet sank deeply into it, it refused to support my weight and poured off the rocks in hissing streams. My mountaineering experience told me that I was beaten immediately I encountered that snow. Neither strength nor skill can avail for long in such conditions. Common sense told me that I was beaten, but I was still determined to climb as far as possible, so commenced to ascend the rocks.

At every step I had to shovel the loose snow away with my arms, in an endeavour to expose satisfactory footholds. It was a desperately slow and fatiguing business. Possibly these rocks are not difficult to climb when free of snow and there are plenty of holds to be seen, but I could find very few holds then, and those I did find sloped so much that I had the uncomfortable feeling that at any moment my feet might slip outwards.

An hour passed. I had made no more than fifty feet of height. At such a rate of progress, even supposing I had the strength to continue, it would be impossible to reach the summit of Mount Everest that day, and to risk being benighted was not to be considered for a moment. I might have continued a little farther, but I am confident that had I done so the margin of strength necessary to retreat safely might have been over-stepped.

I remembered coming to a halt, overcome by a feeling of hopelessness and weariness. My limbs were trembling with exertion, my breath coming in short quick gasps, my heart pounding my ribs unmercifully. It was the limit. I remember, too, after a rest, which eased for the time being the clamour of heart and lungs, looking downwards and outwards. I was alone. There was no sign of my companion. I seemed engulfed in a profound and awful silence. I trod the very boundaries of life and death on the topmost pinnacle of the earth's surface. I saw peaks and glaciers stretching away at my feet, thousands of feet beneath; the brown Rongbuk valley, and the sandy plateau of Tibet checkered with blue cloud shadows stretching endlessly northwards into the fastnesses of the Gobi Desert and Central Asia. It was an experience awe-inspiring and magnificent beyond words, but I was scarcely in fit condition to appreciate it; I was tired, worn out by the effects of altitude, a poor dulled nerveless object, incapable of appreciating anything but my own bodily and mental sickness. I thought only of retreat, of escape from that dungeon-like place with its imprisoning walls into which the sun poured merciless rays which seemed to dry, wither, and scorch me, even though the air temperature was many degrees below freezing.

Near my highest point I was nearly overtaken by disaster. It seemed a small incident at the time, I was too dulled by fatigue and lack of oxygen to appreciate its significance, but I know now that I had a narrow escape. A small hold beneath my feet suddenly broke away, and for a moment my feet went with it. All the way up I had been using my ice-axe on every possible occasion and at that moment had the point jammed in a crack. Thus I was able to support myself instantly and check the slip before it had properly begun.

Descending was altogether an easier matter than ascending,

and only a few minutes were occupied in climbing down the fifty feet of rocks which had taken an hour to surmount. I recrossed the great gully and halted on the ledge for a breather.

And now I must recount the first of two strange experiences that befell me that day. All the time that I was climbing alone, I had the feeling that there was someone with me. I felt also that were I to slip I should be held up and supported as though I had a companion above me with a rope. Sir Ernest Shackleton had the same experience when crossing the mountains of South Georgia after his hazardous open-boat journey from Elephant Island, and he narrates how he and his companion felt that there was an extra 'someone' in the party. When I reached the ledge I felt I ought to eat something in order to keep up my strength. All I had brought with me was a slab of Kendal mint cake. This I took out of my pocket and, carefully dividing it into two halves, turned round with one half in my hand to offer my 'companion.'

The second experience was bizarre, to say the least of it. It was in all probability an hallucination due to lack of oxygen, which affects not only the physical powers but the mental powers also. I was making my way back towards Camp Six when chancing to look up, I saw two dark objects floating in the blue sky. In shape they resembled kite balloons, except that one appeared to possess short squat wings. As they hovered motionless, they seemed to pulsate in and out as though they were breathing. I gazed at them dumbfounded and intensely interested. It seemed to me that my brain was working normally, but to test myself I looked away. The objects did not follow my gaze but were still there when I looked back. So I looked away again, but this time identified by name various details of the landscape by way of a mental test. Yet, when I again looked back, the objects were still visible. A minute or two later, a mist drifted across the north-east shoulder of Everest above which they were poised. As this thickened the objects gradually disappeared behind it and were lost to sight. A few minutes later the mist blew away. I looked again, expecting to see them, but they had vanished as mysteriously as they had appeared. If it was an optical illusion, it was a very strange one. But it is possible that fatigue magnified out of all proportion something capable of a perfectly ordinary and rational explanation. That is all I can say about the matter and it rests there.

It was not easy finding my way back to Camp Six across the wilderness of slabs, and it was a relief when at last the little tent came into view. Shipton was safely there, and after a hot drink we talked over the situation. We were both of us very loath to spend a third night at the camp, which for two men was very uncomfortable. At the same time, I was too tired to descend to Camp Five. It was arranged, therefore, that Shipton, who had had a long rest and had completely recovered, should descend, leaving me behind. I am not sure now that it was a wise decision. It would have been better for us to have remained together, but at the time we both welcomed it. Accordingly, Shipton set off down to Camp Five.

The weather was not looking good when he left and grey clouds were beginning to form about Everest, yet neither of us anticipated the storm that broke an hour later. It caught him when he was still a long way from Camp Five, and he had a terrible descent, narrowly escaping being frozen to death in the blizzard. He told me afterwards that at one point he nearly met with disaster. He had let himself down from a rock by his arms on to a slope of snow, when the latter suddenly slid off, exposing a smooth slab destitute of all footholds. To let go with his hands meant a certain slip, and the only alternative was to pull himself back. To any one who has never done it, it is impossible to give any idea of the strength and determination required for an arm-pull at twenty-seven thousand feet. Suffice it to say, Shipton did it, and thereby saved his life. He arrived at Camp Five almost exhausted, where he was welcomed by Birnie who was in support there.

When the storm broke, and I heard the wind roaring past the little tent, I felt anxious for Shipton's safety, and was relieved when, towards sundown, the weather cleared a little.

It was an extraordinary experience spending a night higher than any other human being, but I scarcely appreciated this at the time. I was concerned only with making myself as comfortable as possible, and one of my memories is a grand brew of *café au lait.*

At sundown the wind died away, and I prepared to settle down for the long cold night which at that latitude lasts for nearly twelve hours. But before doing so, I unlaced the flaps of the tent and glanced outside. It was a scene of incredible desolation. All round were great slabs of rocks mortared with snow in their interstices like an immense expanse of armour-plating. Thousands of feet beneath lay a great sea of cloud slowly writhing and twisting in its uppermost billows and, here and there, seeming almost on fire, where it was touched by the rays of the setting sun. There was not a sound. No stone-fall or avalanche disturbed the serenity of Everest. There was silence, an absolute and complete silence; and permeating all, investing all, with a deadly embrace, was the cold, the coldness that reigns in the abysses of space.

The last flare from the sun was illumining the rocks as I laced up the tent and snuggled deeply in my sleeping-bag. The lull in the weather was only temporary, and later the wind rose, but I was not aware of it; I slept the clock round, a sleep of sheer exhaustion.

I knew there had been a wind in the night, because when I awoke next morning I found myself half-buried in snow which had entered through a small hole that Shipton and I had accidentally burnt in the fabric with the cooker. All night long the snow must have poured through like sand in an hour-glass

until it had formed a drift reaching half-way to the roof of the
tent. It had buried the provisions and the cooker, and I had some
difficulty in preparing my breakfast, to which difficulty was·
added the cold, which made it impossible to keep my hands out
of my sleeping-bag for more than a few seconds at a time. It
was one of the coldest mornings I ever remember.

As I lay in my sleeping-bag, I formulated a plan to return
and examine the possibility of a route up the crest of the north-
east ridge in preference to the route I had followed the previous day, but when, after a struggle, I extricated myself from
my sleeping-bag I knew that I was too weak, too worn down
by altitude to do anything more, and that I must retreat as
quickly as possible. This decision was rendered additionally
necessary by the fact that in cooking my breakfast I used the
last of the fuel; another night at Camp Six was therefore out
of the question, for a man cannot exist at twenty-seven thousand
four hundred feet without hot drinks to keep up his bodily
warmth.

My breakfast eaten, I pulled on my wind jacket with many
halts to gasp for breath, packed my few belongings in my
rucksack, and set off down to Camp Five. As I went, I took
one last look at the little tent that had sheltered Shipton and
me, in my case for three nights, so well. It looked strangely
forlorn on the great roof of Mount Everest, the sole evidence
of man's handiwork in an unvarying desolation of rocks and
snow; the highest camp that has ever been pitched.

The morning was calm as I made my way across the Yellow
Band, following an easier route than the one Shipton and I had
taken during the ascent, which had been discovered by Longland during his descent. Having gone for some distance almost
horizontally towards the north-east shoulder, I found that in
order to reach easy ground it was necessary to descend some
two hundred feet of steep rocks and snow. I went down very
slowly and carefully, partly because my legs felt unpleasantly

weak, and partly because the snow was loose and evil to tread. All went well until I was within fifty feet of the easy ground. I had stopped for a moment, undecided as to the easiest route, when, chancing to look to the north-west, I was puzzled to see the slopes of Everest in that direction disappearing behind a curious fuzzy-looking cloud that was advancing with astonishing speed. Before I had time to realize what it meant there came a sudden and terrific gust of wind which nearly blew me away from my holds. Then came another gust and another, and next minute I was clinging on for all I was worth in the midst of furious clouds of wind-driven snow.

Never in my mountaineering experience have I seen a storm approach so quickly and with such unexpectedness. In one instant safety was changed to danger, and an easy descent into one of extreme difficulty. Somehow or other I struggled down to the easy ground. There the wind was, if anything, worse. My head was protected by a woollen Balaclava helmet, but even so it was impossible to face the wind. My goggles were iced up in a few moments and the wind-driven snow and ice particles stung my cheeks like whiplashes. It was lucky that the ground was comparatively easy at that point, otherwise I should undoubtedly have lost my life, for the wind reached a velocity I have never before experienced on a mountain, a strength so tremendous that several times I was blown off my feet like a leaf, and only stopped myself from rolling or sliding with the point of my ice-axe.

Frequently I was reduced to crawling on hands and knees. Even worse, it was impossible to see more than a few yards owing to the clouds of wind-driven snow, and I had to guess which direction to take. The whole hate and fury of the world's highest mountain seemed concentrated on one miserable little human being.

Somehow or other I kept going, and by great good fortune managed to hit off the route. I felt rather than saw a pinnacle to the right that we had passed when ascending. Below it the climber must get on to the crest of the north ridge or, alternatively, descend the complicated face to the west. I preferred the ridge, and made for it as well as I could. But the struggle could not be kept up much longer. The cold was beginning to tell. The battering I was enduring could not last indefinitely. For the first time in my life, I felt my body gradually growing cold all over, and there was a strange, stiff, lifeless feeling in the pit of my stomach. I was numbed through and through, and it was increasingly difficult to think straight. The struggle was becoming intolerable and could not be endured much longer; exhaustion would supervene. I remember dimly seeing rocks at my feet and all about me whirling, writhing clouds of snow streaming endlessly past. I remember struggling on and on for what seemed an interminable age, and thinking dully what a useless business it was; how much easier to sit down and end it. Yet I kept going, and suddenly came to the crest of the north ridge. There was something familiar about the place. Then I remembered. At that point Shipton and I had descended a few feet to a ledge where we had sunned ourselves, away from a slight but chilling wind. It was the only point on the ridge we had seen where it was possible to descend easily.

I clambered down to the ledge. Immediately I got below the crest of the ridge I was out of the wind. I could hear and see its snow-laden gusts roaring across above me. It was the wind that nearly killed me, nothing else, for immediately I escaped from it warmth began to return to my frozen limbs. I beat my hands together and kicked with my feet. Slowly the numbing, deadening feeling left my body, until only my feet and fingers remained without sensation. Both, as it later transpired, were frost-bitten, and I came near to losing one big toe.

I could even feel the sun shining dimly through the clouds of wind-driven snow. Presently I felt warm enough and strong enough to resume the struggle. The worst of the hurricane had passed, yet the remainder of the descent to Camp Five was by no means easy, especially as I got tied up in difficulties among some slabs above the camp. These were easy enough to a fresh man, but to an almost exhausted man proved only just possible. As I was negotiating them I saw two figures emerge from one of the tents at the camp which was now just below. I shouted and waved, but they did not look up and see me. During the descent I had buoyed myself up with the thought of a hot drink at Camp Five, but it seemed that I was to be disappointed, and it was with very bitter feelings that I saw Birnie and Shipton set off down towards Camp Four, leaving me to follow on alone. Later I learned that they were both exhausted, and that Birnie, after a vigil lasting a week at Camp Five, was totally incapacitated by frost-bite; but, at the time, I felt neglected.

Nothing was to be gained by remaining at Camp Five, though I would have stopped had I known that Birnie had very considerately left there a thermos of hot tea, and I continued on down towards Camp Four on the North Col.

I suppose it was exhaustion, for I do not remember feeling tired, but I found that my legs frequently refused to support me, so that every few steps they collapsed beneath me. Fortunately, the weather improved as I descended, and visibility increased to such an extent that I was seen from Camp Four and Longland came up with a thermos full of tea well laced with rum. This put new life into me and I was able to proceed without assistance to the camp.

From *The Adventures of a Mountaineer.*

James Ramsey Ullman:

Smythe's great solo attempt, carrying to approximately the same point reached by Norton, Harris, and Wager, marked the end of the 1933 venture; and with the coming of the monsoon snows the expedition, like those before it, began the long trek back to India. With them, of course, the climbers took the ice-axe that Harris had found, and when its discovery became generally known the whole field of speculation on Mallory and Irvine's fate was reopened.

But it was still only speculation. As Hugh Ruttledge points out in the following discussion, the axe neither proves nor disproves that the lost climbers reached the summit.

HUGH RUTTLEDGE:

I must now revert to the question of the axe which Wyn Harris found on the slabs, one hour's climbing above Camp VI. I have already stated that the maker of it was Willisch of Täsch. Our first thought was that the owner must undoubtedly have been Mallory, for the reason that Willisch is a master craftsman to whom first-rate amateurs like Mallory, who do their climbing without guides and therefore do their own step-cutting, would be likely to go for a really good axe. I have subsequently been informed, however, that a number of Willisch axes were supplied to the expedition of 1924, so it is possible that this one was carried by Irvine. To one of these two it must have belonged, for no other climbers have gone by that route previous to this year. Norton and Somervell traversed by a lower line, on their way diagonally upwards from their Camp VI to the couloir. Some have suggested that this was the axe dropped by Somervell soon after he and Norton turned to descend. But they were much farther to the west when this happened, and Somervell's axe fell straight down the mountain-side and disappeared from view "still going strong." Others proffer the theories that either Mallory or Irvine put down the axe in order to climb unencumbered, or even that it was planted on the summit and blown by wind in the course of time to the place where it was found.

As to the first of these theories, no mountaineer climbing the north face of Mount Everest regards his axe as an encumbrance. It is his best friend and greatest safeguard. He uses it to help his balance on the outward-dipping slabs, to anchor himself when the treacherous gusts are tearing at his legs, to clear a foothold on the snow-covered rocks and, on occasion, to cut steps across hard patches of snow. The second theory is even less tenable. Supposing the axe to have been planted on the summit, for the reasons just given it would not be abandoned there. Even if it were, and supposing that the wind blew it away, it could only fall on one side or the other of the summit ridge; to north or south, to the main Rongbuk glacier, 11,000 feet below, or down the enormous southern face. By no conceivable combination of circumstances could it be carried down the eastern edge of the final pyramid, and almost horizontally eastwards for a distance of about two thirds of a mile.

We have naturally paid close attention to the problem. Firstly, it seems probable that the axe marked the scene of a fatal accident. For the reasons already given, neither climber would be likely to abandon it deliberately on the slabs, and its presence there would seem to indicate either that it was accidentally dropped when a slip occurred or that its owner put it down possibly in order to have both hands free to hold the rope. The slabs at this point are not particularly steep, but they are smooth and in places have a covering of loose pebbles which are an added danger. A slip might easily occur, and would be difficult to stop. We have no means of knowing if Mallory and Irvine climbed roped together; it is not unlikely that they did. But the rope is a poor safeguard, for the climber has no secure foothold on which to brace himself against a shock. Below, the slabs steepen considerably. A fall once begun is likely to continue. Norton has pointed out that anything dropped almost anywhere on the north face is lost for good, owing to the outward and downward dip of the strata. A flat and comparatively light object like an axe might, in this particular place, have failed to gather momentum and therefore have stayed where it was dropped or laid down; and the axe in question resisted the pull of gravity and of the wind for nine years. But the rule rather than the exception would govern the effect of any miscalculation or loss of balance by a climber.

Secondly, the evidence is insufficient to prove whether the accident occurred during the ascent or the descent. Prima facie, a slip would be more likely to occur during the descent. It is known that Mallory preferred to try the crest of the northeast arête, and he may well have taken this line to reach it, even from the old Camp VI on the north ridge. Would he have returned the same way, whether he succeeded in climbing the second step or was forced on to Norton's traverse? If he was forced on to Norton's traverse, the more direct route back would be that adopted by Norton and Somervell, lower down; but Mallory might have preferred to regain the line which he had taken on the ascent and therefore knew to be practicable. If he climbed the second step he would almost certainly return the same way. Odell believes that he saw Mallory and Irvine near the second step while he was ascending from Camp V in support. If he did see them, and if our theory as to the scene of the accident is correct, Mallory and Irvine fell on the descent.

[Here Ruttledge quotes Odell's account (see page 187 ff.) in considerable detail.—*Editor*.]

Later on, Odell says that he saw the first of the two figures actually surmount the step *within the five minutes* of his last glimpse of them.

Now it is highly probable that Odell did see the "second rock step" through the break in the mists. It is not masked from about his view-point. Moreover the "first rock step" does not need to be climbed—it is easily turned on the north face. Therefore, if Odell saw figures at all, they were almost certainly approaching the "second rock step," and one of them may have ascended it.

I am not prepared to say that a man possessed of good sight could not have seen figures on a snow-slope separated from him by a vertical distance of 2,000 feet and a horizontal distance of some 600 yards; it would, I suggest, be vastly more difficult for him to see a single figure climb a dark rock-face, though he might see it arrive at the top, silhouetted against the sky.

More serious is the time question. The four men of this are very doubtful if it can be climbed at all; they are quite sure that no man, however skilful, could climb it in five minutes.

Supposing them to be right, what then did Odell see? I suggest that the incident which occurred during Smythe and Shipton's ascent to Camp VI offers a reasonable explanation. But Odell's firmly-held opinion is entitled to the greatest respect, and perhaps the affair will always remain a matter for conjecture. There exists, at present, no conclusive evidence as to whether Mallory and Irvine reached the summit. If Odell really saw them near the second step so late as 12.50 p.m., the questions arise whether they could possibly have completed the ascent at all, and whether Mallory would have gone on at all costs, regardless of the danger of being benighted. Norton firmly believes that Mallory had a full sense of his responsibility. If, on the other hand, Odell was mistaken, the time-factor does not apply and we know nothing further of the party's movements. We should like to think that they succeeded, for none deserved it better than Mallory, who throughout three expeditions had ever been in the forefront of the battle; or than Irvine, who in his short period of service showed a devotion to duty which could hardly be surpassed.

From *Attack on Everest*.

JAMES RAMSEY ULLMAN:

So far and no farther. . . .

The climbers of 1933 had reached as high as their predecessors, but the last thousand feet of Everest still remained as aloof and untouched as they had been since the beginning of time. And presently more climbers were on the way again, challenging and trying again.

The next expedition—that of 1935—was sent out merely as a reconnaissance party, permission from the Tibetan government having been received too late to make an actual climbing venture feasible until the next year. It was felt, however, that much useful information and experience would be gained from a preliminary survey, and, accordingly, in late May, the fifth Mount Everest expedition set out for the mountain under the leadership of Eric Shipton. The group was smaller than the usual climbing party, including, besides Shipton, H. W. Tilman, L. V. Bryant, Charles Warren, E. H. L. Wigram, Edwin Kempson, and Michael Spender—seven white men in all.

According to plan, the larger part of their work was to consist of the exploration and mapping of the country around Everest, and this task they performed with great success. Not much was expected in the way of actual climbing on the mountain, for the reconnaissance was being conducted in the middle of the monsoon season; but before they were through, Shipton and his companions had a fling at the North Col.

ERIC SHIPTON:

It had been generally supposed that it would be useless to attempt Mount Everest during the monsoon. But there was little practical evidence to support this belief. Before 1933 complete faith had been placed in the advent of a fine spell during the few weeks immediately preceding the arrival of the monsoon, and the exploration of further possibilities was thought unnecessary. This faith however was somewhat shaken by our experience in 1933. Some people expressed the opinion that the monsoon season would offer a better chance of success than the late spring. These ideas were, I believe, based largely upon experiences in the Karakoram and those of the Bavarians on Kanchenjunga in 1929 and 1931. One of our jobs in 1935 was to investigate the matter.

There were two factors: the risk of avalanches on the slopes below the North Col and the condition of the snow on the upper part of the mountain. Regarding the former we had little evidence, and of the latter we had none. In 1922 a disastrous avalanche had overtaken the party attempting to reach the North Col in June. In June, 1933, Crawford and Brocklebank had reported that the slopes were dangerous (Crawford had himself been involved in the 1922 avalanche). On the other hand in 1921 the North Col had been reached safely in September; but with all respect to Mallory's skill as a mountaineer this may have been due more to luck than to good judgment. In the Alps the study of snow conditions has been reduced to an exact science, but we are still very ignorant about Himalayan snow. It was believed that the dangerous conditions prevailing on the North Col in June were caused by the wind blowing the newly fallen snow from the west side of the Col and depositing it at a low temperature on the eastern slopes, thus producing what is known as "wind-slab," one of the most vicious of all conditions of mountain snow. But it seemed reasonable to suppose that these causes might not be operative later in the summer.

When we arrived there towards the middle of July, 1935, we examined the slopes below the North Col with extreme care. Kempson had had wide experience of winter mountaineering in the Alps, and by now I had seen a good deal of Hima-

Ice towers on the East Rongbuk Glacier. *Ewing-Galloway*

Harris and Wager.

Smythe and Shipton.

Everesters.

layan snow conditions. We could find nothing wrong with the slopes. With ten Sherpas it took us three easy days to establish a camp on the crest of the col. On the first of these days we had a slight contretemps with the Sherpas. They had evidently been shaken by the discovery of Wilson's body * and regarded it as a bad omen. So half way up to the Col they refused to go any further. However, a heart to heart talk in camp that evening set the matter right, and after that we had no more trouble.

Warren, Kempson and I and eight Sherpas occupied the camp on the North Col with enough food to last us for at least sixteen days. We intended to push on up the mountain at least to 27,000 feet to see what the conditions were like up there. Actually we were in a position to make a strong attempt on the summit if these had proved to be good. The whole of the north face was plastered with snow and very little rock was showing. At lower levels the heat of the sun and the cold nights would have combined in a short time to pack the snow and provide a splendid surface up which one could climb without difficulty. The weather for the past fortnight had been very fine. But it was thought that practically no melting takes place above about 26,000 feet, and that except where it is subjected to great pressure the snow remains powdery. It was our object to prove or disprove this theory. We had seen in 1933 how difficult it was to climb those upper slabs with even a slight covering of powder snow; a blanket of this substance covering the whole face to a depth of perhaps eight or ten feet would present an impassable obstacle. If on the other hand the snow were to consolidate in the normal manner, the mountain would be a great deal easier to climb during the monsoon than at any other season.

The weather deteriorated and we waited for four days on the North Col. One day we climbed some way up the north-

* See page 250.—*Editor.*

east spur for exercise, but it seemed unwise to establish the higher camps until the weather improved. At length we decided to retreat to Camp III and to wait until the bad spell had spent itself. We had the whole summer before us and it would be best to preserve our condition. So we left tents and stores on the Col and started down. We were disconcerted to find that 200 feet below the crest of the Col the entire surface of the slope had slipped away for a distance of a quarter of a mile and to a depth of six feet. The resulting avalanche had crashed down on to the glacier below. The snow that we had examined with such care, about which we had been quite satisfied and over which we had been blithely working for three days had been completely rotten.

The term "justifiable risk" is used a good deal by mountaineers, particularly when discussing fatal accidents. It is meant to imply that degree of predictable danger to which, according to the general body of mountaineering opinion, a party is entitled to expose itself. But obviously each man must determine his own standard, and there must be a tacit agreement on the matter among the members of any climbing party. Opinions vary widely according to temperament, between those who regard mountaineering as an exact science whose rules must never be broken and the "death or glory" attitude of the climbers of the north face of the Eiger. Particular circumstances, too, will exercise an influence; for example, one is likely to accept a narrower margin of safety on the final pyramid of Mount Everest than during a holiday climb on the Matterhorn. There can be few mountaineers who have not at some time run the gauntlet of some obvious danger for the achievement of a particularly enticing goal. Most of us have done it more times than we can remember. But in making a route up a great Himalayan peak the position is altogether different. Each section of the route has to be traversed not once but many times, and generally by slow, heavily laden men, many of whom are not trained to act correctly in a moment of crisis. One may pass beneath a tottering serac nine times, to be buried by it on the tenth. A competent mountaineer involved in a snow avalanche can often save himself by going through the motions of swimming on his back, but even without an awkward load strapped to his back a Sherpa porter is unlikely to have the presence of mind to do this. I am sure that no one could have escaped from an avalanche such as that which broke away below us while we were lying peacefully on the North Col.

Two things were clear: first that the slopes below the North Col were not safe, and secondly that we were not competent to judge snow conditions at that particular time and place. I am quite satisfied that the avalanche was not caused by "windslab." The eastern slopes of the North Col form a semi-circular basin, unusually well protected from the wind. The mid-day sun in July, only six degrees from the vertical, beats down with tremendous force upon the stagnant air of this blinding-white cauldron. On occasion I have suffered more from the heat on the snow slopes of the North Col, at 22,500 feet, than I ever have on the plains of India. At night it barely freezes. As a result of these conditions, unusual even in the Everest region, the main body of the snow rots to a great depth, while the surface maintains the appearance of ordinary solid névé. This at any rate was my explanation of the great avalanche and if it were correct it was clear that the slopes would remain dangerous throughout the summer. We decided therefore to leave the North Col alone, for a while at least, and to study snow conditions on other mountains in the vicinity. On these peaks we generally found fairly good snow, presumably owing to better ventilation and lower night temperatures. But on the three occasions when we climbed above 23,000 feet conditions changed abruptly at about that altitude and we found ourselves struggling in a bottomless morass of soft snow. By the end of

August, though the snow on the ridges was still good, the upper glaciers were difficult to negotiate. The ice below the surface was rotten and honeycombed with reservoirs of water.

From *Upon That Mountain.*

JAMES RAMSEY ULLMAN:

The world's highest mountain has held a potent lure for many men, but for only one, so far as we know, to the point where he set out to climb it alone. This was an Englishman by the name of Maurice Wilson, who made a short-lived and ill-fated attempt on Everest in 1934. His body was found near the foot of the North Col by the reconnaissance party of 1935, and Shipton here tells his strange and pathetic story.

ERIC SHIPTON:

About three hundred yards above Camp III we found the body of Maurice Wilson, who had attempted to climb Mount Everest alone the previous year and about whom nothing more had been heard. From a diary which we found on his body and from subsequent enquiries we were able to piece together his curious story. He was a man of about thirty-seven and had served in France during the last war. He had developed a theory that if a man were to go without food for three weeks he would reach a stage of semi-consciousness on the borderland of life and death, when his physical mind would establish direct communication with his soul. When he emerged from this state he would be cleansed of all bodily and spiritual ills; he would be as a new-born child but with the benefit of the experience of his previous life, and with greatly increased physical and spiritual strength. Wilson had fanatical faith in his theory. He believed moreover that he had seen a vision in which he had received divine instruction to preach the doctrine to mankind.

Somehow the word "Everest" had featured in the vision, and he thought that it was intended to indicate the means by which he could achieve his purpose. Obviously if he succeeded in reaching the summit of Mount Everest single-handed, the feat would cause no small stir, and his theory would receive wide publicity.

He knew nothing whatever about mountaineering. At the time, however, the Houston Everest Flight was receiving considerable press publicity. Presumably this gave him the idea that if he were to fly a plane as high as he could and crash it on the side of the mountain he would be able to climb the rest of the way to the summit and return on foot. So with this object in view he learnt to fly, bought a small aeroplane and set out for India. At Cairo he was stopped and turned back by the authorities. But eventually he reached Purnea in India where his machine was confiscated. He went to Darjeeling where he stayed for four months, training himself and making secret preparations for his journey to Mount Everest. He got in touch with some of the Sherpas who had been with us the year before and they agreed to smuggle him through Sikkim and into Tibet. He then covered up his tracks by paying for his room at the hotel six months in advance so that he could keep it locked with his things inside, and gave it out that he had been invited by a friend to go on a tiger shoot. It was some time before the authorities discovered that he was missing.

In the meantime, by wearing a disguise and travelling at night he had succeeded in passing through Sikkim and into Tibet. There he travelled more openly, but with practically no baggage and by avoiding the big places he and his three Sherpa companions attracted no attention. When they arrived at Rongbuk he told the abbot of the monastery that he was a member of the 1933 expedition and induced him to hand over a few small items of equipment that we had left there. He had evidently made a good impression upon the old man, who when we visited the monastery in 1935 talked to us a great deal about him. He left the Sherpas at Rongbuk and started up the glacier alone with the complete conviction that he would reach the summit in three or four days. He had with him a small shaving mirror with which he proposed to heliograph to those at Rongbuk from the summit, so as to provide proof that he had actually reached it. He was used to starving himself and intended to live on a small quantity of rice water. It was early in April and he encountered the usual spring gales on the East Rongbuk glacier. He appears to have reached a point somewhere about Camp II before he was forced to retreat, exhausted.

After a fortnight's rest he set out again, this time with the Sherpas. They reached Camp III and the Sherpas showed him a dump of food which we had left about half a mile beyond, and which contained all kinds of luxuries such as chocolate, Ovaltine, sardines, baked beans and biscuits, with which he was delighted. He left the Sherpas at Camp III and went on alone. He had evidently expected to find intact the steps which we had cut in the slopes below the North Col, and he was bitterly disappointed to find nothing but bare wind-swept ice and snow. Though he had an ice-axe, he did not know how to use it and could make little headway up the slopes. He camped alone on the rocks near the dump and set out day after day to renew his fruitless attempts to reach the Col. Though he had plenty of food, he was gradually weakened by the severe conditions. This was clear from the entries in his diary, which became shorter and less coherent towards the end. But he would not give up and still clung to his faith in divine inspiration. The last entry was on the 31st of May, 1934. He died in his sleep, lying in his small tent. This had been smashed by storms, and all the fragments, except the guy-lines which were attached to boulders, had been swept away.

The Sherpas said they had waited a month for him at Camp III. This is clearly untrue for they would certainly have visited the food-dump from time to time and would have found the body. We had two of the men with us in 1935, but one had been attached to Spender's party and the other had been sent down to fetch some stuff from Camp II on the day that we found the body. We buried it in a crevasse.

From *Upon That Mountain.*

JAMES RAMSEY ULLMAN:

Man proposes. . . .

The climbing expedition that marched in toward the mountain in March of 1936 was as carefully planned and equipped as any that has ever set its cap for a great peak. The reports of the 1935 reconnaissance party had been thoroughly studied, equipment had been redesigned and modernized, and the oxygen apparatus was of the newest and most improved type. Also, for the first time in mountaineering history, the climbers were equipped with wireless-telephone sets, designed to provide communication both with the outside world and between the various camps on the mountain.

The climbers themselves were mostly veterans. Ruttledge was again in command, and among his companions were such old Everest hands as Smythe, Shipton, Wyn Harris, Warren, and Wigram. Added to these were a few new climbers, of the first rank, notably J. M. L. Gavin and P. R. Oliver. Of the total group of twelve, no fewer than eight of the men were considered at least potentially capable of reaching the summit.

Seldom has a group of adventurers set out with such high hopes. And seldom has one had those hopes so cruelly dashed.

HUGH RUTTLEDGE:

The Base Camp was reached on April 26—that is to say, thirty-seven days after leaving Gangtok. Owing to cloud, we had not seen Everest from the Pang La, but from the Base Camp it appeared to be in absolutely perfect condition, and this state of things continued for another four days, during which time we were establishing Camp I. On April 30 Smijth-Windham opened wireless communication with Darjeeling and was at once informed that a disturbance might be expected. Simultaneously we had a moderate fall of snow, which incidentally turned the mountain white, and never again did we see Everest as we wanted to see her.

Nevertheless, there was no reason to suppose that we were experiencing anything different from the occasional disturbances usual at this time of year, and the work of establishing camps up the glacier was proceeded with expeditiously. While retaining the old names of camps, in order to avoid confusion, it had been decided to make our real base this time at Camp I, where Smijth-Windham would have his wireless headquarters. The reconnaissance of last year had found a more suitable position for Camp II in the main trough of the glacier at a height of about 19,900 ft. There was no difficulty whatever in reaching this, and it made the carry to Camp III comparatively simple. The condition of the party was so good (we had all arrived at Base Camp free from the abominable sore throats which affected us in 1933) that it was not found necessary to insist rigidly upon four days' acclimatization at each camp. Camp III was fully established on May 7 and 8—that is to say, within twelve days of reaching the base. Meanwhile considerations of our general fitness and of the prevailing mild weather had persuaded us to advance our programme by a week, so that we now aimed at establishing the N. Col by May 15. This programme was actually adhered to. Camp III was placed about 500 ft. higher and at least half a mile nearer the N. Col than on previous occasions, in a position which rendered a carry to the top of the N. Col not too exacting. The character of the slopes had changed obviously since 1933 but was not dissimilar to that of last year. The ice wall which gave so much trouble on the last expedition seemed to have doubled in height, and there were avalanche débris below it; accordingly it seemed preferable, after a reconnaissance by Smythe, Shipton and Warren on the 9th, to make a direct ascent of about 500 ft. away to the right, N.W., and then traverse along apparently easy slopes about half-way up, finishing with the steep climb direct to the crest.

Snow prevented a resumption of work until the 13th, when Smythe, Oliver, Gavin and Wigram, with 10 selected porters, made the whole route up to the crest, having to cut steps afresh and fix ropes where necessary. This was an extremely hard day's work, but was so successful that next day Wyn Harris and Kempson were able with very little difficulty to escort 46 porters, half of whom had never been on an ice slope before, and establish Camp IV on the crest.

Everybody returned to Camp III the same evening, but on the morning of May 15 Smythe and Shipton occupied Camp IV with 56 men, of whom 42 remained to establish the higher camps. Thus the first part of our work had been accomplished with no set-back and with nothing like the hardship of 1933, and on exactly the same date as in that year we were in position to commence the assaults on the summit.

Unhappily the weather now became completely unfavourable. We had not to contend with the violent gales of 1933; indeed, there was a complete absence of the N.W. wind which alone could remove the snow from the N. face. Day after day was unhealthily warm, what slight wind there was coming from an easterly direction. Snow and yet more snow continued to accumulate. Morning and evening Smythe telephoned down to me by wireless that conditions were getting worse and it would be quite unprofitable to tire out the porters in an attempt to establish Camp V. On the morning of the 18th Smythe gave his opinion, supported by Shipton, that it would be useless to hold the camp any longer for the present; there would be no benefit in acclimatization from staying any longer at such an altitude, and some of the less experienced porters were showing signs of strain. He thought it better to come down that very evening. This he proceeded to do, using every mountaineering precaution to ensure safe descent, especially on the dangerous slopes of the traverse; and it was an immense relief to have the whole party down safe.

Clearly the mountain would be out of condition for at least several days, and it was necessary to decide whether the expedition should be kept in the comparative discomfort of Camp III or taken down for a change of scenery and occupation at Camp I. Next morning orders were given for the descent, and it became at once evident that everybody's condition and spirits improved.

But the arrival at Camp I was not an unalloyed pleasure. On the 20th the wholly unexpected news came through on the wireless that conditions favourable for the formation of the monsoon in the S. of the Bay of Bengal were evident. This was a frightful shock, because up to this time there had not been the slightest reason to suppose that the monsoon was going to arrive earlier than its normal time, say about June 15; indeed, the very cautious and tentative forecast made at Alipore in February had indicated that we might even expect a fairly late monsoon. After considerable discussion we decided that there was just a chance of forestalling the arrival of bad weather by returning up the glacier at once and making an assault. There was always the possibility that what is called the *Choti Barsat* might expend its first fury on the Darjeeling foothills and never reach Everest at all. Everything was ready on the N. Col, and at least one party might have time to attempt the summit.

We were back in Camp III by the 24th, only to find ourselves completely weather-bound there. In fact, the monsoon rushed up from the S. of India to the Everest region in four days, a phenomenon, I believe, never experienced before and one which can be attributed only to the failure of the N.W. wind to stem it.

The N. Col slopes were obviously out of commission, and I find from my diary that it was their uncompromising appearance which induced me at this period to throw out the tentative suggestion that we might examine the W. side of the N. Col. We all knew that Mallory had condemned this approach in 1921, and those members of last year's reconnaissance who saw it thought that little could be done there, so the matter was dropped for the present. But a wireless report that a severe storm might be expected, and the already sufficiently unpleasant conditions, resulted in the second retirement to Camp I on the 28th, on which day a moderate blizzard accelerated our descent. The next morning, however, we woke to find for the first time a strong N.W. wind blowing. This was on May 29. Hope at once revived, and an excursion on the main Rongbuk Glacier below Camp I revealed the very pleasant spectacle of the snow being blown in great sheets off the N. face of the mountain. At the same time the daily weather report indicated that the monsoon was weakening and also showing a tendency to drive off eastwards towards Assam. There could hardly be two opinions as to the inference to be drawn: the party welcomed with delight the proposal to go up the glacier again at once, and on the 30th we reached Camp II. Our optimism was short-lived: the N.W. wind showed every sign of weakening and of veering to the E.; heavy snow fell at Camp II; the mountain resumed its mantle of white, and we were unable to make any progress until the morning of June 3, on which day the wireless completed its tale of woe by announcing considerable activity not only in the Bay of Bengal but also in the Arabian Sea. For the moment, however, the N.W. wind resumed its activities and it was decided at least to see what was happening on the N. Col. Smythe, Shipton and Kempson made a cautious examination of the lower slopes on the morning of the 4th, finding conditions apparently very much better than might have been expected: so much so that it was thought justifiable, if the utmost precautions were taken, to attempt to reoccupy Camp IV with an assaulting party next day.

This plan was very carefully organized with a view to avoiding danger from avalanches. The whole climbing strength of the party was to be employed, the climbers working in pairs for fixed periods of time and the porters being divided into small parties which were to be moved in succession as the route was made. Smythe would accompany each party of climbers and would use his discretion throughout the operations as to the advisability of further progress. Shipton would control the advance of the porters. After a cold night the advance began very early on the morning of June 5. Wyn Harris and Kempson tackled the first 500 ft. straight up, but before long came upon the débris of a small avalanche which must have fallen some days before. After careful discussion with Smythe they completed their section and were succeeded by Warren and Wigram, who with Smythe reached a crevasse which marked the beginning of the traverse. Oliver and Gavin halted the leading porters a little further down, and Shipton was still further below with the remainder. The ascent up the first 500 ft. had been fairly straightforward in spite of the warning conveyed by the avalanche débris, but an examination at close quarters of the slopes of the traverse left no doubt that further progress along this route would be suicidal. Smythe, now thoroughly roused, made the bold decision to attempt a route straight up to the crest. From his position he could not clearly see the difficulties ahead: two very steep bands of ice separated by an unpleasant snow slope, and equally unpleasant snow under the crest—altogether some 400 ft., possibly more, of extremely difficult going. Fortunately a realization of the impracticability of this route came after a few steps only had been cut, and Smythe quite rightly gave up the attempt. It is certain that, even had the climbers reached the crest, porters could not possibly have been taken up by that way. Things looked so bad that Shipton from his place lower down anticipated Smythe's order to start the porters downwards. The descent was conducted with great skill, with a safe return to Camp III.

All that evening and next day the N.W. wind blew with tremendous force, our one really violent gale this year. Inside the shaking tents argument, that certain by-product of such conditions, raged upon the question of advance or retreat. Smythe, despite the anxious time he had been through, was convinced that this wind would remove the snow and give us a chance. The upshot was that on the morning of June 6 Wyn Harris asked me to let him and Shipton have a final look at the slopes, just to see what the actual effect of the wind had been. Nothing could be done during the fury of the morning, but during a temporary lull just after lunch the two men set off. We did not suppose that they would get far, but they made unexpectedly rapid progress up to the crevasse at the beginning of the traverse, finding this part of the slope swept fairly clear. After a short pause, during which they roped up, Shipton led out on to the traverse across what seemed to be good, hard and safe snow. Wyn Harris behind him had just left the crevasse when there came a crack some 200 ft. up and the snow on which they were standing began to slide towards the 400-ft. ice precipice not far below them. Shipton was immediately upset on to his back as the slope began to split up into ice blocks, and was carried down helplessly among them. Wyn Harris made a desperate effort and jumped back to the lower lip of the crevasse, jamming in his axe as he did so. He had to let go the coils of the rope, as his left hand was crushed against the axe-head, and he was upset in his turn; but he instantly recovered his footing, rammed the haft of the axe into the snow with the rope round it, and managed to hold his ground at the extreme edge of the avalanche. Just when it seemed that the straining rope must pull the axe out of the snow, the avalanche slowed down and stopped close to the edge of the precipice. That Wyn Harris could by his action alone have stopped the fall of many hundreds of tons of ice is unthinkable, but there may have been a slight easing off of the slope just before the final drop and it is possible that Wyn Harris, by taking his own weight and to some extent that of Shipton and the surrounding blocks of ice from the avalanche, contributed to arrest its motion. Certainly he did the right thing at the critical moment. The party pulled itself together and descended without further adventure.

This was, of course, the last straw. The wind had removed a great deal of snow from the eastern slopes, but a great deal more had almost certainly come over from the W., to form wind-slabs. Clearly there was nothing more to be done on this side, and orders were at once given for evacuation and descent to Camp I.

From *The Alpine Journal*, vol. 48, 1936.

JAMES RAMSEY ULLMAN:

One last try the Everesters were to make before the clouds of war descended on the world. This was in 1938, and, although notable work was done against heavy odds, it left the campaign against the world's summit pretty much *in statu quo*.

Perhaps the most interesting feature of the expedition was that it was much smaller than the previous ones, a widespread reaction against large and unwieldy parties having developed among Himalayan climbers as the result of previous experiences. H. W. Tilman, who had been on the reconnaissance of 1935, and had since been one of the conquerors of Nanda Devi, was the leader, and his party of six consisted, with one exception, of tried veterans. These were Shipton, back for his fourth attempt, Smythe and Warren for their third, Oliver for his second, and the old 1924 campaigner, Odell, now well into middle age, yet back for another fling after fourteen years. The newcomer was Peter Lloyd, who had been with Tilman (as had Odell) on Nanda Devi and who subsequently more than held his own in formidable company.

Darjeeling—Tibet—Rongbuk—the glaciers. The route was the same, the pattern was the same. . . . And so, too, in the end, was the outcome.

H. W. Tilman:

Our first sight of the mountain was a severe shock. It was white with snow and a cloud plume was blowing from it in the reverse of the usual N.W. direction. But none of us was really convinced that this betokened the monsoon, or believed that we should not still be given a chance. On reaching Camp 3 on the 18th [of May] the drastic change in conditions was even more evident; a foot of snow now covered the ice of the glacier, and water lay in pools ready to hand where before we had had to melt ice.

When clouds poured over the Rapiu La from the S. early next day another nail was driven into the coffin of our hopes. But after a short tour of inspection Odell and Oliver reported the snow of the lower slopes in good condition. Lloyd was sickening for his turn of 'flu, but on the 20th four of us and four Sherpas set out to prepare the route to the North Col. Oliver got off first with two men, the rest of us following an hour behind owing to some indecision about taking up loads. A heavy fall of séracs just to our left at the foot of the slope reminded us that delay is sometimes dangerous. Our route lay slightly to the right of the centre of the snow cirque forming the approach to the Col, and though it was rather too well adapted to act as an avalanche chute the snow was good and the climbing easy until within about 300 ft. of the top. Here a sudden steepening in the slope forced us out to the left on a long traverse before an easier angle allowed us to climb up directly. Oliver and his men, who had done all the work so far, were suspicious of the snow on the traverse and waited for us to join them before they embarked on it, carrying a rope for fixing. A short way out they got bunched and the snow avalanched. The Sherpa who was in front was clear of the cleavage, which was about two feet deep, and the light line for fixing which we were paying out got mixed up in their rope, so that we easily held them. As the incident was not serious I did not report it at the time, but the popular Press got wind of it and passed it on to readers with their usual happy accuracy. Meteorologists must have been interested to hear that we had been 'carried away by the monsoon,' and glaciologists that the party had been 'nearly caught by the tail of the glacier,' both these nasty mishaps taking place on the 'North Column.'

Part of the traverse having thus been made safe, Odell and I took over the job of cutting and stamping a track in the steep, soft snow and fixing a rope. It was so hot that we did not do very much before returning to camp at 4 p.m., where we found Shipton and Smythe who had crossed the Lhakpa La that morning. They had watched our performances and were relieved to see us coming down. It snowed steadily that evening for several hours, and the roar of avalanches was heard throughout the night. This heavy snowfall, accompanied as it was by muggy weather, gave rise to fresh discussion of plans. It seemed that the slopes would now be unsafe for three or four days, and that if the west wind, on which our main hopes depended, came, the probable formation of wind-slab on the lee side might make them dangerous for an indefinite period. From now on, the risk of an avalanche in one form or another was always at the back of our minds. Well aware of the queer behaviour of these slopes in other years, we began to turn our thoughts to a route up the W. side which had been warmly recommended by the 1936 party, who, however, did not go up it. We decided that Shipton, Smythe, and half the porters should go round there. We did not know that it would go, and the old route might still be used if caution was exercised; but although the contemplated division left both parties weak in porters it did promise that one or other would reach the Col.

A cold, windy night followed by a bright cloudless day made us drop the plan for the moment, and an examination of the slopes next day showed that their condition was good enough to warrant another start. On the 24th all the Europeans (except Lloyd who went down to recuperate) and 26 porters went up to the Col. Shipton and Smythe finished the remainder of the route, the others fixed ropes, and by midday all were up. Loads were dumped on the site of the 1936 camp, where the apex of a Pyramid tent just showed through the snow. Next day Smythe and I, starting early, took 15 more laden porters up, reaching the dump by 10 A.M. We sat there for a little, glumly noting the significantly adverse features. The mountain was white, heavy clouds billowed up on either side from the Loh La and the Rapiu La, the air was still, and the snow underfoot deep and soft. Even so, we were not quite convinced that the monsoon was established; as with a man marrying for the second time, hope triumphed over experience. After more discussion it was decided that Shipton and Smythe should withdraw to Rongbuk to await better conditions, and that we others should occupy the Col in order to examine the snow higher up. Uncertain whether the W. side route would go, we were reluctant to commit ourselves to it until forced; meanwhile it was no use keeping more people at Camp 3 than necessary. Nevertheless, when more snow fell the following afternoon we reverted to our first plan and on the 27th those two, with 15 porters, went down to Rongbuk, intending to return by the western route when conditions on the mountain improved. A day later Odell, Oliver, Warren, myself and 13 porters went up to occupy Camp 4. It was hot and muggy, and taking every precaution we crossed the traverse one by one. The eight porters who went down were instructed to come up next day if no snow fell, but as a foot of snow fell that night nothing was done. More snow fell on the 29th, but on the 30th we had scrambled eggs for breakfast and sprang into activity. Oliver went off to examine from the end of a long rope the snow at the top of the western side, and the rest of us began ploughing up the N. ridge in knee-deep snow. Before starting we saw the porters leaving Camp 3 to come up, but a prolonged bellow from us was heard by them and acted upon with almost indecent haste. They returned to camp.

Warren gave the 'closed' type oxygen apparatus a trial with unlooked-for results. As it seemed bent on suffocating him, he did not wear it long. This type weighs 35 lb. and pure oxygen is breathed by means of a mask. In the 'open' type weighing 25 lb., of which we had two, a tube in the mouth supplies oxygen; and air, such as it may be, is breathed through the nose. It was on the sole advice of Finch that I took the latter type, and though neither type is pleasant either to contemplate or to wear, the comparative success of one and failure of the other was instructive. Accompanied by a Sherpa I pushed on to about 24,500 ft., but it was clearly no use trying to occupy Camp 5 yet. When we retreated next day a suggestion that two of us should go down by the W. side was not popular, owing to Oliver's account of the snow.

On June 1 we were at Camp I, and the following morning Oliver and I walked up to Lake Camp, two miles up the main Rongbuk Glacier, where Shipton, Smythe and Lloyd now were, on their way to the W. side. The weather had changed; for 48 hrs. a strong W. wind had been driving low clouds before it, and through breaks in the flying scud we could see snow being whirled off the N. face in a very cheering manner. A wind like that threatened to form wind-slab on the lee slopes, so bowing to Smythe's reiterated warnings we decided to concentrate on the W. side. Shipton's party, which I now joined, was reinforced to a strength of 17 porters, and the others were to follow us as soon as some necessary loads had been brought down from Camp 3. After one intermediate camp at the corner we marched up the short glacier leading from the main Rongbuk Glacier to the foot of the W. side of the North Col. The height of this West Camp 3 must be about 21,500 ft., the same height as Camp 3 itself. The wind was still blowing, though less strongly, and the rocks of the Yellow Band high above us on our right looked hopefully free from snow. That their appearance from below was deceptive we were about to learn.

As we walked up to the foot of the slope next morning, the most phlegmatic might have found himself remarking on the fact that the way led over the débris of an avalanche of no ordinary magnitude. It was recent, possibly having fallen on the day when I expressed an earnest wish to descend the W. side, and the immediate result was to leave the first 500 ft. of our route bare ice. Having cut up this we had to cut across it to the left on a traverse that allowed little safeguard for the porters; beyond it we reached snow which was still in place and might at that early hour remain there if our pious hopes were fulfilled. On the whole, I see little cause for surprise that other parties have not made use of this route. We reached Camp 4 at 11 A.M. after a long plug up snow that continually let us through. A sun surrounded by a double halo peered wanly through a glassy sky, but no violent weather followed these alarming signs.

Next morning, June 6, we started for Camp 5, Lloyd wearing the 'open' type apparatus. The snow on the lower part of the N. ridge was now board-hard, thanks no doubt to being wind-swept, but in spite of the good going two of the porters succumbed to altitude at about 25,000 ft., and the others seemed far from happy. While yet some 300 ft. below the Camp 5 site (25,800 ft.) they were so affected by a sudden snowstorm that they wished to dump the loads and go down. After much talking better feelings prevailed and by 4 P.M. all were up. Leaving seven porters with Shipton and Smythe, Lloyd and I took the rest down. The two abandoned loads were brought up that evening by two of the Camp 5 party—a very fine piece of work.

Nothing was done next day owing to wind, but on the 8th Camp 6 was occupied. It was gruelling work, making a route up fairly steep rock, mostly snow covered. The climb of 1400 ft. to 27,200 ft. took 8 hrs. and the seven Sherpas, who stuck nobly to their task, only got back to Camp 5 very late and very tired. Shipton and Smythe started next morning, but they were out too early and had to go back to the tent to warm up. When they finally left the scree patch on which the tent was pitched they found themselves almost at once in thigh-deep powder snow. The futility of persevering was only too plain, so they returned to camp and thence down to Camp 5.

After an off day Lloyd and I took three sick men down by the W. side, and then, on the day the first pair were coming down, we started up with six porters, one of whom gave in halfway. From the N. ridge we watched Odell, Oliver, Warren, and two Sherpas coming up the W. side and met the seven porters returning from Camp 5. It was like Snowdon on a bank holiday. We were a queerly assorted pair because Lloyd was using the 'open' type apparatus, but there were not enough cylinders for two of this kind to be used throughout, as Lloyd was doing, and the 'closed' type was useless. At 3 P.M. we reached Camp 5, where Shipton and Smythe were, on their way down. Their account of conditions higher up put the summit out of the question, so we decided to go for the summit ridge and to work along it as far as we could, if possible to the Second Step. Two of our porters were persuaded to stay, the rest went down. A gale in the night made the double-skinned Pyramid tent flap so furiously that sleep was impossible.

Leaving at 8 A.M., helped to some extent by the tracks of the first party, though the wind had filled most of these, we reached Camp 6 soon after midday. Lloyd led while I followed, roped with the two porters. He arrived some 30 min. before us, evidently receiving more benefit from the oxygen as we gained height. For the short distance we went next morning he again went better than I did, but perhaps that is no criterion. What I did hope and expect was that the oxygen would give him sufficient 'boost' to climb the rock wall which, as will be seen presently, so easily defeated us. Lloyd is a chemist, so perhaps not unbiassed, but he was satisfied that when using oxygen less effort was required and that consequently he was less fatigued. We sent the men down, collecting snow for cooking, and turned in, for the wind was already rising. We ate pemmican with equanimity if not with gusto. At night it blew hard and again we slept little.

Starting at 8 A.M., fanned by what seemed a gentle zephyr from the W., we had not reached the steeper ground above the scree before my hands were numb and Lloyd complained that his feet were in almost the same state. We retreated to the tent and waited until 10.30 before trying again. As our objective was the summit ridge immediately W. of the N.E. shoulder, we had to climb a steep rock wall some 50 ft. high. Not liking the look of this from closer up, we turned half-right towards an upward-sloping snow corridor, but there a few thigh-deep steps in powder snow were enough to send us back to our first choice. There were three or four possible lines up the rock, all of which we tried with an equal lack of success. Each looked simple enough, but the smooth outward-sloping rock, sometimes snow-covered, easily withstood our irresolute attacks. While I was reconnoitring the fourth and last possibility, which might have 'gone,' though it meant a 'shoulder,' we saw Angtharkay and Nukku approaching the tent with more oxygen cylinders. Had we been short of an excuse for ceasing operations here was one, so down we went. If we had succeeded in gaining the ridge about 200 ft. above us, we should have been 1200 yds. from the Second Step and about a mile from the summit. Progress along the ridge would not have been easy and the Second Step looked most formidable. It will be a lasting regret that neither was tried.

From *The Alpine Journal*, vol. 51, 1939.

6

Wings

Everest from the Air

We now know a method of mounting into the air, and, I think, are not likely to know more. The vehicles can serve no use till we can guide them; and they can gratify no curiosity till we mount with them to greater heights than we can reach without; till we rise above the tops of the highest mountains.

Dr. Samuel Johnson

James Ramsey Ullman:

Many men have looked upward at the summit of the highest mountain. In recent years a few have looked *down* upon it.

Aviation, to be sure, is a vastly different proposition from mountaineering, and in itself has no place in this book. But the actual flights that have been made are an integral and important part of the Everest story. Man plodding doggedly afoot and man soaring at three miles a minute through the substratosphere present as extreme a contrast as can be found in the range of human locomotion, and it is part of the fascination of Everest that we find these extremes converging, as it were, towards its summit.

The first air expedition, elaborately planned and equipped, took place in April, 1933, and was signally successful. Like the climbing expeditions, it was a British venture, led by the Marquess of Douglas and Clydesdale (later the Duke of Hamilton *) and Air-Commodore P. F. M. Fellowes of the Royal Air Force. Two flights were made—one on April third and one on April nineteenth, with a flight over Kanchenjunga intervening—and on each occasion two planes participated. The base of operations was the town of Purnea, in northern India, and not the least of the fliers' contributions was the first detailed description of the heretofore almost unknown southern side of the mountain.

The account that follows is of the first flight and was writ-

* The same Hamilton onto whose estate Rudolf Hess parachuted on his bizarre flight to England in May, 1941.

ten by L. V. Stewart Blacker, Chief Observer and Photographer
of the party.

L. V. STEWART BLACKER:

A few minutes after we left the ground I had to busy myself with my routine duties. At the start of all high-altitude
flights, a number of vital checks must be made, and to avoid
the chance of omitting any I had compiled a list. No less than
forty-six separate jobs were included, and though each one
was trifling in itself, none could be omitted without risk to the
eventual success of the work. It was the more necessary to prepare such a list since we were inhaling oxygen the whole time,
and one of its effects on the human mind seems to be to create
a tendency to concentrate on the idea or task that is uppermost to the exclusion of everything else. As most of the forty-
six tasks were small details, it was all the more necessary to
have them down in writing, so that each observer could con-
sult his list at any particular time during the flight, and thus
ensure that every piece of work had been done by the appropriate time. The flight might be ruined, for instance, by omis-
sion to remove the caps from the lenses of all the cameras, and
in this dusty climate they had to be left on till the last moment.

The leading aircraftman photographer was responsible in
the programme for removing all these caps, counting them
and reporting to the observer the moment before the chocks
were removed from the wheels.

Everything passed off without incident as the two great machines soared up through the haze over the brown plains,
except that just for a moment the dynamo refused, as electri-
cians put it, to build up. This is a temperamentalism to which
all dynamos are liable. So, almost in a panic, I had to take off
the cover of the cut-out of the electrical system, undo the
screws with my thumbnail, pressing the platinum contacts to-

gether by hand. All was well, the generator behaved perfectly throughout the flight, and a supply of current kept us warm from first to last.

By the time the initial batch of these tests was completed we had been flying for some ten minutes, and for the next half-hour I had nothing to do but to sit conning over and recapitulating in my mind my duties. This part of the journey was the more humdrum because the plains and foothills below were almost lost to view owing to the thick dust-haze which had, unfortunately, on that day, chosen to rise to a phenomenal height. Gradually the dull monochrome of the brown chequer-boards of the ploughed fields of Bihar fused together into a uniform carpet, and every now and then the cluster of tiny rectangular roofs of a village stood out from the scene.

This haze almost invariably ceases at about a 5,000 or 6,000 foot level; [in] the present case its continuance above that height was infuriating in the last degree.

We did not rise clear of it until actually about 19,000 feet, and so the southern ground control, which was the river confluence near Komaltar, was practically invisible to the pilot. He could not find it with sufficient accuracy, a decided misfortune, since it was the point from which the photographic survey was started.

Nevertheless, I was just able to see an infinite tangle of the brown mountains of Nepal, seamed with black forests, and caught occasional glimpses of the swift Arun river in its gradually steepening valley as now and then I opened the hatchway of the floor and looked down through thousands of feet of purple space. We crossed the frontier of this forbidden kingdom at 13,000 feet. Then, suddenly, a little after our craft sprang clear of the haze into the wonderful translucent air of the upper heights, and away to our right an amazing view of Kangchenjunga in all its gleaming whiteness opened out against the blue.

For a few minutes nothing else could be seen against the sky but this.

Fumbling with the catches in my thick gloves, I threw up the cockpit roof, put my head out into the icy slip-stream and there over the pulsating rocker arms of the Pegasus, showing level with us, was the naked majesty of Everest itself. Just a tiny triangle of whiteness, so white as to appear incandescent, and on its right, a hand's breadth, another tiny peak which was Makalu. For some time nothing could be seen above this purple haze but these three incredible white peaks—Everest and Makalu just to the right of the engine, and Kangchenjunga behind the right wing. It was fortunate that the wind from the westward caused the machine to lie with a drift of eighteen degrees, obliquely to our track to the mountain, and thus we had a clear view of our goal straight beneath a point on the under-surface of the upper wing, eighteen degrees from the centre line.

Gyachungkang was masked by the engine, but soon Gauri-sankar showed over the port wing.

I was not long able to remain watching these wonderful sights, for soon the machine soared upwards, unfolding innumerable peaks to right and left and in front, all in their amazing white mantles, but scored and seared with black precipices.

The light on the snow was a wonderful thing in itself. A quality of whiteness, as much more brilliant than the snow to which ordinary human eyes are accustomed, as that snow is more vivid than the unclothed landscape.

Somewhat to our dismay, there streamed from the crest of Everest away towards its sister peak, Makalu, eastwards, that immense ice-plume which is the manifestation of a mighty wind raging across the summit. Lifting from the prodigious cliff face, countless particles of ice are driven over the summit with blizzard force.

Soon, very slowly it seemed, we approached closer and closer to the big white mountains, and all my time became occupied with work on the cameras.

Now I crouched down over the drift-sight, peering through the great concave lens and adjusted the wires across it. I rotated them carefully and this gave me the angle of drift of eighteen degrees. I passed this to the pilot, who needed it for navigation and then I adjusted the big automatic survey camera, turning it through the same angle in its mounting.

I had to look to the spirit-levels, longitudinal and transverse, and to adjust the tilt of the camera in both senses, until the bubbles rested in the middle of their travel. This required delicacy and judgment as the machine swayed every now and then. The adjustment had to be made in each case just at the moment when the machine happened to be level, neither one wing-tip up or down in either direction, nor pitching. I glanced at the big aluminium actuating-knob, and saw that after twenty seconds or so it turned by itself as the pilot had switched on the current into its motor. The camera was warm, the current was running through it, and all seemed well.

Now, without getting up from a prone position, I could move myself back a little on my elbows, open the hatchway in the floor, and look vertically down on the amazing mountainscape, bare of trees, seamed with great glaciers, and interspersed with streaks of scree and shale. This was the beginning of the range, insignificant enough to our eyes at the height we were, which rises up to the culminating 24,000 feet peak of Chamlang. Then shutting the hatchway and, laboriously taking great care to keep the oxygen pipe unentangled, and myself clear of all the various electrical wires, I could stand up and look again through the top of the cockpit. I caught a glimpse over the pilot's shoulder of the brilliant red light on his dashboard, which flashed for a moment as the camera shutter operated itself.

Up went our machine into a sky of indescribable blue, until we came to a level with the great culminating peak itself.

Then, to my astonished eyes, northwards over the shoulder of the mountain, across the vast bare plateau of Tibet, a group of snow-clad peaks uplifted itself. I hesitated to conjecture the distance at which they lay in the heart of that almost trackless country, for by some trick of vision the summits seemed even higher than that of Mount Everest. The astonishing picture of this great mountain itself, whose plume for a moment seemed to diminish in length, and with its tremendous sullen cliffs, set off the whiteness of Makalu, was a sight which must for ever remain in one's mind.

I had been hard at work with the cameras first exposing plates, uncapping dark slides, winding and setting the shutters to seize a series of splendid views. The scene was superb and beyond description. The visibility was extraordinary and permitted the whole range to be seen on the western horizon. It seemed that the only limit to the view along the mountain was that due to the curvature of the earth's surface. The size of the mountains stunned the senses; the stupendous scale of the scenery and the clear air confounded all estimates of size and distance. So I went on, now exposing plates, now lifting the heavy cinema camera to run off fifty feet or so of film. I crouched down again, struggling to open the hatchway, to take a photograph through the floor. Everything by now, all the metal parts of the machine, was chilled with the cold, the cold of almost interstellar space. The fastenings were stiff and the metal slides had almost seized. I struggled with them, the effort making me pant for breath, and I squeezed my mask on to my face to get all the oxygen possible. I had to pause and, suddenly, with the door half-open I became aware, almost perceptibly, of a sensation of dropping through space. The floor of the machine was falling away below us. I grasped a fuselage strut and peered through my goggles at the altimeter needle.

It crept, almost swung, visibly as I looked at it in astonishment, down through a couple of thousand feet. Now I had the hatchway open and the aeroplane swooped downwards over a mighty peak of jagged triangular buttresses, which was the South Peak.

Below us loomed an almost incomprehensible medley of ridges, ranges and spurs of black rocks, with here and there the characteristic yellowy-red of Everest showing through. We had suddenly lost two thousand feet in this great down-draught of the winds, and it seemed as though we should never clear the crags of the South Peak on the way to Everest now towering in front of us. However, the alarm was short-lived, for our splendid engine took us up through the great overfall. Again we climbed; slowly, yet too quickly for one who wants to make use of every moment, our aeroplane came to the curved chisel-like summit of Everest, crossing it, so it seemed to me, just a hair's breadth over its menacing summit. The crest came up to meet me as I crouched peering through the floor, and I almost wondered whether the tail skid would strike the summit. I laboured incessantly, panting again for breath to expose plates and films, each lift of the camera being a real exertion. Every now and then my eyes swam a little and I looked at the oxygen flow-meter to find it reading its maximum. So I bethought myself of the little cork plugs I had whittled down to fit the eye apertures of the mask. Tearing off the heavy gloves and fumbling with cold fingers, I managed to stuff them in.

Now I had worked my way up again to a standing position, with the cockpit roof fully open and its flaps fastened back. I had my head and shoulders out into the slip-stream, which had become strangely bereft of its accustomed force. I was astonished for a moment till I suddenly remembered that the wind here only weighed a quarter as much as at sea-level. Now I could take photographs over the top of the machine much aided by these fortunate cork plugs. Without them, if the aviator has his head sideways in the slip-stream the oxygen tends to be blown from his mask and the flow stopped before it can reach his mouth, in much the same way that a trout may be drowned by pulling him upstream against the lie of his gills.

Thus almost, and indeed before I expected it, we swooped over the summit and a savage period of toil began. The pilot swung the machine skilfully again towards the westward into the huge wind force sweeping downwards over the crest; so great was its strength that, as the machine battled with it and struggled to climb upwards against the downfall, we seemed scarcely to make headway in spite of our 120 mile an hour air speed. I crammed plate-holder after plate-holder into the camera, releasing the shutter as fast as I could, to line it on one wonderful scene after another. We were now for a few moments in the very plume itself, and as we swung round fragments of ice rattled violently into the cockpit.

We made another circuit and then another as I exposed dozens of plates and ran off my spools of film. We could not wait long over the mountain-top for the oxygen pressure gauge needle in my cockpit was moving downwards, an ominous sign. We had no very exact idea of the length of time our return journey would take with that violent wind blowing, and fuel was needed for emergencies. After a quarter of an hour or so, which seemed perhaps on the one hand like a lifetime from its amazing experiences, and yet was all too short, we turned back. Soon we saw this wonderful view with serried peaks, row upon row, in fairy beauty, surmounted by Everest and Makalu almost grotesquely outlined by the aluminium-coloured fabric of our rudder. We came back towards the terrific Arun gorges over a bewildering medley of peaks, ranges and spurs, interspersed with broad grimy glaciers littered with moraine, scree and shale. These peaks must be a great height and yet they seemed insignificant enough to our eyes.

Camp IV on the Col.

Ewing-Galloway

So near yet so far. Powder snow on the slabs leading toward the summit.

160 miles home passed surprising quickly, the journey marred by the discovery that the second film in the ciné-camera had become frozen despite its warm jacket, and was so brittle that I could not reload. My oxygen mask, too, plugged as it was with cork stoppers, had become a solid mass of ice. Steadily we came down, gradually losing height with the throttle of the engine fairly well open to guard against the carburettor freezing. It was in another struggle that I managed to change the magazine of the survey camera and adjust it to the drift now coming from the opposite side of the aeroplane.

Soon the semi-circle of gleaming peaks faded from our sight as the straight line of purple dust-haze rose to overwhelm it.

From *First Over Everest.*

JAMES RAMSEY ULLMAN:

Far different from the carefully planned 1933 expedition was the flight made in 1942 by Col. Robert L. Scott, Jr., an American flier then on wartime duty in the C.B.I. theater of operations. Flying alone in a P-43A fighter plane, Scott set off on his astonishing junket not only without authorization but also without special preparation of any kind; in fact, simply on a whim during the course of a routine test flight. It is hard to imagine a more dramatic demonstration of the development of aviation over a period of a few years.

COL. ROBERT L. SCOTT, JR.:

My course was away from the river as I pointed the nose of the fighter towards the great peaks that were now coming up over the curve of the earth. Even at the high altitude I had reached—over 25,000 feet—I could only gasp at their greatness. Now, as I swept my head around and made my pictures, in one glance I took in an area that must have had more than a thousand-mile diameter. In one sweep my eye passed from the steamy depths of the Assamese jungle, to the Naga Hills, ten to twelve thousand feet high; then from these mere foot-hills to the distant snows of the Himalayas—the roof of the world.

Now, straight ahead, I saw Kanchenjunga, with three of its five peaks visible. On ahead to the West, summit after summit pointed into the purpling sky. There was Makalu, rearing up to 27,790 feet on the other side of Kanchenjunga. Kanchenjunga and Chamo Lhani were between Makalu and the great one—Everest. The greatest of mountains was still muddled together in its multitude of spires; so that from my distance I could not yet pick out the highest point of land on this earth.

With the turbo on full we climbed on, above twenty-six thousand feet. Far to the West, I saw where the Himalayas end, and above the heat haze of India there appeared other peaks in other mountain ranges far away in the Punjab. One of these I recognized as Badrinath, itself nearly 28,000 feet high. The entire range of the Great Himalayas now appeared like the giant vertebrae of some greatest of animals from which during countless centuries the flesh had gone. Below me it stretched, from Burma, some four hundred miles be-hind me to the East, to that peak near Badrinath, far out to the West. Approaching Kanchenjunga, I circled that impressive 28,150-foot pyramid and then wove in between it and the slightly lower peaks to the West. Continuing my color pho-tography as the sky darkened in the substratosphere, I silhouet-ted the snow-covered pinnacles against the purpling sky.

On I went, now, to the peaks of Makalu and Chamo Lhani, keeping the little fighter climbing steadily, winding in among the saddles between the mighty hills. Even in the lethargy that comes with oxygen starvation—or aëroembolism, as the flight surgeons call it—I was proud of the loud American engine that was pulling me on and on to the top of the world. Looking at those massive, snow-covered spires, I respected the magnitude of nature and the magnificence of the Himalayas, and I perceived the insignificance of man. Then, as my position above it all impressed itself on me, I realized that, after all, man had perfected that steadily purring engine which was carrying me on and on above the greatest of mountains. Perhaps, then, man in all his insignificance deserved a little credit too.

Rising along, without the proximity of lofty lesser peaks, Kanchenjunga is truly the most beautiful of mountains. Though a full thousand feet lower than Everest, it sweeps up in isolation from a fourteen-thousand-foot plain for another fourteen thousand feet in a graceful pyramid, commanding the chain of the highest mountains in the world.

The little fighter and I "topped out" over Makalu. On the other side, towards Everest, I saw Kamet. Then peak after peak met my gaze. There was Chamo Lhani, Chomiomo, Kanchenjau, Cho-oyo at 26,870 feet, Gyachung Kang, Lhotse (the South peak of Everest)—until finally and with reverence, as though I had saved the greatest for last, my eyes centered on Everest, in Tibet called Chamolang, the Sacred One.*

I guess my real reason for finally yielding my eyes to the great mountain alone was that by now it was the only summit above me—the others had gradually sunk beneath the mounting altitude of the little fighter plane. Now even Everest was slowly giving way, and I headed directly for that mass of reddish yellow rock, all of it covered with snow and ice except where the everlasting winds of the upper air had torn the covering away. At 30,000 feet and just South of the center pyramid, I saw the "plume" of Everest, formed by snow being blown from the summit. On this day it pointed to the South, borne by a North wind, and the sun shining through it made a rainbow that was beautiful.

* Still another variant, both in the Tibetan name and in its translation. —*Editor.*

Above Everest now, I withstood my temptation to fly close to the big peak on the down-wind side—there were bound to be terrible down-drafts there, and I had respected lesser down-drafts of lesser peaks in lower parts of the world. Passing directly over the South peak, Lhotse, I photographed Everest against the sky, and as I opened the glass canopy of the plane I felt the chilling blast of the wind. I noted then that my thermometer registered 22 degrees below zero, which though cold is nowhere near the temperature one would experience at an equal altitude anywhere else than in the Himalayan region. For there the warm monsoon winds out of the Indian Ocean are raised rapidly by the slope of the earth, and thus the troposphere is evidently higher.

On we climbed, with my turbo moaning its din among the Himalayas. Everest fell farther below, and there came the feeling of exhilaration that I was higher than the highest of mountains—and still climbing. Circling, I set my course toward the peaks forming the northern Tibetan border—the hills of Arma Dreme (according to my map) and the distant Kwenlun Mountains. My effort was to get that ship as high as it would climb and yet leave me sufficient oxygen to get me back to a safe free-breathing level—and at the same time have enough fuel to reach my selected refueling field to the South, in Cooch Behar. Finally, at 37,000 feet as indicated on my altimeter— which is over forty thousand, probably 44,400 feet true, calibrated from temperature and pressure corrections—I passed the point where for the sake of my heart and lungs it was best that I go home.

Already I could feel the aëroembolism symptoms to such a degree that I wanted to yell at myself one minute, beat myself over the head the next, and pat myself on the back in another. It's a peculiar kind of "jag" the high altitude flyer gets on, and it's best to be careful. I surely didn't want to fall suddenly asleep and dive down to be a permanent resident among the

Lamas in Tibet. Anyway my eyes could no longer see well enough to appreciate the beauties of the mountains, and the reduced pressure was causing extreme discomfort in my stomach. Even with the oxygen regulator on "full" I gasped frequently, and when I raised my camera it seemed to weigh tons. Then I got to where I couldn't remember whether or not I had heard the camera mechanism run. You see, at that altitude the oxygen that we carry in the ship, even if you get it to your lungs, is only partially absorbed by the blood. Anyway, as I opened the canopy the cold air hit me in the face and revived me enough to enable me to make my decision to go on down.

The temperature gauge on the dashboard was now minus fifty and on the peg. It had to be lower than fifty below, and that is cold anywhere. Though my camera had been hung over the cockpit heater, I know that it had been frozen at times and didn't run. Below me now were mountains marked on the map with the familiar phrase: "Territory unexplored and unadministered." Probably some peak in that chain would be higher than Everest—who knows?

I passed over Everest and took my last pictures from the highest altitude that I reached—approximately two miles above the great mountain. To the North I saw, five hundred miles away, the summit of Ulugh Muztagh, itself over 26,000 feet. Around it I could see the desert haze from the sands of Chinese Turkestan. To the West now, and behind the top of Aling Kangri (over 25,000 feet) and Kamet (26,500), the real Western Himalayas, I could see the summits of Saser Kangri and Distaghil Sar. One mountain of this range was the 28,240-foot bulk of Badrinath.* To the North of these I saw the desert of Kashgar, almost five hundred miles from me. To the South appeared the hills of Shilong, nearly four hundred miles away,

* Earlier, Col. Scott refers to Badrinath as "nearly 28,000 feet high." There is no Himalayan peak of such a height that is generally known by this name. Perhaps he is referring to K2, in the Karakoram.—*Editor.*

and around them were the boiling clouds of the approaching monsoon season. Back in the East—the direction from which I had come—was the top of Namsha Barwa, another five hundred miles distant, where the Naga Hills met Burma. On this Spring day, as I spiralled down my eyes must have covered millions of square miles, from my vantage point above the highest peak.

Just to ease a brain that was rapidly growing "befuddled" from altitude, I tried to fire my guns, but they were frozen. Circling in a power dive to exactly thirty thousand feet, I passed directly over Everest and into the "plume." Immediately I was thankful that I had heeded my better judgment of the earlier hour and had not flown close to the down-wind side below the summit. For I was sucked down in the most violent down-draft I have ever experienced.

As the nose of the ship went into the "plume" area, it felt to me as though some gigantic hand had reached up from old Chamolang and was drawing us roughly towards Nepal, the country directly beneath. My camera cracked me in the chin. My maps from the map-case flew all over the cockpit. I got the nose pointed down towards Asia as quickly as I could, got the prop in low pitch, fought the maps out of my eyes—and almost before I realized it we were out of the down-draft, sailing smoothly along at 25,000 feet, at least five miles South of the big peak. Even in that time we had lost almost a mile of altitude.

Gaining complete control of the ship, I circled for more photography, and climbed once more for a view of the North Col, the point where the best efforts at climbing Everest have failed.* Out there now I could see that place, at about 28,000

---

* This, of course, is incorrect. Judging from what immediately follows, Col. Scott is referring not to the North Col but to the eastern summit ridge.—*Editor.*

feet above sea level, where man had been forced to turn back, beaten by Nature and the elements. I thought of the months that those hardy men had worked to condition themselves and and to fight that high-altitude walk over the 18,000-foot passes from Darjeeling across Sikkim, through these perpetual hills— to a failure here in the very shadow of success, barely a thousand feet below the summit. Personally, I want to do all my Hima- layan mountain climbing right behind the steady drone of "A Loud American Engine."

Fuel, oxygen, and film about gone, I turned now through the saddle of Everest's main peaks—the West promontory and Chamolang—and saluted with reverence the highest point on the earth's surface. I tried to salute by firing the two fifty- calibre guns into the glacier, but once more they failed to dis- charge. So I just waggled my wings and dove for my refueling base to the South.

With an aching head but with real exhilaration, I buzzed the Maharaja's palace and landed at Cooch Behar. Then, with adequate hundred octane fuel, I went on back East to the Brah- maputra, up past Tezpur, with my glance going back occa- sionally on my old friends, the Himalayas. The great pile of snow-covered summits seemed closer to me now, for I seemed to know them. Everest, with its ocherish-brown color accen- tuating the yellow sandstone band that traversed it, was back there already over two hundred miles away, still commanding the horizon and in reality the rest of the world. Closer to me and over the saddles of the great ones, every now and then I could see the jagged Nyonna-Ri range and the snows of Arma Dreme. Appearing now as another great mass superimposed on Everest, was the pyramid of Makalu, and from there my eyes swept across a hundred lofty peaks. Looking them all over, I tried to name them without reference to my map. Last of all my gaze centered in admiration on the massif of Kanchenjunga.

I had covered the highest range in the world. I had made the trip of over a thousand miles from our base up the Brahmaputra by Lhasa and Everest to Cooch Behar in five hours and ten minutes. My route had been over territory which was probably the most inaccessible in existence. Certainly it was forbidden, not only by nature, but, as I later found out to my sorrow, by the very religion of the people.

For shortly after I landed in Assam, came the usual letter that has dogged me throughout my military career. "You will explain by indorsement hereon why you flew over Everest and crossed the country of Nepal."

You see, on the thread of this "reply by endorsement" there hangs many a tale. To dodge the veiled girl back in Galata, I had crossed the Black Sea to Varna and from Rumania had entered Russia. That had precipitated a letter from the Adjutant General, who demanded a reply by endorsement telling why I, an officer in the American Army, had entered the USSR—a country then not recognized by the U.S.A. Later, in each year, I had had to make the same written reply explaining why I had exceeded the maximum flying time of five hundred hours a year.

There had been many letters, but this one in far-off India had me guessing. I had flown a routine test flight and could not understand why it had required an official answer. Later it came out that the British authorities in India had complained to the U.S. Headquarters in Delhi about the flight for two reasons. First, that a plane flying over Nepal, from which independent country came the fine little Gurka soldiers, offended the religion of the people. Secondly, the entire incident had been discovered from the fact that a Calcutta newspaper had published a story that had been given world-wide publicity. This correspondent had dwelt on the ease with which my little fighter had climbed the 29,002 feet * to the top of Everest and on up two miles above the highest of peaks, but he had closed his article with what the British considered a slap at their ability. It was this classic ending:

"While it required the British Government many months of planning and the expenditure of some hundred thousands of pounds to fly over Everest in 1927,† it merely required an American Aviator, Colonel Scott, about five hours of his morning on a routine test flight and the consumption of a few gallons of aviation gasoline."

Of course I blush when I think that my gallant newspaperman did not consider the difference in the advancement of aviation between the years 1927 and 1942. Oh, well, with the letter answered, apparently to the satisfaction of all concerned, I am still at large, and permitted to fly and to breathe a purer air on high. And there are some magnificent memories locked within me, memories of nature's rocky masterpiece there in the tops of the Himalayas.

From *God Is My Co-Pilot*.

* Col. Scott is here using the old figure, not the revised one, which is 29,141.—*Editor*.
† The year was 1933, and the flight was privately financed.—*Editor*.

7

How? When?

The Problems

By my troth, here's a weather is able
to make a man call his father whoreson.

Greene: *Friar Bacon and Friar Bungay*

JAMES RAMSEY ULLMAN:

The shadow of wings has fallen across Everest. Camera shutters have clicked, and the lineaments of its summit have been made known to the world. But the men in the planes a few hundred feet above it were no closer to *standing* there than if they had been at the opposite end of the earth. It is one of the great and satisfying things about a mountain that it can never be conquered in the laboratory or machine-shop. When Everest is won it will be won by mountaineers.

And the mountaineers, far from being discouraged by the long record of failure, are still planning, preparing, hoping. Nine years have elapsed since the last expedition, and a few more will probably pass before the next is politically feasible. When the curtain rises again a new generation of Everesters will hold the stage. To their exploit they will bring improved equipment, a few new scientific and technological aids, and a detailed foreknowledge of the problems that will confront them. But those problems themselves will be the same as in the past. Everest, the antagonist, will be the same.

The experiences and conclusions of the earlier climbers, therefore, are not merely of interest in themselves, but form the very cornerstone on which all future expeditions will be based. Climber and porter personnel, transport, route, acclimatization, weather, the use or non-use of oxygen: these will remain, as they have been since the beginning, the fundamental components and problems of the enterprise. On some of them, among old Everesters, there is virtual unanimity of opinion; on others, wide variance. But on one question—the ultimate question—they are all agreed. Man can climb Everest, and some day *will*.

GEORGE LEIGH-MALLORY:

It might be supposed that, from the experience of two expeditions * to Mount Everest, it would be possible to deduce an estimate of the dangers and difficulties involved and to formulate a plan for overcoming the obstacles which would meet with universal approval among mountaineers. But, in fact, though many deductions could hardly be denied, I should be surprised to find, even among us of the second party, anything like complete agreement either in our judgment of events or in our ideas for the future. Accordingly, I must be understood as expressing only my personal opinions. The reader, no doubt, will judge the book more interesting if he finds the joint authors disagreeing among themselves.

The story of the first attempt to climb the mountain in 1922 will leave no doubts on one point. The final camp was too low. However strong a party may be brought to the assault, their aim, unless they are provided with oxygen, must be to establish a camp considerably higher than our camp at 25,000 feet. The whole performance of the porters encourages us to believe that this can be done. Some of them went to a height of 25,000 feet and more, not once only, but thrice; and they accomplished this feat with strength to spare. It is reasonable to suppose that these same men, or others of their type, could carry loads up to 27,000 feet. But it would be equally unreasonable to suppose that they could reach this height in one day from the camp on Chang La at 23,000 feet. No one would be so foolish as to organise an attempt on this assumption. Two camps instead of one must be placed about the Chang La; an-

* This summation of Mallory's was written after the expedition of 1922. —*Editor*.

other stage must be added to the structure before the climbing
party sets forth to reach the summit.

But how exactly is this to be done? It is to this question that
one would wish to deduce an answer from the experience of
1922. It is very unlikely that any future party will find itself
in the position to carry out any ideal plan of organisation.
Ideally, they ought to start by considering what previous performances might help or hinder the aim of bringing the party
of attack in the fittest possible condition to the last camp. What
ought they to have done or not to have done, having regard
to acclimatisation? It is still impossible to lay down the law
on this head. After the first Expedition, I supposed that the
limit of acclimatisation must be somewhere about 21,000 feet.
It now seems probable that it is higher. One of the physiologists
who has been most deeply concerned with this problem of
acclimatisation considers that it would probably be desirable,
from the physiological point of view, to stay four or five days
at 25,000 feet before proceeding to attempt the two last stages
on consecutive days. Those of us who slept at Camp V for the
first attempt would certainly be agreed in our attitude towards
this counsel. The desire to continue the advance and spend another night at a higher elevation, if it persisted at all for so long
a time at 25,000 feet, would be chilled to tepidity, and the
increasing desire to get away from Camp V might lead to retreat instead of advance. The conditions must be altogether
more comfortable if the climbers are to derive any advantage
from their rustication at this altitude. It would not be impossible, perhaps, if every effort were concentrated on this end,
to make a happy home where the aspiring mountaineers might
pass a long week-end in enjoyment of the simplest life at 25,000
feet; it would not be practicable, having regard to other ends
to be served by the system of transport. But it might be well
to spend a similar period for acclimatisation 2,000 feet lower
on the Chang La. There a very comfortable camp, with perfect

shelter from the prevailing wind and good snow to lie on, can easily be established. Noel actually spent three successive nights there in 1922, and apparently was the better rather than the worse for the experience.

No less important in this connection is the effect of exertions at high altitudes on a man's subsequent performance. We have to take into account the condition of the climbing parties when they returned to the Base Camp after reaching approximately 27,000 feet. With one exception, all the climbers were affected in various degrees by their exertions, to the prejudice of future efforts. It would seem, therefore, that they cannot have had much strength to spare for the final stage to the summit. But there was a general agreement among the climbers that it was not so much the normal exertion of climbing upwards that was in itself unduly exhausting, but the addition of anything that might be considered abnormal, such as cutting steps, contending with wind, pushing on for a particular reason at a faster pace, and the many little things that had to be done in camp. It is difficult from a normal elevation to appreciate how great is the difference between establishing a camp on the one hand and merely ascending to one already established on the other. If ever it proves possible to organise an advanced party whose business it would be to establish at 25,000 feet a much more comfortable camp than ours in 1922, and if, in addition, a man could be spared to undertake the preparation of meals, the climbers detailed for the highest section of all would both be spared a considerable fatigue and would have a better chance of real rest and sleep.

The peculiar dangers of climbing at great altitudes were illustrated by the experience of 1922. The difficulty maintaining the standard of sound and accurate mountaineering among a party all more or less affected by the conditions, and the delays and misfortunes that may arise from the exhaustion of one of the party, are dangers which might be minimised by a supporting party. Two men remaining at the final camp and two men near Camp V watching the progress of the unit of assault along the final ridge, and prepared to come to their assistance, might serve to produce vital stimulants, hot tea or merely water, at the critical moment, and to protect the descent. It is a counsel of perfection to suggest providing against contingencies on this lavish scale; but it is well to bear in mind the ideal. And there is, besides, a precaution which surely can and will be taken; to take a supply of oxygen for restorative purposes. The value of oxygen for restoring exhausted and warming cold men was sufficiently well illustrated during the second attempt in 1922.

The question as to whether the use of oxygen will otherwise help or hinder climbers is one about which opinions may be expected to disagree. Anyone who thinks that it is impossible to get up without oxygen can claim that nothing has shown it to be impossible to get up with its aid. For my part, I don't think it impossible to get up without oxygen. The difference of atmospheric pressure between 27,000 feet and the summit is small, and it is safe to conclude that men who have exerted themselves at 27,000 feet could live without difficulty for a number of hours on the summit. As to whether their power of progress would give out before reaching 29,000 feet, it is impossible to dogmatise. I can only say that nothing in the experience of the first attempt has led me to suppose that those last 2,000 feet cannot be climbed in a day. I am not competent to sift and weigh all the evidence as to whether, how much, and with what consumption of gas it was easier to proceed up the slopes of Mount Everest with oxygen so far as Finch and Bruce went on that memorable day. But I do venture to combat the suggestion that it is necessarily easier to reach the top in that manner. I think no one will dispute the statement that the final camp for the second attempt was too low, as it had been for the first, to enable the oxygen party to reach the summit.

With the same apparatus it will be necessary in this case also to provide a second camp above the North Col. And the question for the moment will ultimately be, is it possible to add to that immense burden of transport to 27,000 feet the weight of the oxygen cylinders required?

The weather in all probability will have something to say to this problem. The Expedition of 1922 was certainly not favoured by the weather. There was no continuous spell of calm fine days, and the summer snows began a week earlier than the most usual date. One wonders what sort of weather is to be expected with the most favourable conditions on Mount Everest. It is conceivable that a series of calm fine days sometimes precede the monsoon. But when we consider the perpetual winds of Tibet at all seasons, it seems unlikely that Mount Everest is often immune from this abominable visitation. It is far more likely that the calm day is a rare exception, and only to be expected when the north-westerly current is neutralised by the monsoon from the South-east. The ill-luck of 1922 may probably be computed as no more than those seven days by which the monsoon preceded expectation. With so short a time for preparations and advance, we were indeed unfortunate in meeting an early monsoon. And it is hardly possible considerably to extend the available time by starting earlier. There was only the barest trickle of water at the Base Camp on May 1, 1922, and the complications involved by the necessity of melting snow for water, both here and at all higher stages, for any considerable time, would be a severe handicap. But it must be remembered that the second attempt was made a week before the monsoon broke. Time appeared short on the mountain chiefly from the threat of bad weather and the signs showing that the majority of days were, to say the least, extremely disagreeable for climbing high on the mountain. If others are confronted by similar conditions, they too will probably feel that each fine day must be utilised and the attack must be pressed on; for the fine days past will not come back, and ahead is the uncertain monsoon.

A final question may now be asked: What advantages will another Expedition have which we did not have in 1922? In one small and in one large matter the next Expedition may be better equipped. It was disappointing, after so much time and thought had been expended upon the problem of foot-gear, that nothing was evolved in 1922 which succeeded in taking the place of Alpine boots of well-known patterns. The great disadvantage of these sorts of boot is that one cannot wear crampons with them at these high altitudes, for the strap bound tightly round the foot will almost certainly cause frost-bite; either different boots or different spikes must be invented if the climbers are to have crampons or their equivalent. It is essential that they should be so equipped to avoid the labour of step-cutting, and the lack of this equipment might well rob them of victory on the steep final slopes below the summit. This matter of foot-gear is not so very small, after all. But a still more important one is the oxygen apparatus. It is conceivable, and I believe by no means unlikely, that a different type of cylinder may be used in the future, and capable of containing more oxygen, compared with the same weight, than those of 1922. A 50 per cent. improvement in this direction should alter the whole problem of using oxygen. With this advantage it might well be possible to go to the top and back with the four cylinders which a man may be expected to carry from a height of 25,000 feet or little higher. If a second camp above the North Col becomes unnecessary in this way, the whole effort required, and especially the effort of transport, will be reduced to the scale of what has already been accomplished, and can no doubt be accomplished again.

The further advantage of a future Expedition is simply that of experience. It amounts to something, one cannot say how much. In small ways a number of mistakes may be avoided.

The provision of this and that may be more accurately calculated according to tried values. The whole organisation of life in high camps should be rather more efficient. Beyond all this, the experience of 1922 should help when the moment comes towards the making of a right plan; and a party which chooses rightly what to do and when to do it, and can so exclude other possibilities as to be certain that no better way could be chosen, has a great advantage. But, when all is said as to experience and equipment, it still remains true that success requires a quality. History repeats itself, perhaps, but in a vague and general fashion only where mountains are concerned. The problem of reaching the summit is every time a fresh one. The keen eye for a fair opportunity and resource in grave emergencies are no less necessary to the mountaineer everywhere, and not least upon Mount Everest, than determination to carry through the high project, the simple will to conquer in the struggle.

From *The Assault on Mount Everest: 1922.*

JAMES RAMSEY ULLMAN:

One fact that the Everest expeditions have proved is that men—or at least some men—can live at earth's highest altitudes. True, none (unless it be Mallory and Irvine) have yet gone above 28,100 feet; but four surviving climbers are known to have reached that height, several others have fallen only slightly short of it, and there appears to be no doubt that, given favorable conditions, some of them would have been capable of reaching the highest point on earth.

It is that "favorable conditions," of course, that is the great imponderable. Comprising every aspect of an expedition—material, organizational, psychological—it includes, perhaps most essentially of all, the physical condition of the individual climbers. As we have seen repeatedly in the preceding pages, men do not approach the summit of the world in anything like the bodily state they enjoy at sea level. And they could not even so much as begin to approach it, were it not for the marvelous ability of the human organism to adapt and acclimatize itself to strange environments. The past Everest expeditions have provided an immense mass of data on acclimatization—indeed this has probably been their outstanding contribution to scientific knowledge. But it is an even greater understanding of the process, in all its varying individual aspects, that remains as one of the major requisites for the conquest of the mountain.

SIR FRANCIS YOUNGHUSBAND: *

Time after time the climbers have failed to reach the summit of Everest. Immense preparations have been made in England. Intense thought has been given to the project. Hundreds of local men have been engaged in transporting the climbers to the mountain. And the climbers themselves have been ready to endure the severest physical strain and run every risk—even the risk of losing their lives. Yet the mountain remains unconquered.

But if the expeditions have failed in achieving their supreme object they have not been wholly fruitless of results. The climbers have not reached 29,000 feet; but three times they have reached 28,000 feet. And this is an advance of more than 3,000 feet upon anything which had been achieved before. It gives promise that it is only a matter of time before the last thousand feet will be climbed.

And in the process of climbing to 28,000 feet the climbers

* Though never actually on the mountain, Younghusband was one of the foremost of Everesters, from the earliest days to his death in 1942. Guiding spirit of the earlier expeditions and longtime chairman of the Mount Everest Committee, he wrote voluminously about the various attempts and was perhaps the outstanding authority on the overall problems involved. *Everest: the Challenge,* from which the following excerpt is taken, was written in 1937, when its author was seventy-four.

have unwittingly given evidence of one scientific fact of great importance—the fact that the human organism can adapt itself to the atmospheric conditions prevailing at the highest terrestrial altitudes. Life is one long process of adaptation of the living being to its surroundings. But that adaptation can only be effected within certain limits. The human organism can adapt itself to a variety of surrounding conditions. But it cannot adapt itself indefinitely. If the temperature is too low or too high the organism succumbs. So also is it with altitude. If a man were suddenly transported to an altitude of 50,000 feet, or even 29,000 feet, above sea-level he would die. On the other hand, practical experience has shown that if he is not transported suddenly to a great height, but ascends slowly, he can gradually adapt himself to the conditions of high altitude. The only question has been, how high would be the altitude to which men could thus adapt themselves? When De Saussure ascended Mount Blanc, which is less than 16,000 feet in height, he and his companions puffed and blew and made very heavy going of the altitude. Nowadays nothing is thought of it. And when the Everest expeditions were started, though it was known that man could ascend to anyhow the 25,000-feet level, for the Duke of Abruzzi had reached 24,600 feet, it was still very doubtful whether he could, without the aid of oxygen, ascend to even 26,000 feet; and scientific men predicted that he probably would be unable to sleep at 23,000 feet—and if he could not sleep at that altitude there seemed to be little prospect of his being able to reach the summit. But the expeditions have proved that man can adapt himself to the conditions at even the 28,000-feet level. Further, they have shown that men can carry light loads as high as 27,400 feet. And Smythe slept soundly for thirteen hours at that height.

This fact that man can adapt himself to the highest terrestrial altitude conditions is one very valuable result of the Everest expeditions. We know something about ourselves—something to our advantage—which we did not know before.

And what a change in men's views this is may be judged when we look back on Mallory saying after the first expedition that he supposed that the limit of acclimatization must be somewhere about 21,000 feet; and on Somervell (a medical man as well as a climber) saying, when the expedition of 1922 started, that he was personally of opinion that nobody could exist without oxygen at a height above 25,000 or 26,000 feet.

Now it has been discovered that if the higher altitudes are not rushed, but approached gradually, the human body, with its proverbial capacity for adapting itself to varying conditions, will adapt itself to increasing deficiency of oxygen in the air. The airman who flies over Everest has no need to adapt himself, for enough oxygen to make up the deficiency is carried with him in the aeroplane, and all he has to do is to suck it in during the few hours which it takes to fly over Everest from the plains of India and return there. But the climber, if he were to trust to such artificial supply of oxygen, would have to carry it on his back in a most cumbersome apparatus. And the value of the discovery that man can adapt himself to the deficiency of oxygen lies in the fact that he can climb to the highest altitudes without carrying this apparatus. He can do without it and yet reach the 28,000-feet level.

He can only do this, however, if he approaches the higher altitudes by slow degrees. He must not rush the mountain. He must give his body time, slowly and gradually, to adapt itself to the new conditions. The previous expeditions had gone at it too fast, and they suffered in consequence. They had headaches, they got blue in the face, they became irritable, they lost their appetites, they panted, they felt lassitude, they could not concentrate their minds, they became generally miserable. Even Somervell spoke of peevishness at 22,000 feet, and at 27,000 feet he cared very little whether he got to the top or not. Ruttledge, profiting by his experience, gave his expedition more time. He conducted the march across Tibet, and the establishment of camps on the East Rongbuk Glacier and the North Col, 23,000 feet, at such moderate speed as would allow the maximum possible number of climbers to reach an attacking position unstrained and at the very top of their form. He believed that if only they would take their time in going up the East Rongbuk Glacier they would arrive on the North Col with plenty of reserve in hand. So no impatience, or spell of fine weather, was allowed to turn them from the predetermined plan of spending at least four days at every camp on the way up the East Rongbuk Glacier in order that their bodies might accustom themselves to the progressive decrease of oxygen in the air they breathed.

Their efforts, Raymond Green, the medical officer of the expedition, considered, were rewarded to a remarkable degree. There was absence of serious respiratory distress. Except in the case of one slow acclimatizer, disordered breathing passed off rapidly. Of the fourteen climbers, thirteen reached the North Col without having experienced serious discomfort. Above the North Col proper acclimatization was made impossible by the weather and by the nature of the ground. Yet even the distress in breathing felt by the climbers was not great. And what is very remarkable, considering what we were told of the climbers on previous expeditions requiring seven or eight or nine breaths between each step at the higher altitudes, climbers on the 1933 expedition needed only two or three breaths to a step—even above 27,000 feet—and found frequent halts unnecessary. Their appetites were excellent, and at the highest camps they were clamouring for substantial food in face of the delicate fare provided. Headaches were uncommon. They slept well. As we have seen, Smythe, after his climb to 28,100 feet, slept for thirteen hours in the tent at 27,400 feet. Lassitude was less. They were occasionally irritable, one is glad to hear, in case they might be thought too angelic. But only those who went above 27,000 feet experienced any mental deterioration. And, in general, they are reported as being "remarkably fit, cheerful, and energetic, even at Camps above the North Col."

With the porters the same improvement was noted. They were ready to go to the highest camps. There was no difficulty in making them start in the morning, even under the worst conditions. And there were no cases of mountain sickness.

How is it that this acclimatization or accustoming of the human body to the progressive decrease of the oxygen in the air it inhales takes place? The most important way is by an increased ventilation of the lungs. There has to be deeper breathing. The first deep breathing of the ascending climber is probably caused by the direct effects of oxygen-lack. But this renders the respiratory centre in the brain more susceptible to changes in the acidity of the blood. And at the same time it washes carbon dioxide out of the blood and so lowers its acidity. This has to be rectified. And the kidneys have to rectify it by secreting more alkali and so making the blood more acid again. The kidneys only learn this function slowly. But when they do acclimatization has taken place. This process of acclimatization is assisted by an increase in the number of red corpuscles, whose function it is to carry oxygen. And possibly there may be active secretion of oxygen by the lung epithelium. By these chemical changes in the body does it adapt itself gradually, and within certain limits, to the changing conditions.

And the condition of the climbers in 1933 at 28,000 feet was so good that in Raymond Green's opinion there is little doubt of their capacity, in good condition, to climb Everest without oxygen.

Nevertheless, the benefits of acclimatization do not meet all the necessities of the situation. Even the most acclimatized Everest climber is not as fit as a climber on Mont Blanc. From the snow, the cold, the contending with blizzards, the labour of cutting steps in ice, the having for any reason to push on at a faster rate, the discomfort of tiny tents, the want of fresh food, the monotonous and badly-cooked food, and even from acclimatization itself—from all these causes deterioration sets in and the time comes when the climbers lose their appetite and weight, and become less energetic. In all probability prolonged shortage of oxygen is directly or indirectly the most important cause of this deterioration, says Raymond Green, and acclimatization, itself originally due to oxygen-lack, may carry deterioration with it as a noxious by-product.

The good effects of acclimatization are, therefore, to some extent counterbalanced by the bad effects of deterioration, and if climbers stayed too long at the higher altitudes deterioration might outweigh the good of acclimatization. But for the short periods it is alone possible to remain on the upper part of Everest, the advantages of acclimatization are very apparent.

It is not only the bodies of individual climbers that have become acclimatized to the supreme altitudes: their minds also are becoming acclimatized. When nothing was known for certain about accessibility of the summit, when no one knew whether a man, with or without the aid of oxygen, could climb at such altitudes as 28,000 and 29,000 feet, when we knew nothing about the state of the mountain itself, the climbers' minds were full of uncertainty. Now, as the result of our expeditions, men know the mountain, and their minds are thoroughly acclimatized to the 28,000-feet level. On two expeditions men have reached it. There is no uncertainty about it. It is now regarded as the starting-point for the real climb. And this acclimatization of the mind, as well as of the body, will be of great value to the climbers on their next attempt to reach the summit.

It will also be of value to all others who attempt to reach the summits of other peaks. The fact that men have actually climbed to the altitude of the highest peaks next after Everest

—to the altitude of Kangchenjunga and K2—will help to acclimatize the minds of climbers of all lesser heights. In regard
to the effect of altitude their minds will be at rest.

The experience gained on Mont Blanc is being repeated on
Mount Everest. Men still feel certain altitude effects in climbing Mont Blanc, but they accept the discomfort as all in the
day's work, and do not take them so seriously as De Saussure
on his first climb did. It is the same with the Everest climbers.
The last expedition, fortified with the knowledge that Norton
and Somervell had reached 28,000 feet, went at the mountain
with a far greater assurance than their predecessors. They suffered, but they did not bother unduly about the suffering. And
this greater composure of mind reacted on the body. They
went more easily about their task.

From *Everest: the Challenge.*

JAMES RAMSEY ULLMAN:

Closely related to the question of acclimatization is that of
the use or non-use of oxygen, and no other aspect of the
Everest adventure has aroused such diverse—sometimes, indeed,
violently opposed—opinions. Roughly, a third of the climbers
are unequivocally pro-oxygen, another third unequivocally
anti-, and the remainder somewhere in the middle. And the
argument still rages as volubly as ever—if not on the mountain
itself, then in the pages of books and alpine journals.

Those who advocate oxygen have only one reason: that it
helps. Those who oppose it, however, take their stand on two
grounds: the physical one that it is more nuisance than it is
worth, and the ethical one that it is not a legitimate part of
mountaineering. To the nonmountaineer, this last objection may
seem arbitrary and far-fetched, but among climbers themselves
—and the Everesters in particular—it is a very real issue indeed.
And each side has strong and valid points to make. On the one

hand, it seems only reasonable for man to use all his knowledge and skill in the enterprises which he undertakes. On the other, it will unquestionably be a prouder and more satisfying achievement if he can gain the world's summit with the aid of his two legs and two lungs alone.

Mallory, as we have seen, was no great partisan of "English air," but his objections were based largely on the cumbersomeness and unreliability of the 1922 apparatus, and one wonders what his attitude would be toward the vastly improved gear available today. As for the others, the five excerpts that follow give a fair idea of the range of opinion. If nothing else, they show that Everest has not yet been climbed even in theory, much less in fact.

N. E. Odell: *

The results of the Second Expedition to Mount Everest in 1922 went to show that two schools of thought prevailed from the experiences of the high-climbing parties. The one maintained that oxygen was not only desirable but necessary if a party were going to reach an altitude much greater than that made by the climbers who essayed to attain the summit without its use that year. It went further and said that "on any further attempt upon Everest oxygen will form a most important part of the climber's equipment." The other school of thought held that "the chances of climbing the mountain are probably greater if oxygen be not used," since the oxygen prevents the degree of acclimatization in the individual that should be acquired, and in the event of its failure endangers the party's return.

In addition there were certain members who adopted a middle view and said that the case was not proven, and provided

---

* Odell was in charge of the oxygen apparatus and supply on the 1924 Expedition.

the apparatus could be lightened, and that the organization would allow of sufficient porters being available to carry up supplies, benefit would no doubt accrue from its use: at any rate oxygen should be available in case of need.

From what has been said earlier it will have been seen that the attempts on the summit, aided by oxygen, were reduced last year * to one—the last fatal one, and the merits of the oxygen in this case we shall never know. It has been explained also, more especially by Norton, that the extremely bad weather conditions and the consequent shortage of available porters had precluded the transportation of oxygen supplies sufficiently far up the line to admit of an oxygen attempt earlier. This emphatically was the main reason, though a secondary one, as mentioned above, may have been that not the entire party had complete faith in the resurrected apparatus. But if we had had at the outset the serviceable apparatus we expected, and conditions had allowed of oxygen supplies being carried to the North Col at an earlier stage in the proceedings—an event which would at the same time probably have prevented our proving as we did what acclimatization could accomplish—then there is no doubt that oxygen would have been in evidence in earlier attempts. It must not be thought therefore that as a party we were prejudiced against oxygen.

After our first repulse from Camp III by blizzards, on our return there Geoffrey Bruce and I used oxygen in an attempt to reach the North Col under very bad conditions of snow. On that occasion I was feeling somewhat unfit, but thought that the oxygen would give the necessary bracing needed: instead it gave so little effect and the apparatus proved such an irksome load that I was glad to hand the outfit over to a

* 1924.—*Editor.*

porter to carry. Bruce could similarly derive no benefit from it, and this was the more remarkable since he had used it to such apparent advantage when accompanying Finch in 1922. At this time we had been living at altitudes up to and over 21,000 feet for nearly three weeks, with visits to 22,000 to 23,000 feet, and so must necessarily have undergone a considerable degree of acclimatization.

Later in the campaign, when I was in charge of Camp IV on the North Col and lived there for eleven days, not sleeping below 23,000 feet save once, I had the truth, as well as the value, of acclimatization fully brought home to me. It is unnecessary to reiterate the details of my climbs from this camp to over 27,000 feet, except to mention again that on my second ascent to that altitude I used oxygen from Camp V at 25,000 feet, but at rather over 26,000 feet I felt I was deriving so little benefit from it that I turned it off and did not use the gas again. I had been using a relatively small quantity only, rather more than 1 litre per minute, but before switching it off I gave myself a full 2 litres or more per minute, and really the only advantage I seemed to gain from it, was a more or less imagined slight relief of fatigue in my legs. But when I had reached Camp VI and dumped the apparatus, and set off again on my search for the missing party, I felt able to progress altogether better than when I had been breathing oxygen, a contributory factor to this being, no doubt, that I was without the bulk and awkwardness of the apparatus. On the descent of the mountain I was so far unaffected by the altitude as to be able to go from Camp VI to V in about one hour, and from the latter to Camp IV in about thirty minutes, partly glissading near the North Col.

I only venture to give these results and figures to show how real is the capacity for acclimatization to these extreme altitudes, and there seems no reason at all to suppose that this important physiological capability, other things being equal, should not be possible at an altitude equivalent to that of the top of Mount Everest, and perhaps considerably more. I say other things being equal, though realizing this is scarcely likely at any time to be the case, temperature especially altering for the worse, that is of course decreasing as one gets higher; in addition chemical changes and reactions of the blood become more acute. But our evidence has shown us emphatically that one can live and feel fit for an indefinite period at 23,000 feet, and an altitude below this can no longer be considered, as Finch maintained, the upper level of true acclimatization. Somervell considers that acclimatization may take place at 24,000 feet, but in the present state of our knowledge I think no upper limit can be given. If this acclimatization is as real as we seem to have found it to be, then the advantage of carrying a heavy and bulky supply of oxygen is very dubious. It is important to remember in Finch's case that he has accustomed himself during his Alpine career to carry very heavy loads, and this alone must be very contributory to his ability to be at ease with a heavy oxygen apparatus. But the main point, without doubt, is that he derived the benefit he did from the oxygen on account of his not being acclimatized. He and Geoffrey Bruce had come straight up from the Base Camp and been but five days at Camp III before starting their high climb.

It is not a question of whether or not the top of the mountain can be reached without oxygen, but what, considering all the circumstances of the case, is the way most likely to succeed, and which is to the greatest extent within the powers of the average climber. In our opinion the individual's inherent capacity for acclimatization is likely to serve him better than doubtful adventitious aids.

From *The Fight for Everest: 1924*

T. Howard Somervell:

Without allowing time for acclimatisation to take place, it is probable that nobody—that is, unless some *lusus naturae* exists—will reach the summit; if artificially supplied oxygen be used, the acclimatisation may not be necessary; but the danger of an attempt by non-acclimatised men with oxygen apparatus is that a breakdown of the apparatus might lead to serious consequences, while a fully acclimatised man is probably just as capable of standing a height of 29,000 feet, unaided, as you or I would be able to stand the height of Mount Blanc to-morrow. When the Expedition of 1922 started I was personally of opinion that nobody could exist at a height about 25,000 or 26,000 feet without oxygen; but since we have proved that this can be done, it seems that the chances of climbing the mountain are probably greater if oxygen be not used. For the apparatus, and the spare cylinders required, necessitate the use of a large number of coolies; while in an attempt without oxygen only three or four coolies are required for the camping equipment and the food at the highest camp.

Therefore it seems that the best chance of getting to the top of Mount Everest lies in the sending out of some nine or ten climbers, who can remain at a high camp, become thoroughly acclimatised, and then make a series of expeditions up the mountain, three or so at a time, as continuously as weather conditions will allow. By adopting these tactics the number of possible attempts up the mountain can be increased; and it seems to me that the chances of climbing to the summit lie in the multiplicity of possible attempts rather than in any other direction. It were better to prepare for a number of attempts each by a small but acclimatised party, rather than to stake all on one or two highly organised endeavours, in which oxygen, and a large number of coolies, are used. It is only a small pro-

Looking up. Everest from the Indian foothills. *Brown Bros.*

Looking down. The surrounding ranges as seen
from 28,000 feet. *Wide World*

The white ramparts of Asia. The Everest group seen from ninety miles to the south. Everest itself is the second peak from the left. Makalu, to its right, appears higher because it is nearer the camera.

portion of coolies who can get up to the heights of 25,000 or 27,000 feet, and they should be used for any one attempt as sparingly as possible. During the war * we all had our ideas of how it should be run, and they were generally wrong; the above plan is the writer's idea of how to climb Mount Everest, and it may or may not be right, but is enunciated for what it is worth.

From *The Assault on Mount Everest: 1922.*

HUGH RUTTLEDGE:

Readers may well have been forcibly impressed by the speeds attributed to the oxygen party of 1922. The fact that they could climb at 1,000 feet an hour to Camp V, and at 900 feet an hour above that, would appear to afford a very strong argument in favour of the use of oxygen. Unfortunately the experiences of one party do not provide an adequate basis on which to build a general theory of action.

The following points may be noted:

1. Finch appears to have used oxygen continuously from Camp III upwards.

2. An accident to the oxygen apparatus carried by Geoffrey Bruce occurred at about 27,300 feet and nearly produced a disaster.

3. Odell used oxygen in the course of his ascent in support of Mallory and Irvine in 1924. Its effect on him was so very slight as to make it doubtful whether it was worth while carrying the apparatus.

4. Greene, in the course of his climb to Camp V after only one day's acclimatisation at Camp IV [in 1933], made a trial of one of Finch's cylinders on the north ridge, and obtained considerable relief from it.

* Somervell is referring to the First World War, though his statement would obviously apply just as well to the Second.—*Editor.*

5. Smythe, on the other hand, having descended from his high climb, used an apparatus experimentally at the North Col, only to find that it gave him a sore throat. It did not appear to improve his condition in any way.

We may perhaps justifiably conclude that a climber will receive little or no benefit from the use of oxygen at an altitude to which he has acclimatised himself in the natural way.

On the other hand, if the tactics proposed in foregoing paragraphs are adopted, the climbers will always be, to some extent, ahead of their acclimatisation when at work above the North Col, though we know that a camp can be established and occupied for a considerable time above 27,000 feet without danger of collapse. Apart from the difficulty of transporting oxygen in any quantity to high camps, I think it is advisable for the assault parties to attain such acclimatisation as is possible at least as far as 27,000 feet. But we should do well to consider the advantages of the use of oxygen above that, especially if an even more efficient apparatus can be devised. The dangers from deterioration and from bad weather are so great that speed is essential. Wyn Harris's suggestion that an apparatus might be used to help men over the difficult part in the neighbourhood of the great couloir is worth examination. I would go farther. A party might begin using it when leaving Camp VI and might have a better chance of reaching the summit. They would probably suffer less from cold, and would be able to make more rapid progress. Having reached Camp VI without this aid, they should incur little risk of collapse if the apparatus failed.

I know that there are many who would still prefer to attempt to climb the mountain without oxygen; but the odds against success in any conditions are so heavy that I am inclined to recommend the use of every available means.

From *Attack on Everest.*

GEORGE I. FINCH:

The task of climbing Mt. Everest is at last being generally recognized as one lying very close to the limit of human endeavour. As such it calls for the exercise of every advantage that the wit of man can devise. We cannot afford to give anything away. The question of the possibility of the summit being reached without oxygen should be relegated to the mental lumber-room with any future 'ethical' searchings. The question of the additional risks which the use of oxygen may or may not involve is immaterial; such risks must just be accepted. The only material question is simple—namely, do the advantages of oxygen counterbalance the disadvantages of the extra weight and equipment? This was clearly and indisputably answered in 1922 when a weak party using oxygen went further on the mountain than a much stronger party meeting with distinctly less adverse weather conditions.

In 1922, the oxygen equipment, though sound in principle, was cumbersome and heavy. With the resources now available, a compact apparatus supplying oxygen at a rate sufficient to increase the total oxygen partial pressure to the equivalent of a height of 15,000 ft. and containing 10 hours' supply need weigh no more than 20 lb. Thus, two felt-jacketed Vibrax steel cylinders charged to 180 atmospheres and each containing 750 litres of oxygen at N.T.P. weigh about 14 lb. A robust combined pressure gauge, flowmeter, reducing valve and flow valve of the type used in flying weighs less than 2lb. The only additional requirement is half a pound of rubber tubing and bag. A complete apparatus, therefore, holding sufficient oxygen for at least 10 hours at altitudes above 25,000 ft., need weigh only 16-17 lb. These figures should suffice to show that the open type of oxygen apparatus has become an indispensable part of the Everest climber's equipment. Of the so-called closed type of apparatus there is little to be said. It is, indeed, at fault fundamentally, in that it makes no use of the always available supply of oxygen from the atmosphere. Thus, foredoomed to failure on *a priori* grounds, it also failed on the mountainside.

If oxygen is to be the key to success on Everest, the use of oxygen supplies on the mountainside must be properly organized. In future, there must be no weakening of an expedition by splitting it into two parties on the question of oxygen. There is no room for divided opinion. The whole expedition must be organized with a view to pushing the attacking party up to a starting-point as high up the mountain as is practicable and properly equipped with all requisite supplies. Between the high starting-point and the summit small depots of a few cylinders each should be established, the furthest being laid, if possible, at say 28,000 feet on the edge of the great gully. Nor is there room for two types of oxygen apparatus. The choice must be made and adhered to. In the face of facts of actual experience this should not be difficult. The finer points and details of the oxygen outfits, together with consideration of the advisability of doping the oxygen with carbon dioxide, are questions to be discussed and settled by a competent committee, long before the expedition sets out.

From *The Alpine Journal*, vol. 51, 1939.

H. W. TILMAN:

The 'closed' type oxygen apparatus from which some expected so much was a failure.* Its weight, complexity, and the necessity for a mask are against it. In theory it was to have the effect of reducing the climber to sea-level conditions, or rather better, so that had it answered expectations the climbing of the mountain would hardly have been worth the fuss that would undoubtedly have been made. The oxygen enthusiast hopes

* In 1938.—*Editor.*

to abolish fatigue, breathlessness, cold, the numbing mental
and physical effects of high altitudes—those things, in fact,
which the mountaineer delights to struggle against and which
together make the climbing of Everest such a formidable task;
but at the same time he considers the climbing of the mountain
with these handicaps removed as meritorious as the climbing
of it under natural conditions. To my mind there would be no
finality about a successful oxygen climb, it would only inspire
a wish to do it without. Would the Alpine Club recognize such
a climb? Would it matter a hoot, reply the gas brigade, if it did
not? They refuse to see any difference between using nailed
boots, warm clothing, snow glasses and (*horribile dictu*) sleeping draughts, and the use of oxygen. If the stuff could be taken
as pills, they say, then you would use it quick enough. Perhaps we should; pills, at any rate, one hopes, would not weigh
25 lb., but in my opinion it would be a confession of defeat.
Meantime, until the pills are forthcoming, let us continue being
illogical. We are an illogical people, and mountaineering is an
illogical amusement which most are content to have as it is. To
put the matter on the lowest possible moral grounds, I am not
convinced on this year's showing that the advantages conferred
by using oxygen outweigh the ethical objections to its use.

From *The Alpine Journal*, vol. 51, 1939.

JAMES RAMSEY ULLMAN:

During the recent war years, of course, the effects of altitude
on the human organism were exhaustively studied by the air
forces of the combatant nations. One of the most elaborate ex-
perimental stations was the U. S. Navy Research Laboratory at
Pensacola, Florida, where a series of interesting high-altitude
experiments were carried out under the direction of Dr. (then
Lieutenant-Commander) Charles S. Houston. In addition to
being a physician, Dr. Houston is one of the foremost American

mountaineers, having climbed in Alaska and on Nanda Devi and acted as leader of the 1938 expedition to K2. His Navy work, to be sure, was concerned with fliers rather than with climbers; but many of his findings were as applicable to the second as to the first, and at war's end he conducted an experiment, called "Operation Everest," which was specifically geared to mountaineering conditions.

The following article by Dr. Houston, which appeared under the original title *29,000 Feet*, is written from the mountaineering point of view and presents a compact summary of what is known to date about the physiology of the body at great altitudes.

CHARLES S. HOUSTON:

Until a man actually stands on the summit and returns to tell about it, no one will know for certain that Everest can be climbed. But ignoring the technical climbing problems, one can speculate on the physiology involved and perhaps reach certain conclusions.

The war has made high-altitude flight a commonplace. Ten or fifteen years ago 30,000 ft. was a remote and seldom attained height; today tens of thousands of military plane crews have flown even higher. Before the war there were perhaps a dozen steel altitude chambers in the entire country, while today hundreds of them are in constant use. All military flying personnel are trained for altitude flight by at least one simulated "flight" in these chambers to altitudes of 30,000 ft. and higher.

It is not surprising, in view of this extensive altitude experience, to find that our knowledge of the body's response to altitude has increased enormously. Not that we have discovered many new facts which Paul Bert, Barcroft and others did not know thirty or fifty years ago—we have merely polished up, refined, and learned to understand them better. Having spent the past four years in altitude training and research, I should like to try to apply some of these facts to climbing.

When the military pilot takes his altitude training "flight" in an altitude chamber, he may be allowed to remove his oxygen mask at 30,000 ft. or thereabouts. Within a few seconds he begins to fumble over simple tasks, becomes ludicrously and pathetically "drunk" and in less than two minutes loses consciousness. After two or three breaths of oxygen he has recovered completely, none the worse but much the wiser. The higher the altitude, of course, the quicker his collapse, but even as low as 18,000 ft. his condition is far worse than at sea level. His nails are blue from lack of oxygen, and he feels sleepy, dizzy, perhaps hilarious. Even simple problems baffle and irritate him, and his judgment is poor, his emotions unstable. He is certainly far different from the acclimatized mountaineer who feels little effect as high as 23,000 ft.

The difference is, of course, due to acclimatization—that delicate adjustment of the body to oxygen lack. Most climbers who reach altitude slowly, working as they climb, are eventually able to spend weeks above 20,000 ft. and perform strenuous physical work. On the other hand, the unacclimatized man taken in a few minutes or hours to high altitude from sea level, has only minutes of rapidly failing consciousness as is dramatically shown in the table [p. 318].

A complete discussion of the intricate processes of acclimatization is obviously beyond the scope of this paper, but among the many changes which occur, three may be mentioned briefly: The red blood cells increase in number, thereby providing more transportation to carry oxygen from lungs to tissues. The volume of breathing is increased in an effort to bring more oxygen deep into the lungs and thence into the blood. And finally, the increased breathing, by "blowing off" carbon dioxide (carbonic acid gas) makes the blood more alkaline, which

DURATION OF CONSCIOUSNESS AT ALTITUDES

Altitude	Acclimatized Man	Unacclimatized Man
20,000 feet	weeks*	30 minutes
23,000 feet	weeks	15 minutes
25,000 feet	at least 10 days	8 minutes
26,000 feet	at least 5 days	7 minutes
27,000 feet	at least 3 days	5 minutes
28,000 feet	several hours	3 minutes
30,000 feet	?	1½ minutes

* Remember that these figures represent the time that climbers have actually spent at these altitudes *without* losing consciousness.

in turn increases the amount of oxygen which the blood can hold.

At present we have practical means to control only the second and third of these processes. Years ago physiologists knew that over-breathing would decrease the effects of oxygen lack. But if the over-breathing were too great and too much carbon dioxide were lost, the blood became so alkaline that dizziness, pins and needles, and later muscle cramps resulted. Too much over-breathing might thus be worse than lack of oxygen.

Many recent studies have shown, however, that if the breathing is increased only slightly above what the body dictates, it is possible to stand safely between the Scylla of oxygen lack and the Charybdis of carbon dioxide lack. One of the truly dramatic demonstrations developed by aviation medicine is the difference between a man breathing normally and a man over-breathing slightly, at 25,000 ft. The former is incapacitated in five minutes and unconscious in less than ten, whereas the latter can move freely about the plane, perform his work, and remain in good condition for 45 minutes or longer.

It remains for some one to show us whether or not over-breathing will help the acclimatized mountaineer as much as it helps the unacclimatized pilot. In the case of the climber, acclimatization has already increased his breathing somewhat (though individuals differ considerably in this), and how much good he can obtain from further increase is speculative at best. But we do know that the pattern of breathing may be as important as the depth. Smooth rhythmic breathing, with inspiration about equal to expiration, at the rate of twelve to fifteen a minute probably gives the optimum oxygen supply to lungs and blood. Thus the scientists confirm what climbers and distance runners have known for years: smooth rhythmic breathing is of great benefit for optimum efforts.

Are there any methods for predicting or for improving the ability of a man to acclimatize? Aviation medicine has not helped us much in this respect, for acclimatization is really not practical for high-altitude flying, in which the pilot ascends in a matter of minutes to heights which climbers reach in days or weeks. No tests have been developed recently which are better than that by which Harrop, in 1922, predicted which members of a Peruvian expedition would suffer from mountain sickness* and which would not. His method is a bit cumbersome and complicated, however, to apply to any man who is interested in learning his altitude potential. The ability to withstand lack of oxygen in an altitude chamber is no indication of acclimatizing ability, because this process requires weeks rather than minutes. And finally, none of the physical fitness tests can be used with confidence, because fitness and ability to acclimatize are not necessarily linked. However, many small pieces of information, plus the Himalayan experiences of the past ten or fifteen years, indicate strongly that acclimatization is not much better in

---

* It might be well to emphasize once that *mountain sickness* occurs only at altitudes above 10,000 ft. and is due to lack of oxygen. *Air sickness*, like sea sickness or car sickness, is due to rough motion and occurs at any altitude.

youth than it is in middle age. In fact, many men under 21 withstand altitude less successfully than others over 28. There is good reason to believe that 22 to 35 is the optimum age for acclimatization, but that even up to 40 or 45, age *per se* does not decrease acclimatization ability.

The ability to tolerate altitude can, however, be improved by several means, and this may be of considerable help to Everest climbers. The controversy over the best foods for climbers which has raged for years and almost disrupted several expeditions seems to have been fairly conclusively settled recently. It has been shown experimentally that carbohydrates (sugars and starches) increase altitude tolerance by 1000 to 5000 feet—in unacclimatized men. Theoretically the explanation for this effect should also apply to acclimatized men, though the demonstration remains to be made. The reasoning behind this effect is sound, though too complex for this paper. Of course it is well known that carbohydrates are an excellent source of rapid energy. On the other hand, it cannot be denied that men need proteins and fats to replenish constantly breaking down tissues, particularly during hard work.

An ideal arrangement would therefore appear to be a diet which is almost exclusively carbohydrate during the working day, when energy is needed and when any protection will be of help. In the evening, when the day's work is done and the need for oxygen less acute, proteins and fats can be the main part of the meal, to rebuild the body. Finally, quite apart from altitude, other considerations indicate that frequent small feedings (every two hours or so) are far more effective than fewer but larger meals. This is particularly helpful at altitudes where the stomach, laboring under difficulties anyway, should not be overburdened by large meals.

Vitamins on the whole have been oversold to the public. Though these mysterious compounds work wonders in certain specific deficiency diseases, they definitely do not "increase re-

sistance" in the average man. For the climber, on a long expedition, they may, however, be of value, since his diet is by necessity somewhat limited. Furthermore we do know that the
vitamins B and C are indispensable catalysts in the use of oxygen
by the tissues, and bits of evidence, as yet fragmentary, indicate
that altitude tolerance may be improved by adding these vitamins to the diet. This means that the high altitude mountaineer,
in addition to a normal quota of vitamins added to his diet, will
probably benefit by larger doses of vitamin B complex and
vitamin C.

What about other drugs? Years ago ammonium chloride was
proposed, and used, to improve altitude tolerance. The ra-
tionale behind its use was logical, but the effects were disappointing in most cases. Bicarbonate of soda, suggested for
entirely different reasons, is probably no better. No new "secret" drugs studied during the war have been revealed nor is it
likely that any will be found which significantly raise man's
ceiling.

In any discussion of the 28,000 and 29,000 ft. peaks the use of
oxygen is inevitably brought up. In aviation, the pilot knows
that life above 20,000 ft. is impossible for more than a few
minutes unless he breathes oxygen. To the flight surgeon dealing with aviation problems, it seems incredible that oxygen
should not be a *sine qua non* on any major peak. Even in acclimatized men, he argues, oxygen should give an added lift, an
extra source of energy which might get the climber to the top.
Why then have several who used oxygen on Everest claimed
that they obtained little if any benefit from it? Were their statements biased by the bulk and discomfort of the apparatus then
available? Or did the oxygen, in fact, fail to relieve their worst
difficulty—the dreadful shortness of breath which resulted from
the slightest exertion?

Lack of oxygen itself exerts a relatively weak influence on
breathing. A man may lose consciousness and even die without

being anywhere near as short of breath as a distance runner. Breathing is largely contolled by the balance between carbon dioxide and base in the blood. During exercise, large amounts of carbon dioxide, and other acids, are formed which must be neutralized by the blood or blown off through the lungs by deeper faster breathing. After hard work, therefore, we pant to blow off carbon dioxide rather than to obtain more oxygen. As mentioned above, one of the changes which takes place in acclimatization is a loss of carbon dioxide which, over a period of days and weeks, is balanced by a loss of base from the blood in order to maintain the proper reaction, though at a lower level. The net result is that there is a smaller reservoir of base available to neutralize the acids formed during exercise; these acids (particularly carbon dioxide) change the reaction of the blood and cause far more panting than they would were the normal amount of base present in the blood.

Acclimatization, therefore, actually is responsible for our breathlessness at altitude. In fact if the blood contained as little base at sea level as it does at, say 20,000 ft., in acclimatized man, the slightest exertion would cause severe breathlessness, just as it does at altitude. However, this very breathlessness may keep the climber from "committing suicide" by exerting himself too far beyond the supply of oxygen available to him.

This is probably the best available explanation of the failure of oxygen to benefit the acclimatized man, at least to any great extent. Differences from individual to individual may explain why some men did notice some help from oxygen, though most did not. We have the anomalous situation, therefore, in which an unacclimatized man fresh from sea level and provided with a full supply of oxygen will far outclass a well acclimatized climber *with or without oxygen.*

In this air age one cannot resist speculating about the possibility of dropping a climber at base camp with a full oxygen supply. This man could climb at least at the Alpine rate of 1000 ft. per hour and descend at least twice as fast. Allowing seven days to reach 29,000 ft. and return, he would require 168 hours of *continuous* oxygen supply. He would be forced to breathe oxygen for every minute of the nights and days, otherwise he would lose consciousness like the pilots in the altitude chamber. Using any of a number of excellent military oxygen assemblies, his supply of oxygen, plus equipment, would weigh between 400 and 600 pounds, depending on the type used, the man's size, and his physical condition. Yes, it could be done, with elaborate preparations, detailed supply and transport arrangements—and extraordinary luck. The risk would be tremendous, for failure of his oxygen supply for an hour or less at higher altitudes would cost our climber his life.

Can men reach 29,000 ft. (or higher) without oxygen? Until it is actually done the answer will be doubtful at best. But by the best calculations which we know how to make at the present time, we can say that 29,000 ft. is only imperceptibly worse than 28,000 ft. On paper at any rate man can climb to 29,000 ft. and perhaps higher. He will need magnificent physical condition and climbing ability. He must have sound judgment and great perseverance and courage. His food, his creature comforts, and his climbing stages must be elaborately planned. He will probably be as well off without oxygen as with it.

One day a man will do it.

From *The American Alpine Journal*, vol. vi, 1946.

JAMES RAMSEY ULLMAN:

If oxygen is the subject on which there is most controversy, porterage is that on which there is least. There is, one gathers, room for much improvement in the transport arrangements from India in to the base of the mountain. But the work of the Sherpa and Bhutia porters on the peak itself has won the unstinted admiration of every Everester.

Not the least of the satisfactions involved is the fact that this trained and loyal corps of "Tigers" has been developed absolutely from scratch, not a single man of them having ever been on a high mountain before the reconnaissance expedition of 1921. The older generation, to be sure—like that of the climbers themselves—has now passed on. But tradition and pride of achievement have been established in their communities, and it is probable that the quality of future Everest porters will be even higher than it has been in the past.

HUGH RUTTLEDGE:

No praise can be too high for the services rendered by the porter corps of 1933. There can no longer be any doubt whatever that, physically and morally, they are capable of bringing the summit within reach of the climbing parties. The final climb can probably be done from the height and position of the Camp VI of 1933, but a still better chance would be afforded if this camp could be placed just below the first step at a height of about 27,800 feet. The form shown by the porters allows of the belief that they are capable of carrying as far as this, even from the site of our Camp V. The position of the latter cannot, we think, be improved upon; but the camp itself might well be more solidly constructed.

In calling upon the porters to carry to 27,400 or perhaps to 27,800 feet, we must see to it that they are under escort both up and down; for the dangers of climbing above Camp V demand it. This requires an act of self-sacrifice on the part of at least one among the climbers. I am confident that a volunteer will never be called for in vain. It is essential that every climber should be capable of independent action on the mountain; morale is a plant of tender growth, and the porters must have confidence in the ability of the man to whose care they are entrusted.

Norton has always, and rightly, laid stress upon the importance of getting to know the porters individually and of learning their language. The party of 1933 did its utmost in this
respect, though linguistic ability was not universal. It was found
that, if only the porters liked and trusted a climber, they would
follow him anywhere even though his powers of communication were limited. Personal influence is by no means in direct
proportion to capacity for speech. The latter, however, is obviously a valuable asset, and will always increase the standard
of performance and improve the safety factor at a crisis.

In the matter of climbing Mount Everest the Sherpa and
Bhutia communities have now developed an esprit de corps
which ensures that any future expedition will have no difficulty
in obtaining a fine body of men.

From *Attack on Everest.*

JAMES RAMSEY ULLMAN:

Mark Twain might well have been speaking of Everest when
he said that everyone talks about the weather but no one does
anything about it. The accounts of every expedition are full
of rueful "ifs" . . . *If* the wind had slackened. *If* the monsoon
had held off. *If* it had not snowed or blown or stormed. . . .
Had the climbers been able to *do* something about it, or even
been blessed with good fortune at a few crucial points, Everest
would long since have been climbed. (Frank Smythe, for one,
ascribes his failure to reach the top in 1933 directly, and solely,
to the powdering of early monsoon snow on the slabs of the
north face.)

True, there are many things that can be, and have been, done
to minimize the effects of storm and cold. Enormous pains have
been taken to time the operations so that they would have the
optimum chance for success. But in the last analysis the weather
is a matter of luck, and luck is a gift which Everest rarely and
reluctantly bestows.

SIR FRANCIS YOUNGHUSBAND:

All this,* however, though very pretty on paper, may be utterly impossible in practice. The weather may absolutely preclude it. For an assault on Everest ample time for the most deliberate and leisurely movements is required. Plenty of time is necessary for acclimatization, for the establishment and stocking of higher and higher camps. But this sufficiency of time is precisely what Everest weather does not allow. Even on a perfectly fine, cloudless day, out of the blue will come a raging tempest, driving the snow on the mountain in whirring swirls which may put a stop to operations for days. Then, ever in the background, is the monsoon.

The weather it is that decides. And in the weather the deciding factor is the precipitation of snow upon the steeply outward-facing slabs of rock on the approach to the final pyramid. The Everest climbers seem able to ride out the most terrific blizzards and to put up with the severest cold. But once even a sprinkling of snow has settled on the mountain they are brought to a standstill. And this is the more surprising because the Bavarian expedition on Kangchenjunga climbed right through the monsoon season, with snow constantly falling. If they could climb on Kangchenjunga through several feet of snow, why could not the Englishmen climb on Everest with only a sprinkling?

The answer is that the very fact that it was only a sprinkling constituted the danger. The snow on Everest was not enough in itself to give sufficient hold. It was just enough to make going on the slabs dangerous. It covered the footholds. Mountaineers, steady in control and in fine physique, might get over that difficulty. But *returning* mountaineers, with little control of

* The detailed plans of organization.—*Editor.*

themselves and in the last stage of exhaustion, might be in the utmost peril on these outward-facing snow-sprinkled slabs.

This precipitation of snow is the decisive factor in weather. When is it most likely to occur? It does not occur in the winter, for in that season the strong west winds are powerful enough to blow away the snow as fast as it falls. But there is a period of the year when these prevailing west winds diminish in power, and when the clouds coming up from the Indian side precipitate an increased amount of snow. The snow wins against the wind. Monsoon conditions have set in. On Kangchenjunga this may not greatly matter. On Everest it is decisive.

What, then, an Everest expedition has to determine is when these monsoon conditions may be expected to set in. And this cannot, of course, be done with any precision. But with the experience of four expeditions to guide them, an approximate estimate may be made. It may be assumed that the monsoon will begin to prevail at the earliest at the end of May, and, at the latest, in the middle of June. Round about the first of June— a week or two on either side—the wind will weaken and the cloud increase. Snow will lay faster than it is swept away; and the slabs will become too dangerous for climbers to venture on. This seems to be the rough conclusion to which climbers have come. And what a future expedition has to plan for is to reach the summit before this critical point is arrived at. They must be on the mountain while the wind is in the ascendant and before the snow has got the upper hand. It will be colder then. It will be vastly unpleasant. But it will be safer.

Can an expedition reach the mountain thus early in the season? Wager, who made a special study of the weather, and who was himself one of those who climbed highest, thinks that it can. The 1933 expedition started from Darjiling earlier than its predecessors, but Wager thinks that it is both possible and desirable that the next expedition should start even earlier—a month earlier. "The glacier camps and Camp IV on the North

Col could then be occupied a fortnight earlier," says Wager, "and those who acclimatize quickly might attempt the mountain on any days of relatively calm weather which happen in the last half of May. . . . At this early time," he adds, "climbers would be liable to more severe winds and cold than in June, but they would certainly find the mountain free from snow. The slower acclimatizers, kept definitely in reserve at low glacier camps, would make their attack on the mountain if, as happened in 1924 but unfortunately not in 1933, there should be good weather in the first ten days of June."

As to the chances of success, Ruttledge says: "When we can synchronize four consecutive days of fine weather with the perfect simultaneous acclimatization and training of six men, perhaps two climbers will reach the summit."

This is a rather too nicely-calculated estimate, for it is quite certain that six perfectly trained and acclimatized climbers will never meet with *four* perfect days on Everest, and at that rate the mountain will never be climbed. But Ruttledge himself is sure it will be. So there must be a flaw somewhere.

Perhaps Bauer's* words about the possibility of climbing Kangchenjunga—a mountain 800 feet lower but far more difficult—might be applied to Everest. If men attempt it at all, they must be optimists.

Anyhow, we onlookers at the mighty drama now being enacted cannot help rising to this optimistic note. We have seen the mountaineers overcome so many obstacles, and show such pertinacity and adaptability, that we are confident they will rise triumphant. We have been appalled at the ferocious malignity of the mountain, the devastating snowstorms, and the frightful cold. The operations have had to be more lengthy, and the mountain itself has proved more difficult than we had originally supposed. But we have been impressed by the re-

* Leader of the German Kanchenjunga expeditions of 1929 and 1931. —*Editor.*

sourcefulness of the mountaineers, by their ability to rise to the occasion and adapt themselves to severer conditions, and by the advance which they have made in mountaineering technique. We also note the improvement which has been made not only in the spirit but in the mountain-craft of the Himalayan porters. Everest has done something more than merely hurl back her assailants. She has stung them into developing their resources. She has called forth the unsuspected best within them.

All this makes us estimate the climbers more highly than they estimate themselves, and gives us confidence that even if Everest is only moderately lenient they will succeed.

From *Everest: the Challenge.*

JAMES RAMSEY ULLMAN:

Every Everest expedition to date has attacked the mountain by the route recommended by Mallory after the 1921 reconnaissance, the only even minor variant being the 1938 party's ascent to the North Col from the west instead of the east. There has, to be sure, been occasional talk of trying the peak from another side altogether. But the 1935 reconnaissance confirmed the judgment of 1921, and it is all but certain that future attempts will be along the old Col-Northeast Ridge route that has now become classic ground.

On this route, all Everesters are agreed, there are only two sections which present formidable climbing difficulties: the snow-slopes leading to the North Col, and the steep slabs immediately below the summit pyramid. The problem below the Col—as has been repeatedly, and once disastrously, demonstrated—is the danger of avalanche, and the best route to the crest varies with the snow conditions from year to year. Near the summit there are the two alternatives of Mallory's ridge route and the long traverse across the face blazed by Norton and subsequently followed by Harris, Wager, and Smythe. In spite of repeated failures, most of the climbers still believe that the latter offers the better chance for success.

LT. COL. E. F. NORTON:

The approach to the final pyramid appears to be the only other place entailing any danger,* except perhaps when new snow is lying. Here there are two possible routes; the first, which Mallory always favoured, and which he followed in his last climb, is by the crest of the Northeast Arête.

There was always the doubt that a feature in this route, which we called the second step, might cause considerable difficulty; it presents a vertical face to the south and east, but seemed surmountable, though evidently steep, to the north. Mallory and Irvine were last seen on the top of the step, and so must have climbed it; but this is not quite sufficient to guarantee this route, as they may well have fallen from it on the descent.

From the point where they were last seen to a point some 300 feet below the summit it is all steep, but almost certainly easier than the place they had just surmounted; the last 300 feet is obviously easy.

The alternative route which I favoured, and which Somervell and I followed, is roughly parallel to the crest, but 500 feet to 1,000 feet below it on the north face. This route becomes steep and rather dangerous, though nowhere difficult—if I may so differentiate—in, and just west of, the big couloir, which cuts off the final pyramid from the great north-east shoulder of the mountain. For a short distance, perhaps 200 feet, the going is very steep, and composed of overlying slabs approximating to the general slope of the mountain; there is always apt to be a sprinkling of snow here, which conceals the foot-

* Besides the North Col snow-slopes.—*Editor.*

holds and constitutes the principal danger of a slip, for, sheltered as it is from wind and sun, the snow is powdery (of the
consistency of coarse salt) and nowhere supports the foot.

About 200 feet above the point I reached, all of which is of
the steep slabby rock I have described, you emerge on to the
face of the final pyramid, and, as far as we could judge from
the Base Camp, there should be no further difficulty up to the
summit.

Thus by either route there is some steep climbing at about
28,200 feet, steeper than anything on rock below; this factor
must not be forgotten in estimating times both in ascending
and descending, for over portions of it it may be necessary to
move one at a time on a belayed rope.

From The Fight for Everest: 1924.

HUGH RUTTLEDGE:

The experiences of 1933 confirmed an opinion which first
took shape in 1924, that Mount Everest is, in a technical mountaineering sense, a difficult mountain. Norton, whose favourite
climbing ground in Switzerland is not dissimilar in formation to
the upper slopes of Mount Everest, with the added disadvantage
of loose rock, was the very last man to exaggerate the obstacles.
He considered that the climbing for perhaps 400 feet on either
side of the couloir, and in the couloir itself, was difficult, and,
in a greater degree, dangerous; and that both difficulty and
danger were greatly increased by the presence of powder snow
on the slabs. The point is that, although the work is not of the
kind found on "severe" routes in the British mountain districts
or the Chamonix Aiguilles, it nevertheless requires delicate
and accurate balance. Overhangs, or places requiring strong
arm-pulls, would not be negotiable at all at such an altitude;
but smooth, small outward-sloping ledges, which have to be
traversed by climbers whose co-ordination of mind and muscle

has necessarily been impaired by altitude, constitute a difficulty of a high order when masked by snow.

The reconnaissance made by Wyn Harris and Wager afforded evidence, which to my mind is conclusive, regarding the comparative merits of the routes favoured by Mallory and Norton respectively. The conditions on May 30th were sufficiently good to permit accurate judgment of the practicability of the second step. One cannot go so far as to say that a rock-climbing expert might not climb, or turn, this step in good conditions at Alpine levels; but I am satisfied that if Wyn Harris and Wager, both of them first-rate mountaineers, turned away from it, future parties will be well advised to leave it out of their calculations. If, after arrival at Camp VI, they should find the slabs rendered temporarily impassable by a sudden fall of snow, they might make a further examination of the second step. But this should not, I think, be included in the plan of assault.

I would strongly recommend single-minded adherence to Norton's route, which offers a practical certainty of success in good conditions. Provided that you can synchronise the arrival of two parties at the top of their form with the absence of snow and three, or preferably four, days of consecutive fine weather, I believe that the summit will be reached by Norton's route.

From *Attack on Everest*.

FRANK S. SMYTHE:

Under the conditions prevailing in 1933, Everest is impossible by any route. Under better conditions, when the rocks are free of snow, Brigadier Norton has shown that it is possible to traverse the "tiles" with comparative ease. It would appear, however, that the best route is not to traverse the couloir high, but as low as possible. Apart from the fact that the general inclination of the yellow band is slightly concave and that the lower it is traversed the easier it is, it is better to avoid the steep buttress, and this can be done by keeping low down and turning it at its base where the subsidiary couloir bifurcates with the great couloir. If the subsidiary couloir held good snow, it could then be climbed direct to the breach, but if it held bad snow, as is extremely likely, it should be possible to climb the rocks at the side of it, or alternately to traverse out of it on to the snow ridge bounding it to the west. Whichever route is followed, something more than an ordinary effort will be required before easier ground on the face of the final pyramid is reached.

Wyn Harris has suggested that oxygen apparatus giving off a large quantity of gas for a short time should be used for this bad section of the climb. Camp VI should be pitched on the scree ledge under the first step. Thence carrying oxygen but not using it, the climber will make a gradually descending traverse across the yellow band to the great couloir. He will then don the apparatus and climb as rapidly as possible to the breach in the black band. Once through this he will leave his apparatus and proceed without it. Any oxygen left over could be employed to help him during the descent. In addition, a long length of very light cord could be taken and fixed to pitons above and below the steep 300 feet between the great couloir and the breach: this might prove invaluable, for there is no doubt that those who climb Everest even in the best conditions are going to be "all in" after their tremendous effort. One disadvantage of pitching Camp VI under the first step is that the exhausted climber returning from the summit will be required to ascend over 100 feet to the camp; but this disadvantage will be more than compensated by the saving of time on the way to the summit and the carrying of the oxygen apparatus downhill instead of up before it is used.

Both mentally and physically it is going to require a supreme effort to climb the last 1,000 feet, and anything that can stimulate the climber's flagging mental and physical energies should be employed. In all probability the summit can be reached by an acclimatised man without oxygen, but the odds against him are great. The difficulty of the mountain, the evil effects of altitude, the possibility of being benighted, the risk of sudden storms and the dangers of exhaustion are so serious that oxygen should be taken if it can aid the climber. Prior to 1933 there were those to whom the thought of it was abhorrent. I confess to a similar prejudice. There seemed something almost unfair in climbing what was then thought to be an easy mountain by such artificial means. I doubt whether there is a member of the present expedition who now thinks thus, for Everest has been proved to rely for its defence not only on bad weather and altitude, but on its difficulties too; it allows of no latitude; it defends with every means in its power, and its weapons are terrible ones; it is as exacting on the mind as it is on the body. Those who tread its last 1,000 feet tread the physical limits of the world.

From *Attack on Everest.*

JAMES RAMSEY ULLMAN:

The preceding discussions of the many problems of Everest were written over a period of almost two decades. Over this span a great wealth of experience was accumulated and new methods and techniques were developed; on certain specific points, notably the use of oxygen, there is wide variance of opinion. Yet the interest and significance of the various conclusions reached lie not in their differences but in their basic similarity. The years passed; the climbers changed; but Everest and the problems of Everest remained the same.

Thus, Ruttledge, summing up after the expedition of 1936, is still concerned with the same fundamentals as was Mallory in 1922. Acclimatization, weather, porterage, route of ascent—

these and the other physical aspects of high mountaineering
—may be called the constants of the Everest adventure, in which
succeeding expeditions repeat the pattern of the old. The vari-
ables are to be found in the climbers themselves, their *modus
operandi*, their point of view. And in the ensuing discussion of
the 1936 attempt Ruttledge concentrates largely on this organizational aspect of the venture, which has become the subject
of much disagreement among the climbers in recent years.

HUGH RUTTLEDGE:

Six expeditions, including the Reconnaissances of 1921 and
1935, have now visited Mount Everest. Each has made its contribution to the common stock of experience, but not one has
been able to place a climber on the final pyramid, and still the
difficulties and dangers of the last thousand feet or so are matter
for conjecture. Four men—Norton in 1924, Wyn Harris,
Wager and Smythe in 1933—have reached a height of about
28,100 feet, when exhaustion and bad snow conditions forced
a return; the expedition of 1936, certainly not inferior in
strength to any of its predecessors, and equipped with the hard-
won experience of fifteen years, got no further than the first
expedition of all.

In these circumstances it is natural that the public in general,
and mountaineers in particular, should ask themselves two
questions: first, *is* the summit attainable at all; second, are our
methods sound? I think that all men qualified to give an opinion will support me when I answer the first question in the
affirmative. There is not one iota of evidence to the contrary.
The four men who reached 28,100 feet were all handicapped
by circumstances which will not necessarily recur: Norton was
prematurely exhausted by the struggle to establish Camp IV in
very bad weather; by the necessary rescue of porters marooned
there; by the effort to get the men to carry up to the higher

camps; and by the fact that his highest camp could not be placed high enough to bring the summit within reach on the final day. Wyn Harris and Wager and Smythe had equally bad weather on the glacier and the North Col, but better protection through improved equipment. Their assaults were delayed by events over which they had no control, and when they were able to ascend deterioration had already set in and the weather was unfavourable. Again, Wyn Harris and Wager, unsure of the best route to the summit, lost time in prospecting alternate ways. Smythe in his turn had to climb alone, and to negotiate bad snow on the higher slabs. Lastly, all these four men were inadequately equipped in respect of high-altitude tents and food. Therefore they were capable of still finer performance and, with better resources and less previous strain, might have reached the summit.

The psychological factor is all-important, and has definitely changed for the better. Climbers and porters are now perfectly sure that they can place a camp at about 27,800 feet, on the snowslope below the First Step. The worry of uncertainty about this has now gone for ever. Equipment of every kind is now so good that the problems of shelter and food are practically solved. The tactical necessity of saving the climbers from excessive labour in the early stages is appreciated, and the selection and training of the assaulting parties are understood. The one still incalculable factor is the weather. Here the element of luck must come in—without luck I think that Everest cannot be climbed. In good weather I am certain it can. Whether oxygen must be used I do not know. Sir Leonard Hill and Captain G. I. Finch are convinced that it is both necessary and efficient. Some of our best climbers insist that the mountain can be climbed without it, and that the dangers from breakdown of apparatus and from carrying the weight across difficult slabs outweigh any possible benefit. The tests of the Royal Air Force on their pilots indicate that oxygen-lack at very high altitudes causes quite sudden insensibility. I advocate that oxygen be taken to the highest camps for use at the discretion of the climbers. Given all equipment, and the right weather, and sent up when they are at the top of their form, they should reach the summit.

Now for the second question: Are our methods sound? Controversy is focused chiefly on the season for operations, and on the numbers and composition of personnel. The former point I have already discussed, and would merely repeat here that I think the period between spring and summer is the best—indeed the only—one; and that too early an arrival is fraught with danger. The matter of personnel requires full and dispassionate consideration. One difficulty is to dissociate the genuine needs of the enterprise from our personal preferences. I have so often heard men say: "But a small expedition is so much more easy and pleasant." Of course it is—my own happiest memories in the Himalaya are of small parties—but that is not the point. Pleasure and facility are not the criteria. An Everest expedition is not like a holiday climb in the Alps. We have to decide, not what we like, but what will give the greatest efficiency.

Many mountaineers, including some who have distinguished themselves on Mount Everest, believe sincerely that large expeditions are inherently inefficient.* The chief reasons advanced in support of this belief are: unwieldy and slow transport; the strain of contacts between too many climbers whose nervous systems are already affected by altitude; overlapping of work, loss of speed and mobility; adverse effect on the economic and social system of Tibet; and an objectionable publicity. In some cases there is yet another reason which should be mentioned: a partly subconscious resentment at the inclusion in the party of men who are not potentially capable of reaching the summit. It is thought that their work, however useful and however

* See page 358.—*Editor.*

essential in a large expedition, can be dispensed with in a small one. The holders of these views allege that not a single large expedition to the Himalaya has ever succeeded in achieving its purpose.

I should like to take the last assertion first, and to say that it is special pleading which begs the question. No expedition, large or small, has yet climbed a peak higher than 25,660 feet; so the superior efficiency of a small party on one of the real giants remains to be proved. I yield to none in my admiration of the comparatively small expedition which climbed Nanda Devi last year*—they were magnificently efficient for their purpose and they succeeded. But I submit that it is unsafe to infer that the same numbers and the same methods would succeed on Mount Everest, where the really serious difficulties only begin at an altitude greater than that of the summit of Nanda Devi. Again, on the latter mountain the climbers did their own carrying, their Sherpa porters having failed them. I am absolutely convinced that the European members of an Everest party should not—probably they could not—carry loads up to the highest camps.

So much for analogy; let us now examine the other arguments. No one knows better than I do the difficulty of procuring and of expediting transport for a large expedition across Tibet. But this difficulty can be overcome, as it was in 1936; and it is not a brake on efficiency, because a party is unlikely to benefit from a very rapid march to Everest, and from arrival with indifferent acclimatisation.

The strain of contacts is and should be negligible in parties of twelve or so, especially where the men know each other well. There must, of course, be a certain amount of give and take, and there is no room for the egoist; but most Englishmen under-

* 1936.—*Editor.*

stand and can apply the team spirit which should survive such a test.

Overlapping of work does not occur where the leader knows his business—on the contrary, there is plenty of work for every man, even in a large party, with no occasion for him to trespass on his neighbours' domains.

The question of having none but potential summit men deserves a fuller treatment; and with it should be linked the question of leadership. It is only natural that men who are to face the dangers and endure the hardships of the assaults should consider themselves capable of framing their own tactics and working out their own salvation, especially when they already know most of the ground on which they will have to work. I have every sympathy for this view, and will only enter the caveat that tempers are short at high altitudes and men become critical of one another. Sometimes, therefore, a non-climbing leader may be able to take a more dispassionate view of a situation than the protagonists, and to help them to recover their lost equilibrium. It has been suggested that there should be no officially recognised leader, but that the Alpine precedent should be followed according to which decisions are informally arrived at and occasion produces the natural leader. I am afraid this would bring about chaos on Everest, where circumstances may often demand instant and authoritative orders.

Again, it must be sorrowfully admitted that our best high-altitude climbers do not include a single linguist. I wonder if they realise how often potential trouble has been averted by, for instance, Morris's* ability to discuss matters with porters in their own language. So long as things are working smoothly, a smattering may suffice; but there is real danger in having no one within reach who can do better than that.

I have already ventured the opinion that two doctors should

* Capt. C. G. Morris, a member of the expeditions of 1922 and 1936. —*Editor.*

accompany an Everest expedition. It may be a positive advantage that one of these is unlikely to go higher than the North Col.

Lastly, if wireless reception and transmission are required you must have a specialist, who might well be trained also in the science of meteorology. He will have no leisure for climbing. Of course, several men think that wireless transmission is unnecessary and that the reception of weather reports from India —which can be done by anyone—is sufficient for all needs. Certainly transmitting apparatus increases transport difficulties. It would be easy to argue on either side; for my part, I am inclined to think that contact with the outer world both ways is worth maintaining. A situation might easily occur in Tibet where it was necessary to invoke the assistance of the Government of India.

The question of publicity has been, so far, spliced to that of finance. Big expeditions cost a lot of money, and such is the outer darkness in which we live at home that wealthy individuals consider the climbing of Mount Everest unworthy of support. But newspapers require news, especially in the silly season, and there is reason to suppose that the general public takes more interest in these adventures than it used to do. If money is obtainable from newspapers and not from private subscription, we are forced into the limelight, however much we dislike it; and, unhappily, exciting headlines and a tendency to "improve upon" sober despatches are a part of much modern journalism. This is where the advocate of a small party becomes really eloquent, knowing full well that his opponent is now in the same box with him— "Reduce your numbers," he says, "and your expenses drop at once to a figure which can be met by private subscription. You are aware that most people of taste object to sensationalism, as you do yourself; conduct your affairs in a respectable obscurity, and sufficient support will be

forthcoming. Reject, if you must, all my other arguments; from
this one you cannot escape with dignity."

It is, indeed, a strong argument—a shot between wind and
water. Let us suppose that it has gone home, and consider the
implications. Some, for instance, would like a party of six Europeans, all potential summit men. We can, undoubtedly, collect
six of the very best; our budget will be extremely modest and
we will probably be able to raise sufficient funds without both-
ering our heads about publicity. The transport organisation is
easy. Perhaps thirty porters will suffice for the mountain. Progress across Tibet will be rapid, and immediate advantage can
be taken of fine weather to establish the North Col. The six
climbers, all supremely competent, able to rely upon one another, and well acclimatised by previous service, will be able
to select their moment and deliver at least two, and probably
three, formidable assaults, with the assistance of the very pick
of the Sherpa and Bhutia porters. No one is redundant; perfect
economy of effort has been achieved; the chances of success
are good.

I readily admit the symmetry of this plan, and the possibility
of success if all goes well, but it reminds me of Wellington's
remark about the French Marshals' campaigns in the Peninsula:
that they resembled a beautiful piece of leather harness, which
served only so long as nothing broke, whereas his own could
easily be repaired with rope. Things do not always go according to plan on Everest. What *might* happen to this party of six?
We may assume that they all arrived fit at the Base Camp—
larger parties have achieved that. At that point two might fall
sick; this happened in 1933. Then four would have to go on
and make the camps up the glacier and establish the North Col.
If they met weather like that of 1924 and 1933 they would be
tired men by the time this work was done. An interval for rest
might be necessary, during which time the weather might be
perfect for the ascent, only to break the moment the invalids

rejoined and the others were ready again. With the menace of the approaching monsoon in their minds the party would make desperate efforts to establish the high camps and deliver the assaults; during this time two men might break down, and the survivors would have to carry on knowing that they had no supports on the North Col or elsewhere, in case of bad weather or of accident to themselves or to porters. In all probability no one could be spared to accompany porters down from the highest camp—they must fend for themselves, in fine weather or in foul. If a camp were cut off by a blizzard; if a man so much as sprained his ankle, no relief could come; each assault party must rely on its own resources to win through.

While accepting the possibility of a smaller expedition than has hitherto been thought necessary, I do plead for adequate reserves. The case for climbers only is perfectly rational, but I would never agree to less than eight; to take less seems to me an unjustified gamble. I should not envy the position of a leader who on returning home was obliged to report, "We had splendid weather in May and early June, but at that time I had not enough fit men available to carry out the assaults."

From *Everest: the Unfinished Adventure.*

JAMES RAMSEY ULLMAN:

The 1936 expedition, of which so much had been expected, was a bitter disappointment to all concerned and led to a general reappraisal of problems and methods. Ruttledge, as we have seen, remained in favor of a large and elaborately equipped expedition, but several of the younger men, notably Shipton and Tilman, felt strongly that a far smaller group would have a better chance of success, and the party which they led out to the mountain in 1938 consisted of only seven white men.

This last try, it is interesting to note, carried to approximately the same height as the very first, in 1922. This was higher

A world of snow and stone. Camp II, on the glacier *Wide World*

The loads go up. A column of Sherpas threading their way
through a forest of seracs.

King of the Blizzard. Everest impregnable, blanketed in monsoon snow

The challengers. Mallory and Norton on the northeast ridge.

than the mark set in 1936, and lower than those of 1924 and 1933; and, so far as practical results are concerned, the matter of large versus small expeditions remains a moot, and hotly debated, question.

ERIC SHIPTON:

One day Mount Everest will be climbed; of that there can be little doubt. It may be achieved at the next attempt; there may be another twenty failures. From the evidence we have at present it would appear that success will demand a combination of circumstances which in the very nature of the conflicting components is not common. In the spring northerly gales render climbing on the north face practically impossible. These gales are neutralised by the advent of the monsoon currents blowing up from the south. The monsoon however deposits powder snow upon the mountain which again renders the steep upper rocks unclimbable. This snow neither melts nor consolidates, and the only agent which clears it away is the north wind. We have always relied upon a short period of quiet weather immediately preceding the monsoon precipitation. But was it reasonable to assume that such a period is the rule? Our experiences in 1933, 1936 and 1938 would certainly suggest that this is not the case. From an examination of photographs taken during the attempts in 1922 I should say that there was far too much snow on the rocks to have permitted a crossing of the Black Band. Only once, then, in June, 1924, has the upper part of the mountain been found in a condition which offered any real chance of success. Unfortunately the climbers were then already too exhausted to take full advantage of their opportunity. Nevertheless I believe that the pre-monsoon period is the only possible one.

But there are those who hold that the winter (November, I think, is the month advocated) is the right time for attempting to climb Mount Everest. As far as I know this view is not shared by anyone who has climbed high on the mountain. The risk of frost-bite even in June is deadly at that great elevation. The noon altitude of the sun over Mount Everest in November is only about 43 degrees, which means that the rocks on the north face would be in shadow for all but a very few hours of the day, and it is doubtful if sunlight ever reaches the upper part of the Great Couloir during the winter months. The cold would be intense, far worse than anything that we have hitherto experienced up there; the slightest breeze would inevitably result in severe frost-bite. All the Sherpas with whom I have discussed the matter are agreed that October and November are months of heavy wind during which they experience great hardship in crossing the passes from Nepal to Tibet. However it would be foolish to dogmatise. The mountain should certainly be attempted in the winter by those who believe in the plan, so long as they have a clear understanding of what they are up against and are determined not to allow their disappointment to get the better of their sense of proportion, which is very liable to happen on Everest. Actually we had intended in 1938 to stay there throughout the winter, so as to examine the conditions. But we evolved another plan which unfortunately did not materialise.

I believe that the best way of tackling the job would be to obtain from the Tibetan Government permission covering five consecutive years in which to run a series of small expeditions. Each should include four mountaineers with wide Alpine as well as high altitude experience; its main object would be to attempt the mountain in the usual pre-monsoon period, but it would also have secondary scientific objectives, among which physiological research might well take pride of place. Such a series would not be expensive to run, as the bulk of the equipment could be dumped at Rongbuk on the first occasion for use of the subsequent expeditions. It would not be necessary to

have the same party each time, though it would be as well for
one man to remain in charge during the whole period, so as to
co-ordinate the scientific work and to accumulate first-hand
experience of conditions on the mountain. It is probable that at
least one of the five consecutive years would provide the fairly
late monsoon which appears to be a necessary condition for
that period of calm weather and snow-free rocks experienced
in 1924. Four thoroughly competent climbers with proved
ability to go high would be ample to take full advantage of such
an opportunity. In addition, with careful organisation, an ambitious programme of valuable scientific work could be undertaken. Winter conditions on the mountain could also be investigated.

With regard to the tactical plan to be adopted on the upper
part of the mountain, I am convinced that it is a mistake to keep
men for too long on and above the North Col. I believe that
in 1933 too much emphasis was laid upon acclimatisation. Admittedly many of us were forced to live above the North Col
for longer than had been intended; but the whole policy had
been one of slow advance. When we returned to the Base Camp
we were terribly emaciated. It was a standing joke that we
looked like a collection of famine-stricken refugees. In 1938 we
were far fitter both while on the mountain and when we returned. For this reason alone I should be opposed to attempting
to establish a third camp above the North Col, and there are
many other strong objections. It has been amply shown that the
establishment of two high camps can be a simple and rapid operation. No doubt a better site could be found for Camp VI than
that used in 1933. I believe that under good conditions the
porters could carry from Camp V to the foot of the First Step
where Wager and Wyn Harris found a good place for a camp.
From there to the Couloir is a very short distance. If in good
conditions the climbers could not reach the summit from such
a camp it is doubtful if they could ever do so.

The wide interest which the Mount Everest Expeditions aroused among the non-climbing public, the great confidence of each successive expedition in its ability to reach the summit and the fact that several parties have been forced to turn back when success was apparently almost within their grasp, have caused a good deal of perplexity and perhaps have made the repeated failures seem rather foolish. To see the matter in its true perspective it is well to remember that in spite of all the attempts that have been made during the last sixty years upon the giants of the Himalayas by climbers of many nations, not a single mountain of 26,000 feet has yet been climbed. Most prominent among these attempts were the repeated, desperate and sometimes disastrous German efforts to climb Kangchenjunga and Nanga Parbat. There were no fewer than five German expeditions to Nanga Parbat in the nineteen-thirties. On the first of these in 1932, the climbers appeared to come so close to their goal that when I discussed the prospects of the second attempt in 1934 with the leader he appeared to regard its success almost as a foregone conclusion, in much the same way as we had assessed our chances on Everest in 1933. It would seem almost as though there were a cordon drawn round the upper part of these great peaks beyond which no man may go. The truth of course lies in the fact that, at altitudes of 25,000 feet and beyond, the effects of low atmospheric pressure upon the human body are so severe that really difficult mountaineering is impossible and the consequences even of a mild storm may be deadly, that nothing but the most perfect conditions of weather and snow offers the slightest chance of success, and that on the last lap of the climb no party is in a position to choose its day.

In this connection it is not irrelevant to reflect upon the countless attempts to climb the Matterhorn before the summit was finally reached in 1865—attempts by the best mountaineers, amateur and professional, of the day. Compare the two problems. The Matterhorn could be attempted on any day in each successive summer; attempts upon the summit of Everest have been launched on, at the most, two days of a few arbitrarily chosen years. The upper part of the Matterhorn could be reached in a single day from a comfortable hotel in the valley so that the same party could set out day after day to attempt the climb, gaining personal knowledge and experience of the problem with each successive effort; no man has yet succeeded in making more than one attempt upon the summit of Everest in any one year—few have tried more than once in a lifetime. Climbing on the Matterhorn is an experience of supreme mental and physical enjoyment; life on the upper part of Everest is a heavy, lifeless struggle. The actual climbing on the Matterhorn is no more difficult than that on the last two thousand feet of Everest. To-day the Matterhorn is regarded as an easy climb for a competent party in reasonably good conditions. And yet year after year it resisted all the efforts of the pioneers to climb it; many proclaimed it to be unclimbable. It was certainly not that these men were incompetent. The reason must be sought in the peculiar, intangible difficulty presented by the first ascent of any peak. How much more should we expect this factor to play a part in the defence of the great peaks of the Himalayas!

No, it is not remarkable that Everest did not yield to the first few attempts; indeed, it would have been very surprising and not a little sad if it had, for that is not the way of great mountains. Perhaps we had become a little arrogant with our fine new technique of ice-claw and rubber slipper, our age of easy mechanical conquest. We had forgotten that the mountain still holds the master card, that it will grant success only in its own good time. Why else does mountaineering retain its deep fascination?

It is possible, even probable, that in time men will look back with wonder at our feeble efforts, unable to account for our repeated failure, while they themselves are grappling with far more formidable problems. If we are still alive we shall no doubt mumble fiercely in our grey beards in a desperate effort to justify our weakness. But if we are wise we shall reflect with deep gratitude that we seized our mountaineering heritage, and will take pleasure in watching younger men enjoy theirs.

From *Upon That Mountain.*

8

Why?

The Men and the Motives

Have we vanquished an enemy?
None but ourselves.

George Leigh-Mallory

James Ramsey Ullman:

"The chances of a given party to reach the summit in a given time are fifty to one against."

Thus Mallory, speaking in London after his return from the reconnaissance of 1921, and to date his odds have stood the test of twenty-six years and seven attempts. What the future holds, no one, of course, knows. But this much—and this only—is sure: that men will go on struggling for Everest, if they have to try fifty times, or five hundred.

And now, to be sure, we are back again to the inevitable and imponderable question:

Why?

It is not only the nonclimber or the armchair cynic who asks; the Everesters themselves, most of them deeply thoughtful and intelligent men, have repeatedly examined their minds and hearts, searching for the motives that drive them on—and up. None, to be sure, has ever found the whole answer. Any more than man can find the answer to why he falls in love or listens to music or looks up at the stars. But this much we do know about ourselves—and this much the Everesters know about their own adventure: that the supreme and most precious moments of human living, however much they may appear to depend on the body and senses, are primarily experiences of the spirit. The men who try to climb Everest are aspiring, consecrated men. If we understand that we understand their exploits—far better than if we read a hundred treatises on technical mountaineering.

351

Frank S. Smythe:

Of recent years there have been many expeditions to the highest peaks of the world. These expeditions have cost large sums of money and have resulted in the loss of not a few lives. To mention three disasters: in 1922 seven porters were swept to their deaths by an avalanche on the slopes of the North Col of Mount Everest; in 1924 Mallory and Irvine failed to return from an attempt to reach the summit of the same mountain; in 1934 four Europeans and six porters perished in a blizzard on Nanga Parbat. What is the good of it? ask some. Is it worth while? query others. Some people who question and query thus are animated by a genuine desire to gather information and instruction; others do not wish to understand and are actuated by a desire to exercise their powers of destructive criticism or to extol their "common sense" which, in many instances, is merely an aphorism for their ignorance. The force that drives man towards the summits of the highest hills is the same force that has raised him above the beasts. He is not put into this world merely to exist; he is put there to find love and happiness, to express and to create. Some achieve happiness best by seeking out the wildest and most inaccessible corners of the earth, and there subjugating their bodies to discomfort and even to peril, in search of an ideal which goes by the simple word "discovery," discovery not only of physical objects but of themselves. To condemn another's ideals, however foolish they may seem at first sight, unless there is something inherently evil in them, is to stand yourself condemned of a retrograde narrow-mindedness.

An Alpine peak of whatever difficulty may be scaled by anyone possessing sufficient strength and skill, but the Himalayas, by virtue of their height, interpose a new factor. To climb them a man must, in addition to strength and skill, possess a body which is so constituted as to be able to exist in the rarefied atmosphere of high altitudes. But even these qualifications, necessary though they are to success, are not sufficient. In all work which involves a considerable output of physical and mental force, if it is to be performed successfully, a man must cultivate a mental attitude commensurate with such work and which is in phase and sympathy with it. It is essential to safety and success on the highest hills to approach them rightly. I would go so far as to say that it is unlikely that the strongest and most skilful mountaineers can reach the highest summits of the world unless they concentrate their whole mental force, as well as their physical energies, towards that end. That is the strength, the power and the charm of the highest hills; they demand something much finer and greater than mere physical and technical ability. They are problems set, not for brutes or angels, but for ordinary thinking men, for mountaineers who can turn an inward and a contemplative eye upon the glories of the hills.

Many clouds of falsehood have been woven about the highest hills. Unfortunately, no pursuit has been so misinterpreted as has mountaineering. The harm done is very real, inasmuch as one effect is to present an entirely false picture to those who have yet to "discover" the hills, or who are ignorant of the motives underlying mountaineering. One evil result has been to presuppose a competitive aspect in mountaineering. That this does exist to some extent none will deny, but there are many to whom mountaineering is primarily a means of strengthening that happy relationship which exists, or should exist, between man and nature. To the more ignorant and unthinking journalists the highest hills are nothing but "stunts" or "records," words utterly hateful and somehow suggestive of all that is low and vulgar in the present age.

Even worse is the "national" atmosphere surrounding them.

One mountain has become a preserve for British mountaineers; two more are a preserve for German mountaineers. Harm may come to mountaineering as a whole if such a policy of national isolation is persisted in in the future. The highest hills should be free to all without "prior rights" or national prejudices to interpose doubts and jealousies between men and a pursuit whose roots should be around goodwill and idealism.

Another thing that my own experiences on the highest hills have made me realise very forcibly is the wrongness of an approach in a conquering spirit. I have been guilty myself of this loose way of thinking, but the highest hills have taught me that a man cannot conquer Nature. Such a word as "conquest" to express his relationship with Nature breathes of egotism and smacks of a conscious superiority which in itself suggests a lack of affinity with Nature. Nature is not a thing apart, something to be stormed and conquered, it is a part of us, an all-prevailing beauty and magnificence in which we strive to realise ourselves, and in realising learn the true import of existence. The expedition that advertises itself out to "conquer" one of the highest hills sets its seal on unsuccess before ever it sails from Europe. By its own vanity must it fail.

To climb on the highest hills is to realise an akinship with Nature. Penalties and pain may attend such a realisation, but these make the eventual consummation all the more vital and joyful, for it is the immutable law of the universe that only through striving and suffering shall man learn to realise himself, to gain in awareness, to enlarge his moral stature, to discover truth and joy. With gasping lungs and failing strength a man may one day tread the highest point of earth, but he will tread it in no spirit of a conqueror, but humbly and thankfully, knowing that a power has been given to him capable of animating him not only to the full extent of his natural strength, but far beyond that strength.

The greatness of mountaineering on the highest hills lies in the fact that no single man is capable of reaching a summit by his own efforts. It is this that segregates the greatest peaks of the world from peaks of lesser altitude as mental and physical problems. They demand much more than a personal approach. Young Maurice Wilson believed that, unversed as he was in mountaineering technique and in all the manifold problems inherent in the ascent of Everest, he could attempt that mountain alone. He believed that through faith, and faith alone, he could reach the summit. It is a magnificent philosophy, but an impractical one. On practical and humanistic grounds his forlorn attempt was open to severe criticism. It is not expedient to glorify such a wastage of life; yet, supposing that he was actuated by no sordid motives of publicity or material advancement, that in Everest he saw an ideal, a means of establishing through physical toil and suffering a joyous contact with universal forces, then, while deploring his action, I cannot withhold a feeling of admiration for his purpose. It was not mountaineering, yet it was magnificent. Call it madness, call it anything you like, but is there not an element of grandeur in the thought of this young man actuated, perhaps, by a flame of idealism, a desire to express something, to expand consciousness, to escape from fleshly shackles, to rise above all earthly considerations, setting out alone to scale the world's highest mountain, which four elaborate expeditions of experienced mountaineers had already failed to climb? There is something magnificent in this thought, just as there is in the thought of Mallory and Irvine disappearing for ever into the clouds surrounding the final pyramid.

In our present stage of existence it would appear to be an immutable law that "God helps those who help themselves." Some may argue that faith and faith alone supplies all that is necessary. It may be that the practical values and achievements of occultism, as practised so successfully by Christ, have been lost sight of. Sometimes men such as Wilson, deemed mad by those who judge an action by the action itself and the results of it rather than the thoughts and motives that inspired it, try to achieve the "impossible." They die, and if failure and success are calculable in terms of life, death and concrete performance, they have failed. But only God knows whether they have really failed.

Perhaps, as regards the highest hills, it would be more intelligible to say that God not only helps those who help themselves, but helps those who help others; for the essential difference between their problems and most other mountain problems is that whoever is eventually successful in reaching their summits will have achieved no more than his predecessors. The part taken by a summit party is but a minor part of an endeavour which in some cases has occupied men for years. It is essential that the general public as a whole should realise this, otherwise much of the value of an expedition is lost.

Many mountaineers believe in a policy of isolation as regards their mountaineering. They think that it should be kept severely aloof from the knowledge of their fellow-men and that there is something vulgar in accounts of an expedition being published in a newspaper. As already mentioned, it is possible for truth to be so distorted as to be virtually lost, but if it is realised how much a successful attempt to climb one of the highest hills depends on comradeship, goodwill, service, a sense of proportion in estimating values both in the present and in the past, and all those qualities which are so necessary in any community if it is to exist happily, then the highest hills can serve to inspire men, and one meaning, at least, of an expedition becomes plain. Publicity, therefore, of a nature which takes these matters into account, and is not merely concerned to promote sales through sensation-mongering, can be of great national and international value.

It is to be hoped that the highest hills will be ascended without use of oxygen apparatus, the use of which * is inimical to the ideals of mountaineering, even taking into account expediency on the grounds of safety and success. To climb breathing oxygen, in order merely to reach a summit, would be a dreadful anticlimax to the work of an expedition; it would, indeed, be in the nature of an insult to that work. If a mountain is climbed thus, the ascent will not be a genuine one from a mountaineering standpoint, and the mountain will still await a mountaineer who can, by his own unaided powers, overcome the problem set by Nature.

This is no place to discuss other than the broader aspects of the problems set by the highest hills. There is one thing that I have left to the last, not because it is least important (not one thing is more important than another in the whole problem, as all form part of a homogeneous whole), but because it is most worthy of being remembered.

Expeditions to the highest hills rely for the establishing of their camps, and in the transport of equipment, food and fuel, on the services of Sherpa and Bhutia porters. No words of mine can do justice to the courage, hardihood, willingness and cheerfulness of these men. Several have already died in the services of previous expeditions. Without them, success is impossible. They have proved themselves in skill, endurance and other qualities to be splendid mountaineers. They are capable of establishing a camp higher than any yet established and of climbing safely to the highest summits of the world. Would it not be a fitting culmination to the attempts to climb Mount Everest if these men were given the opportunity of standing alongside their employers on the summit?

From *The Spirit of the Hills.*

* This does not mean to say that oxygen should not be used at high camps for therapeutical purposes.

JAMES RAMSEY ULLMAN:

Time and again, both in their deeds and in their discussions, we have seen that the Everesters not only want very much to climb their mountain but also care deeply *how* they climb it. By "how," here, is not meant the practical operations and techniques of mountaineering, but the spirit, the standards, and the values with which they undertake their task.

In his brief favoring the large expedition (see page 335) Hugh Ruttledge confined himself largely to pragmatic considerations. Much of the argument about the size of parties, however, is concerned not with practicalities at all, but with the underlying motives and ideals of the Everest ventures, and indeed of mountaineering in general. Especially has this been the case with the advocates of small expeditions, who feel that the large ones of the past, with their elaborate organization and attendant publicity, have been inimical to the best traditions of the sport. What has happened, they ask, to the simplicity and natural comradeship that is the essence of the mountaineering spirit? Is this sport, or spectacle? An adventure, or a traveling circus?

In the following section two Everesters and one vicarious Everester give their opinions on the subject. And while others may well take issue with various of their points, no mountaineer—and no one who cherishes the pure spirit of adventure—can disagree with their basic belief that Everest should be climbed "right" or not at all.

ERIC SHIPTON:

Opinions vary considerably regarding the optimum size of expeditions. I once asked my friend Dr. Humphreys for his views on the matter. He replied firmly and without hesitation "Three constitutes a large expedition, a party of one may be considered a small expedition." I did not propose anything so drastic for an attempt on Mount Everest, though I have always thought that a party of three climbers would stand almost as good a chance as any larger number. The kind of expedition that I visualized was one consisting of six European members all with considerable Alpine experience and all with a proved capacity for going high, and about thirty carefully selected and specially trained Sherpa porters. I advocated a considerable reduction in the quantity of stores and equipment taken per head, and the total expenditure of somewhere between £2,500 and £3,000, as against £12,000 which was the average cost of each of the previous expeditions (except for the first "Reconnaissance").*

Such an expedition would have the advantage of mobility, with a consequent lessening of the risk of a breakdown in lines of communication. Even at the enormously reduced cost, each porter could be provided with much better and more carefully selected equipment. The climbers would get to know the porters individually in a way that was quite impossible when there were 170 of them; this would lead to a greater mutual understanding and trust. The chances of theft of equipment would be greatly reduced. With a huge caravan of three or four hundred animals, varying from powerful yaks to tiny donkeys, which inevitably become spread out over miles of country, it is exceedingly difficult to prevent looting, and vital equipment is as liable to be stolen as are superfluous stores. In 1933 a considerable number of porters' boots were lost in this way; had the theft been larger than it actually was it might have resulted in the complete breakdown of the expedition. Also the provision of a small number of animals would not disrupt the normal life of the country, which is one of the principal objections of the Tibetan officials to Everest expeditions.

* This was written following the expedition of 1933.—*Editor.*

But it was mainly on psychological grounds that I was opposed to large expeditions. It is vitally important that no member of a party should at any time feel that he is superfluous, or that he is simply there in case someone else breaks down. Such a state of affairs imposes an intolerable strain on everyone, and is bound to lead to friction and a consequent loss of efficiency. This matter is easily overlooked by a leader who has all the interest of the organisation and is constantly busy with his plans. On a scientific expedition each man is, or should be, absorbed in his particular line of research; the party can easily be split up into self-contained units each with its special task and responsibility. But when the sole object of a venture is to reach the top of a particular mountain, the problem is entirely different. It is merely tactless to remind a man that he is lucky to be there at all, and that there are hundreds of equally good climbers at home who would be only too glad to take his place. You cannot argue an expedition into running smoothly, nor avoid a competitive feeling by appealing for the "team spirit." The strongest mountaineering party is one in which each member has implicit confidence in all his companions, recognises their vital importance in the common effort and feels himself to have an equally indispensable part to play. This ideal is no less important on a Himalayan expedition than on an Alpine peak. To my mind it can only be achieved with a relatively small, closely-knit party. Only then can you talk (if you must) about "team spirit." How is it possible, when at least 50 per cent. of the members are destined to remain in reserve, to avoid a feeling of competition? Only a saint would expunge from deep down in his soul all hope of another man falling sick, that he might take his place. How different from the joyous partnership we have known on other climbs!

For my part I loathed the crowds and the fuss that were inseparable from a large expedition. I always had the ridiculous feeling that I was taking part in a Cook's tour or a school treat, and I wanted to go away and hide myself. Of course this did not apply to the few days or weeks when one was actually doing a hard job of work, but unfortunately such spells occupied a very small proportion of the whole time. The small town of tents that sprang up each evening, the noise and racket of each fresh start, the sight of a huge army invading the peaceful valleys, it was all so far removed from the light, free spirit with which we were wont to approach our peaks. And I believe that spirit plays an important part in the success of any mountaineering venture. Remove, then, the impression that one is engaged in a vast enterprise upon which the eyes of the world are focused, realise that one is setting out to climb a mountain, higher perhaps, but fundamentally no different from other mountains, and one will add greatly to one's chances of success, and, more important still, enjoyment.

Then there is the question of finance. The argument here, as I understood it, was that money for an Everest expedition was easy to raise, so why not spend it if it would help? In the first place the mere spending of money does not in itself increase the efficiency of an expedition; indeed it can, only too easily, be a source of weakness by cluttering up the works with a lot of superfluous junk and obscuring the really important issues. For example it would be of more value to supply all the porters with precisely the same equipment—dome-tents, boots, sleeping-bags—as that used by the climbers, than to transport cases of champagne and other luxuries all the way from London to Rongbuk. Secondly, if the money must be spent, there are many profitable ways of doing it. For the difference in cost between a large expedition and one of moderate size, no fewer than a dozen expeditions could be sent to other parts of the Himalayas. These, if properly run, could have a direct bearing upon the main problem of climbing Mount Everest, and could be undertaken during years when political permission to enter Tibet was not forthcoming. There are hundreds of young mountaineers who would give anything for a chance to go to the Himalayas. How much easier would be the work of the Mount Everest selection committees if some of them could be given that chance. Again, the climbing of Mount Everest is as much a physiological as a mountaineering problem. We are lamentably ignorant of the real effects of high altitudes upon the human body, or of the means by which these may be countered. Physiologists have been working for years upon these problems; they have been handicapped by lack of opportunities and subjects for their experiments. It would be possible for a small party of trained physiologists and climbers to camp for a month on the summit of Kamet. The results of their experiments would be as valuable to science as to those who wish to climb the lofty peaks of the Himalayas.

Finally, the disadvantage of large expeditions lay in the fact that the necessity of raising big funds made it difficult to control publicity. The expeditions became invested with a glamour foreign to the fundamental simplicity of the game. It was quite natural that mountaineers should wish to climb the highest peak in the world, or at least be interested in the project. But unfortunately Everest's supremacy among mountains appealed to the popular imagination of a record-breaking age, and gradually the expeditions began to receive a press publicity out of all proportion to the value of the undertaking, and certainly out of keeping with what used to be regarded as "the best traditions of mountaineering." It was claimed that the enterprise symbolised the spirit of modern youth, and that its success would represent a triumph of humanity over Nature. In fact, of course, the first part of the venture was an intensely interesting piece of geographical exploration, and the second an absorbing mountaineering problem—no more, no less; both were on the same plane as any similar project.

I knew a man with a strong claim for a place on the expedition, who said that he wanted to climb Everest so as to make a big name for himself, which would enable him to use his influence in the cause of world peace. A worthy ambition no doubt, but surely it would have been more profitable to devote his energies to the study of political economy rather than to proving himself a mountaineer with an exceptionally large lung capacity or whatever it is that enables a man to climb to great altitudes. This is one example among many of an extraordinary distortion of values which has its roots in the opening of a short-cut to fame. Were it not so laughable it might well be resented by those who find in mountaineering a deep æsthetic pleasure.

It was perhaps difficult for those actually engaged in the expeditions not to be carried away by this flood of notoriety, and it needed a good deal of sober introspection to trace the origin of the nasty taste that began to appear in the mouths of the more sensitive. But I think that the feeling of a large section of mountaineers was summed up by the remark that a friend of mine (not himself a member of the expeditions) once made: "For heaven's sake climb the wretched thing and let us get back to real mountaineering." It seemed a pity that so simple a project should have led to such a feeling.

One of the most unfortunate effects of the Mount Everest expeditions was their influence upon Himalayan mountaineering. In consequence of their elaborate scale, it came to be thought impossible to achieve anything in the Himalayas without an enormous and costly organisation. Many of the expeditions—Italian, German, French, international—which followed the early attempts to climb Everest, were run with an extravagance which made the Everest expeditions appear modest by comparison. Fantastic equipment was evolved, dynamite brought to blow away obstacles, aeroplanes used for dumping supplies on the mountain, all the delicacies known to culinary art were provided to sustain the exhausted climbers, whole populations were uprooted from their homes to carry this stuff up the glaciers—with the consequent risk of famine the following year due to the neglect of agriculture. Needless to say these tactics met with very little success, and not one of the peaks attacked with such ferocity was climbed. But the sad thing was that the lessons taught by the great pioneers of the Himalayan exploration—Longstaff, Conway, Kellas, Godwin-Austen, Freshfield, the Schlagintweits—who achieved so much by the simple but hardy application of their art, were forgotten or ignored.

It is perhaps unfair to blame this cult of mighty Himalayan campaigns entirely on the Everest expeditions, but from talks I have had with the organisers of one of these foreign expeditions, in which I tried in vain to persuade them to adopt a less elaborate plan, I am sure that they based their ideas largely upon the Everest precedent.

These observations are made in no unfriendly spirit, and I hope that they will be regarded as constructive criticism. It was sincerely believed that the job could best be tackled by employing all the resources that money could buy. There are still those who hold this view, though I am narrow-minded enough to believe that they can not have themselves experienced the enormous moral and material advantages of the small, compact expedition. One day men will again turn their eyes towards the high Himalayas; I hope that then this other point of view will be kept in mind.

When all is said, the Mount Everest expeditions have been a good adventure, and I think that most of those who were lucky enough to take part in them have gained much by the experience. For my part, much as I disapprove of large expeditions, I would not have foregone a single friendship that I made in 1933.

From *Upon That Mountain.*

H. W. TILMAN:

I hope it will be accepted now that a small party run on modest lines is as likely to achieve success as a large, expensively run party. Two groups of two were in position at 27,200 ft.—three could have been found if wanted—fit and ready to make a serious bid for the top had conditions been favourable.* To have reached the top would have been more convincing still, but I think enough was done to satisfy candid people that these methods are sound. To judge by some of the parties at work in the Himalaya this season, the saner methods advocated here are already in vogue—the use of an aeroplane by one party being a startling exception. The Americans began it in Alaska, using aeroplanes to carry men and stores to a base, but in their case absence of porters, shortness of season, and remoteness give some excuse. The Germans went a step further by dropping stores on the mountain itself, and the logical step, which may not be far distant, is to drop men as near to the summit as convenient. It will probably be quicker and safer to climb there in the end, but we must move with the times, and the end—which is certainly not mountaineering—justifies the means. Whatever our disagreements may be, surely we can agree not to drop tins, tents, and possibly men on mountains. Everyday life is sufficiently cluttered up with complicated gadgets without our wishing to introduce them into such an essentially simple thing as mountaineering. In that we want more simplicity, not less—small parties equipped with bare essentials, not large, over-organized, over-fed, over-equipped expeditions.

From *The Alpine Journal*, vol. 51, 1939.

* On the 1938 Expedition.—*Editor.*

R. L. G. IRVING:

There are two ways of regarding the conquest of Everest. One is to regard it as a personal adventure undertaken by a small party of climbers with no responsibility to any one but themselves. Such an adventure was the ascent of Nanda Devi by two of Tilman's party. If this view is taken it means a number of attempts by small parties, not burdened with oxygen, but prepared to accept the problem of altitude as a challenge to their own natural equipment, similar to the challenge of the rocks and snow. These small 'irresponsible' parties would be under no contract to supply news of their doings to newspapers. Indeed, they might well be composed of men who considered entire forgetfulness of newspaper headlines one of the benefits to be found in high mountains.

The other attitude to Everest is to regard its conquest as a matter of public or even national importance, for news of which newspapers will pay thousands of pounds to secure copyright. Important men write big words about the tremendous effect on men's minds of placing the mountain under the foot of man, of the impression it will make upon the natives, banishing the superstitious awe of these unconquered peaks. If this subjugation of Everest by man is the end in view, then without question man should employ every scientific means to attain it. It is largely a matter of providing enough cash to put these means fully at his disposal. Oxygen must, of course, be on tap wherever it may be useful as a fillip to the energies or to secure a good night's rest. But why stop at oxygen? Surely the triumph of man over nature is most clearly shown when it is accomplished with the minimum of effort. The obvious method is to employ an airship. A small party could be lowered in a comfortable basket till it gently touched the top of Everest, and the occupants could get out and plant a slippered foot on its rebellious head. This is the simplest method, and it could probably be done for half a million. If the spiritual uplift foretold by some enthusiastic writers results, it would be cheap at the price.

At considerably less cost a rope with an anchor at both ends could be dropped by an aeroplane across the long north-east ridge. If it were dropped just above the Second Step, the rope would not need to be a very long one. The ascending party would follow the ledge used by previous parties below the ridge till they reached the hanging rope. A good pull would wedge it firmly on the ridge or secure it by the anchor on the far side. If any serious difficulties on the ridge between the Second Step and the foot of the final pyramid were suspected, a rather longer rope could be dropped across the ridge near the latter point so as to hang down the great furrow or couloir in the face, which has been already reached by four men. It would be invaluable to the party on the west wall of the couloir and the very steep snow gully beyond. Personally I think that the final pyramid will prove an exceedingly formidable obstacle to men climbing at nearly 29,000 feet and that the airship method, provided the aeronauts do their job efficiently, is much the sounder method. Moreover it would demonstrate, with the most convincing effect, the power of men to dominate nature.

The rope-aeroplane method might be used in the establishment of a *téléphérique* across the North Col, and this would be a useful stage in the complete subjugation of Everest. For I do not feel that its subjugation would be considered complete in the public mind till a hotel is planted on the top with hot water in all the rooms and air oxygenated according to price. That really would impress the natives!

From *Ten Great Mountains*.

James Ramsey Ullman:

A nation, an army, a team, a mountaineering expedition—every collective enterprise—is made of many various elements, but most fundamentally of all it consists of individual human beings. The Everest adventure has been what it has because of the men who lived it.

The reader of this book will long since have formed his opinion about these men. Alike in nationality and background, they were diverse, as are men everywhere, in temperament and character. And yet, on an even deeper level than environment or personality, one cannot but feel that they are alike again; and that what made them alike was Everest itself. Seeking its summit, they were bound together by the closest of all human ties: the sharing of a common dream.

Hugh Ruttledge:

What of the men who climb? An attempt has been made, in the first part of this chapter, to interpret other people's points of view: will any single formula suffice to demonstrate the motives and ideals which send a man to try himself against the mountain? I think not. *Quot homines, tot sententiae* applies no less to the very few who can be chosen than to mankind in general. We speak of a homogeneous party, and strive for the closest possible approximation to that ideal, but that can at its best only imply unselfish team work—the willing self-subordination of each member to the common interest; we cannot deny to each his individuality, and it will be found that in most men of this type that individuality is strongly marked, for they are not exactly gregarious by nature. The sport of mountaineering fosters independence of character.

Reference was made above to the facile and, for its purpose, adequate explanation that men go to Everest because they like doing so. Of course they do—the climbing of this mountain may be fairly regarded by mountaineers as the arrival at Mecca is regarded by adherents of Islam. Selection for the party implies recognition that a man has qualified himself by the hardest preparation and is possessed of exceptional skill and endurance. He will wish, not only to demonstrate that the confidence in him has not been misplaced, but to put to the test, on the biggest of them all, everything that he has learnt of mountains. What could give greater satisfaction to a keen man? I do not mean to convey that, in a technical mountaineering sense, Everest is the most difficult of all mountains; but the fact that five first-rate expeditions have failed is sufficient indication of her quality. This is a challenge to the very best, to be taken up for its own sake.

So much for the motive shared by every man and requiring no embellishment. Even in its best form it cannot be altogether dissociated from personal ambition, which is harmless and even praiseworthy if kept within bounds. I have had the good fortune to find in Everest parties a remarkable absence of this quality carried to the length of egotism. Members would not be human if they did not hope themselves to reach the summit; but I had the impression that, provided they could do well enough to secure or retain the respect of fellow-climbers, they were content—for publicity they cared very little. The proposal has more than once been made—and not in British mountaineering circles only—that the names of those who reach a summit should not be published, on the ground that every man had done his duty and made success possible; so that equal credit was due to all.

When a spirit like this animates men, you have not far to go to find ideals; expressed in conduct rather than in speech. I suppose we have changed very much in this respect; in the seventeenth century men were prone to analyse and proclaim their ideals; they still do so in the East; in the twentieth century it is more usual to find reticence. Matters of the spirit are jealously guarded within, and to the world is presented an appearance of lighthearted flippancy. But there is no disguising conduct, especially when all veneers have been stripped away by the chisel of hardship.

It may be taken as axiomatic that each man has joined an expedition resolved, not only to prove his own capacity, but to think of his companions and of the expedition before himself. The execution of that resolve must depend on ideals which are not formed in a day, but are the outcome of long self-discipline and meditation. From a subjective standpoint he may, if very advanced, be like Kipling's hero, and accept triumph or disaster as equal impostors, regarding his duty as an end in itself. A more positive attitude may be adopted by the man who regards the effort he is about to make as the highest expression of himself, and as a test rather than a demonstration. Another will be sensitive to the age-old belief of the East, that mountains are holy ground, with all that that implies of sacrifice. Yet another will be psychic, seeing visions and dreaming dreams, but ever pressing on, like Tennyson's Ulysses, through the arch of experience towards the ever-fading margin of the untrodden world.

The mere healthy materialist has no place in such company, and I think that Everest will have none of him. When the real strain comes, his appetites will hold him back while the men of ideals go forward, supported at the last by that power of the spirit which surpasses the physical. Bayard in the Middle Ages, Mallory in our time; study them, understand them, and you have the key to Everest.

From *Everest: the Unfinished Adventure.*

JAMES RAMSEY ULLMAN:

A champion, a chevalier, a pure and flaming spirit: Mallory was all of these, as Ruttledge implies. But he was also very much a human being, and his feelings about Everest and the Everest adventure were subject to very human fluctuations. There were times when he looked upon the mountain almost with the passion of a lover; times when he feared it and hated it; times when he wondered if the game were worth the candle. The following excerpts show him in four widely varying moods, of which no one is more valid, more the "real" Mallory, than any other. Nor any less. Taken together, they present perhaps as true a picture as one can find of the greatest of Everesters—and of the relationship of a mountain and a man.

GEORGE LEIGH-MALLORY:

Confidence

The whole difficulty of fitting people in so that they take a part in the assault according to their desire or ambition is so great that I can't feel distressed about the part that falls to me. The gasless party has the better adventure, and as it has always been my pet plan to climb the mountain gasless with two camps above the Chang La it is naturally a bit disappointing that I shall be with the other party. Still, the conquest of the mountain is the great thing, and the whole plan is mine and my part will be a sufficiently interesting one and will give me, perhaps, the best chance of all of getting to the top. It is almost unthinkable with this plan that *I* shan't get to the top; I can't see myself coming down defeated. And I have very good hopes that the gasless party will get up; I want all four of us to get there, and I believe it can be done. We shall be starting by moonlight if the morning is calm and should have the mountain climbed if we're lucky before the wind is dangerous.

Only four marches, starting to-morrow morning, to the Rongbuk Monastery! We're getting very near now. On May 3 four of us will leave the Base Camp and begin the upward trek, and on May 17th, or thereabouts, we should reach the summit. I'm eager for the great events to begin.

Now I must say good night to you and turn into my cosy sleeping-bag, where I shall have a clean nose sheet to-night, one of the two you made to fix with patent fasteners. Considering how much grease my face requires and gets, that device has been very useful.

The telegram announcing our success, if we succeed, will precede this letter, I suppose: but it will mention no names. How you will hope that I was one of the conquerors! And I don't think you will be disappointed.

From his letters in *The Fight for Everest: 1924.*

Apathy

It was our intention naturally in setting out this day to reach the summit of Mount Everest. Provided we were not stopped by a mountaineering difficulty, and that was unlikely, the fate of our Expedition would depend on the two factors, time and speed. Of course, we might become too exhausted to go farther before reaching our goal; but the consideration of speed really covers that case, for provided one were capable of moving his limbs at all he would presumably be able to crawl a few steps only so slowly that there would be no point in doing so. From the outset we were short of time; we should have started two hours earlier; the weather prevented us. The fresh snow was an encumbrance, lying everywhere on the ledges from 4 inches to 8 inches deep; it must have made a difference, though not a large one. In any case, when we measured our rate of progress it was not satisfactory, at most 400 feet an hour, not counting halts, and diminishing a little as we went up. It became clear that if we could go no farther—and we couldn't without exhausting ourselves at once—we should still at the best be struggling upwards after night had fallen again. We were prepared to leave it to braver men to climb Mount Everest by night.

By agreeing to this arithmetical computation we tacitly accepted defeat. And if we were not to reach the summit, what remained for us to do? None of us, I believe, cared much about any lower objective. We were not greatly interested then in the exact number of feet by which we should beat a record. It must be remembered that the mind is not easily interested under such conditions. The intelligence is gradually numbed as the supply of oxygen diminishes and the body comes nearer to exhaustion. Looking back on my own mental processes as we approached 27,000 feet, I can find no traces of insanity, nothing completely illogical; within a small compass I was able to reason, no doubt very slowly. But my reasoning was concerned only with one idea; beyond its range I can recall no thought. The view, for instance—and as a rule I'm keen enough about the view—did not interest me; I was not "taking notice." Wonderful as such an experience would be, I had not even the desire to look over the North-east ridge; I would have gladly got to the North-east shoulder as being the sort of place one ought to reach, but I had no strong desire to get there, and none at all for the wonder of being there. I dare say the others were more mentally alive than I; but when it came to deciding what we should do, we had no lively discussion. It seemed to me that we should get back to Morshead in time to take him down this same day to Camp IV. There was some sense in this idea, and many mountaineers may think we were right to make it a first consideration. But the alternative of sleeping a second night at our highest camp and returning next day to Camp III was never mentioned. It may have been that we shrank unconsciously from another night in such discomfort; whether the thought was avoided in this way, or simply was not born, our minds were not behaving as we would wish them to behave. The idea of reaching Camp IV with Morshead before dark, once it had been accepted, controlled us altogether.

From *The Assault on Mount Everest: 1922.*

Disenchantment

I sometimes think of this expedition as a fraud from beginning to end invented by the wild enthusiasm of one man— Younghusband, puffed up by the would-be wisdom of certain pundits in the Alpine Club, and imposed upon the youthful ardour of your humble servant. Certainly the reality must be strangely different from their dream. The long imagined snow slopes of this northern face of Everest with their gentle and inviting angle turn out to be the most appalling precipice, nearly ten thousand feet high. . . . The prospect of ascent in any direction is about nil and our present job is to rub our noses against the impossible in such a way as to persuade mankind that some noble heroism has failed once again. And the heroism at present consists in enduring the discomforts of a camp at nineteen thousand feet in the company of a band, of whose native tongue I can scarcely understand a syllable, and in urging these good folk to rise before daylight in the most usually vain hope that by the time we have got somewhere something may still remain unhidden by the clouds.

. . . Believe about one-quarter of this mood and supply the others which are beyond me to describe—from your sympathy. . . . The rucksack is packed with to-morrow's provisions; the compass and glasses and aneroid are to hand waiting for the start; and I must to bed soon with the alarm watch

Man proposes—

Ewing-Galloway

The unvanquished. *Ewing-Gall*

under my pillow. . . . The snow? It's a passing shower, we hope, we hope. The peaks will be clear and glorious in the morning.

From a letter quoted in Irving: *The Mountain Way.*

What Price Victory?

It is very natural that mountaineers, particularly if they are members of the Alpine Club, should wish success to the Everest Expedition; for in a sense it is their own adventure. And yet their sympathies must often wobble. It is not always an undiluted pleasure to hear of new ascents in the Alps, or even in Great Britain; for half the charm of climbing mountains is born in visions preceding this experience—visions of what is mysterious, remote, inaccessible.

By experience we learn that we may pass to another world and come back; we rediscover the accessibility of summits appearing impregnable; and so long as we cannot without a tremor imagine ourselves upon a mountain's side, that mountain holds its mystery for us. But when we often hear about mountaineering expeditions on one or another of the most famous peaks in the world, are told of conquests among the most remote and difficult ranges or others continually repeated in well-known centres, we come to know too well how accessible mountains are to skilful and even to unskilful climbers. The imagination falters, and it may happen that we find ourselves one day thinking of the most surprising mountain of all with no more reverence than the practised golfer has for an artificial bunker. It was so, I was once informed by a friend, that he caught himself thinking of the Matterhorn, and he wondered whether he shouldn't give up climbing mountains until he had recovered his reverence for them. A shorter way, I thought, was to wait until the weather broke and then climb the Matterhorn every day till it should be calm and fine again, and when he pondered this suggestion he had no need to test its power, for he very soon began to think again of the Matterhorn as he ought to think. But from the anguish of discovering his heresy he cherished a lesson and afterwards would never consent to read or hear accounts of mountaineering, nor even to speak of his own exploits. This was a commendable attitude in him; and I can feel no doubt, thinking of his case, that however valuable a function it may have been of the Alpine Club in its infancy to propagate not only the gospel, but the knowledge of mountains, the time has come when it should be the principal aim of any such body not only to suppress the propagation of a gospel already too popular, but also to shelter its members against that superabundance of knowledge which must needs result from accumulating records. Hereafter, of contemporary exploits the less we know the better; our heritage of discovery among mountains is rich enough; too little remains to be discovered. The story of a new ascent should now be regarded as a corrupting communication calculated to promote the glory of Man, or perhaps only of individual men, at the expense of the mountains themselves.

It may well be asked how, holding such opinions, I can set myself to the task of describing an attempt to reach the highest summit of all. Surely Chomolungmo should remain inviolate, or if attempted, the deed should not be named. With this point of view I have every sympathy, and lest it should be thought that in order to justify myself I must bring in a different order of reasons from some other plane, and involve myself in a digression even longer than the present, I will say nothing about justification for this story beyond remarking that it glorifies Mount Everest, since this mountain has not yet been climbed. And when I say that sympathy in a mountaineer may wobble, the mountaineer I more particularly mean is the present writer. It is true that I did what I could to reach the summit, but now as I look back and see all those wonderful preparations, the great array of boxes collected at Phari Dzong and filling up the courtyard of the bungalow, the train of animals and coolies carrying our baggage across Tibet, the thirteen selected Europeans so snugly wrapt in their woollen waistcoats and Jaeger pants, their armour of wind-proof materials, their splendid overcoats, the furred finneskoes or felt-sided boots or fleece-lined moccasins devised to keep warm their feet, and the sixty strong porters with them delighting in underwear from England and leathern jerkins and puttees from Kashmir; and then, unforgettable scene, the scatter of our stores at the Base Camp, the innumerable neatly-made wooden boxes concealing the rows and rows of tins—of Harris's sausages, Hunter's hams, Heinz's spaghetti, herrings soi-disant fresh, sardines, sliced bacon, peas, beans, and a whole forgotten host besides, sauce-bottles for the Mess tables, and the rare bottles more precious than these, the gay tins of sweet biscuits, Ginger Nuts and Rich Mixed, and all the carefully chosen delicacies; and besides all these for our sustenance or pleasure, the fuel supply, uncovered in the centre of the camp, green and blue two-gallon-cans of paraffin and petrol, and an impressive heap of yak-dung; and the climbing equipment—the gay little tents with crimson flies or yellow, pitched here only to be seen and admired, the bundles of soft sleeping-bags, soft as eiderdown quilt can be, the ferocious crampons and other devices, steel-pointed and terrible, for boots' armament, the business-like coils of rope, the little army of steel cylinders containing oxygen under high pressure, and, not least, the warlike sets of apparatus for using the life-giving gas; and lastly, when I call to mind the whole begoggled crowd moving with slow determination over the snow and up the mountain slopes and with such remarkable persistence bearing up the formidable loads, when after the lapse of months I envisage the whole prodigious evidences of this vast intention, how can I help rejoicing in the yet undimmed splendour, the undiminished glory, the unconquered supremacy of Mount Everest?

From *The Assault on Mount Everest: 1922.*

JAMES RAMSEY ULLMAN:

As it was with Mallory, so was it too with the others. They did not merely climb Everest; they felt Everest, thought Everest, lived Everest. In the two brief excerpts that follow we are vouchsafed a glimpse into the minds of two of them, high up on the mountain: Somervell at Camp Six with Norton, in 1924; and Smythe, nine years later, just before he turned back from his great summit attempt.

T. HOWARD SOMERVELL:

We struggled up the easy mountain-side, hampered only by our own physical condition and by poor Semchumbi's knee, but most of all by the atmosphere. Norton and two porters went on in front, while I helped Semchumbi by carrying part of his load—only a few pounds, but hard work. At last we reached the others, where we found the camp site being levelled —at a place with good shelter behind a rock, at a height of 26,800 feet. A bit too low, but still—we had done 2,000 feet a day with ease up to now; and there was little more than 2,000 feet left for the morrow.

The three stout fellows who had got our stuff—tent, bedding, and food, nearly 50 lb. in all—up to this height, and without whose aid we would have been at that moment retreating, were sent down to Camp 4 with a note describing their prowess and suggesting reward by suitable gastronomic methods. Norton and I settled down to melt snow for to-night's supper and to-morrow's breakfast, looking out from time to time at our porters bucketing down the mountain-side, and far beyond them at a sunset all over the world, as it seemed—from the rosy fingers of Kangchenjanga in the east, past the far-distant peaks of mid-Tibet, separated from us by several complete ranges of mountains, to Gaurisankar and its satellites in the west, black against the red sky. I remember a curious sensation while up at this camp, as if we were getting near the edge of a field with a wall all round it—a high, insuperable wall. The field was human capacity, the wall human limitations. The field, I remember, was a bright and uniform green, and we were walking towards the edge—very near the edge now, where the whitish-grey wall said: "Thus far, and no farther." This almost concrete sense of being near the limit of endurance was new to me, and though I have often felt the presence of a Companion on the mountains who is not in our earthly party of climbers, I have only on this single occasion had this definite vision of limitation. With it I went to sleep and slept remarkably well, though I woke up at five with my extremely sore throat even worse than before, and with the unwelcome announcement by Norton that the cork had come out of the thermos flask and there was nothing for it but to melt some more snow and make more coffee.

From *After Everest*.

FRANK S. SMYTHE:

The summit was just in view over the rock band. It was only 1,000 feet above me, but an æon of weariness separated me from it. Bastion on bastion and slab on slab, the rocks were piled in tremendous confusion, their light-yellow edges ghostlike against the deep-blue sky. From the crest a white plume of mist flowed silently away, like unending volcanic steam, but where I stood there was not a breath of wind and the sun blazed into the hollow with an intense fierceness, yet without warming the cold air. Clouds were gathering, but they were thousands of feet below me. Between them, I could see the Rongbuk glacier, a pure white in its uppermost portion, then rugged and uneven where it was resolved into a multitude of séracs and, lower still, a gigantic muddle of moraines as though all the navvies in the world had been furiously excavating to no logical purpose. Beyond it, the Rongbuk valley stretched northwards towards the golden hills of Tibet, and I could make out the Rongbuk monastery, a minute cluster of minute buildings, yet distinct in every detail through the brilliantly clear atmosphere. With this one exception, I remember no details. My position was too high, my view too vast, my brain too fatigued to register detail. There was nothing visible to challenge my elevation. The earth was so far beneath, it seemed impossible I could ever regain it. The human brain must needs be divinely inspired to comprehend such a vista, and mine was tied to a body fatigued by exertion and slowed down in all its vital processes by lack of oxygen. Somervell's description of the scene is simplest and best: "A god's view."

More by instinct than anything else, I pulled my camera out of my pocket. The photograph I took is pitifully inadequate.

I cannot enlarge on the bitterness of defeat. Those who have failed on Everest are unanimous in one thing: the relief of not having to go on outweighs all other considerations. The last 1,000 feet of Everest are not for mere flesh and blood. Whoever reaches the summit, if he does it without artificial aid, will have to rise godlike above his own frailties and his tremendous environment. Only through a Power within him and without him will he overcome a deadly fatigue and win through to success.

From *Camp Six*.

JAMES RAMSEY ULLMAN:

High on the mountainside the Everesters paused to look down at the earth beneath them and inward at their own minds and hearts. And back in the valleys of home they still looked inward, trying to understand the force that held them, possessed them, drove them onward and still onward in consecration to a dream.

For that, above all else, is what Everest was to them—a dream. And that is what it will remain as long as man endures, because when his dreams die he will no longer be a man.

SIR FRANCIS YOUNGHUSBAND:

I must say yet one word more about "the good" of climbing Mount Everest. These repeated efforts to reach the summit of the world's highest mountain have already cost human life. They have also cost much physical pain, fatigue, and discomfort to the climbers. They have been very expensive. And there is not the slightest sign of any material gain whatever being obtained—not an ounce of gold, or iron, or coal, or a single precious stone, or any land upon which food or material could be grown. What, then, is the good of it all? Who will benefit in the least even if the climbers do eventually get to the top? These are questions which are still being continually asked me, so I had better still go on trying to make as plain as I can what is the good of climbing Mount Everest.

The most obvious good is an increased knowledge of our own capacities. By trying with all our might and with all our mind to climb the highest point on the earth, we are getting to know better what we really can do. No one can say for certain yet whether we can or cannot reach the summit. We cannot know till we try. But if—as seems much more probable now than it did ten years ago—we can reach the summit, we shall know that we are capable of more than we had supposed. And this knowledge of our capacities will be very valuable. In my own lifetime I have seen men's knowledge of their capacity for climbing mountains greatly increased. Men's standard of climbing has been raised. They now know that they can do what forty years ago they did not deem in the least possible. And if they reach the summit of Mount Everest, the standard of achievement will be still further raised; and men who had, so far, never thought of attempting the lesser peaks of the Himalaya, will be climbing them as freely as they now climb peaks in Switzerland.

And what then? What is the good of that? The good of that is that a whole new enjoyment in life will be opened up. And enjoyment of life is, after all, the end of life. We do not live to eat and make money. We eat and make money to be able to enjoy life. And some of us know from actual experience that by climbing a mountain we can get some of the finest enjoyment there is to be had. We like bracing ourselves against a mountain, pitting our mettle, our nerve, our skill, against the physical difficulties the mountain presents, and feeling that we are forcing the spirit within us to prevail against the material. That is a glorious feeling in itself and a real tonic to the spirit— even when it does not always conquer.

But that is not all. The wrestling with the mountain makes us love the mountain. For the moment we may be utterly exhausted and only too thankful to be able to hurry back to more congenial regions. Yet, all the same, we shall eventually get to love the mountain for the very fact that she has forced the utmost out of us, lifted us just for one precious moment high above our ordinary life and shown us beauty of an austerity, power, and purity we should have never known if we had not faced the mountain squarely and battled strongly with her.

This, then, is the good to be obtained from climbing Mount Everest. Most men will have to take on trust that there *is* this good. But most of the best things in life we have to take on trust at first till we have proved them for ourselves. So I would beg readers of this book first trustfully to accept it from the Everest climbers that there is good in climbing great mountains (for the risks they have run and the hardships they have endured are ample enough proof of the faith that is in them), and then to go and test it for themselves—in the Himalaya, if possible, or if not, in the Alps, the Rockies, the Andes, wherever high mountains make the call.

From the Introduction to The Assault on Mount Everest: 1922.

T. Howard Somervell:

Can we now answer that question—was it worth it? Did Mallory and Irvine lay down their lives in vain? It is a sad thing that they never returned to tell the tale of endeavour, and possibly of conquest. But nobody can hold that lives lost in fighting Nature's greatest obstacles in the name of adventure and exploration are thrown away. *Dulce et decorum est pro patria mori;* and surely death in battle against a mountain is a finer and nobler thing than death whilst attempting to kill someone else. The loss of these splendid men is part of the price that has been paid to keep alive the spirit of adventure. Without this spirit life would be a poor thing, and progress impossible.

From After Everest.

Frank S. Smythe:

Many people ask: 'What is the use of risking life and limb in attempting to climb Mount Everest?' It is not enough to reply that valuable scientific work is undertaken during an Everest expedition, for much of this could be done elsewhere, though science naturally forms one of the interests of an expedition. The real reason behind an expedition is the same spirit of inquiry and adventure that lies behind all mountaineering and exploration. Were man not an inquirer and an adventurer, he would never have risen to his present status. If everything we do in life is to be measured in terms of money, then life would

be a very poor thing. The greater ambitions and desires of mankind are actuated by something deeper and finer than the desire
to amass material wealth.

In mountaineering, and on Mount Everest in particular, a
man sees himself for what he is. He learns the value of comradeship and of service. In the bitter cold and blasting winds he sees
life for the grand thing it is. He learns the value of a superla-
tively fit body, and of a mind inspired by no motives of selfish
gain but by achievement for the sake of achievement. An Everest expedition brings a man into contact with the simple and
happy things of life. The cares of civilization slip away. Seen
from the snows of the Himalayas, war and the threat of war,
the jumble and hurly-burly of speed, noise, and rush, the anxie-
ties and uncertainties of this maelström we call 'civilization,'
appear for what they are worth. Life becomes simple, and simplicity is the soulmate of happiness. Never does a plateful of
soup and mutton taste so well as it does after a hard day's work
in the open. Nature is honest, there is no meanness in her composition, she has no time for fools, there is no place in her code
for weaklings and degenerates. Out of her strength we gather
our own strength. And it is good to be strong, to be able to
endure, not as a brute beast, but as a thinking man imbued
with the spirit of a great ideal. This is what Mount Everest
means to those who have tried to climb it.

From *The Adventures of a Mountaineer.*

During the winter following the expedition of 1922 George Mallory visited the United States on a lecture tour. One evening, after a talk in Philadelphia, a member of the audience approached him and asked the inevitable question: "*Why* do you want to climb Mount Everest?"

Mallory considered a moment and gave his answer. "Because it is there," he said.

Appendices

Appendix I

An Everest Chronology

1849–Discovered by the Indian Trigonometrical Survey and
       listed as Peak XV
1852–Recognized as the world's highest mountain
1860–First Himalayan journeys of the "pundit" explorers
1893–First attempt to organize an expedition to the mountain
1904–British Military Mission to Lhasa
1913–Noel's exploration of the approaches to Everest
1919–Formation, in London, of the Mount Everest Committee
1920–Permission for an expedition granted by the Tibetan
       government
1921–First expedition (reconnaissance)
1922–Second expedition
1924–Third expedition
1933–Fourth expedition
       –First plane flight over summit
1934–Maurice Wilson's attempt
1935–Fifth expedition (reconnaissance)
1936–Sixth expedition
1938–Seventh expedition
1942–Col. Scott's flight over summit

Appendix II

Biographical Notes

(Some sixty white men, all told, have participated in the various Everest expeditions. The following list, however, comprises only a selected group of the more famous climbers, whose names, both as participants and as writers, appear most often in the pages of this book. The dates following their names indicate the years of the expeditions in which they took part.)

CHARLES GRANVILLE BRUCE (1922, 1924), leader of the first Everest climbing expedition, was a soldier and adventurer in the best tradition of the old British empire-builders. Born in 1866, he went out to India as a young man and served there through most of his career, chiefly as officer and finally commander of the celebrated 6th Gurkha Rifles. With them he took part in many of the frontier engagements of the '90's and early 1900's and, during the First World War, in the Middle Eastern and Gallipoli campaigns. A notable all-around sportsman, mountaineering was always his first love, and it is doubtful if any man of his time traveled more widely among the farflung ranges of the Himalayas. He was the natural choice for Everest leader in 1922, and again in 1924, but on the second expedition he was taken ill during the trip across Tibet and had to return to India, while Norton took over. The Mount Everest Committee offered him the leadership again in 1933, but he was unable to accept. Bruce retired from the Army in 1936 with the rank of Brigadier General and died three years later, at the age of seventy-three.

JOHN GEOFFREY BRUCE (1922, 1924), a younger cousin of the General, also followed an Army career. Born in 1896, he attended Rugby School and went from there into active service in the First World War. Sent out to India, he served with a Gurkha regiment, where he became familiar with the Himalayan hill-tribes and their various dialects. He was a "walker" rather than a climber, and was attached to the expeditions primarily as transport officer and overseer of porters. He proved himself a first-class mountaineer, however, and in 1922, together with Finch, established a new altitude record of 27,200 feet. He remained in the Army through the 'twenties and and 'thirties, served in the Second World War, and emerged from it a Major General.

GEORGE INGLE FINCH (1922) is a research chemist by profession and throughout the Everest campaigns has been the outstanding advocate of the use of oxygen. Born in Australia in 1888, he was brought to Europe as a child, attended schools in England and Switzerland, and as a young man climbed widely throughout the Alps. Following the First World War, in which he served with the Royal Artillery, he was selected for the Everest expedition of 1922; and he and Geoffrey Bruce, using oxygen, climbed to the then record height of 27,200 feet. Since 1936 he has been professor of chemistry at the University of London.

PERCY WYN HARRIS (1933, 1936) was born in 1903, went through Cambridge (it is interesting to note how greatly Cambridge preponderates over Oxford among the Everesters), and then entered the Civil Service. While serving in Kenya Colony he did his first high climbing on the great African peaks—much of it in company with Eric Shipton. But he had done no Himalayan climbing prior to his participation—and remarkable performance—in the Everest attempt of 1933. Through the past decade and a half he has continued his Civil Service career in various parts of the world.

CHARLES KENNETH HOWARD-BURY (1921), the leader of the first reconnaissance expedition, was not a mountaineer in the technical sense, but had traveled widely through the Himalayas and other parts of Central Asia. Pursuing an Army career, he attended Sandhurst, served in the First World War, and was taken prisoner by the Germans in 1918. He was a member of Parliament in 1922-24 and again in 1926-31, and since then has held various appointive political offices.

ANDREW COMYN IRVINE (1924), who climbed with Mallory to death in the clouds, was, at twenty-two, the youngest of all Everest climbers. He had, however, made a remarkable record as an undergraduate at Oxford, where he had been an oarsman on the crew and an outstanding member of a university-sponsored expedition to Spitzbergen in 1923. He was possessed of a magnificent physique and great youthful enthusiasm, and his selection as Mallory's climbing-partner for the final summit try is ample proof that he had qualified as a real Everester.

GEORGE HERBERT LEIGH-MALLORY (1921, 1922, 1924) remains, almost a quarter of a century after his death, the most famous, and probably the greatest, of Everest climbers. Born in 1886, he attended Winchester and Cambridge and after graduation from the university embarked on a career of teaching at Charterhouse School. He began his mountaineering career while still a schoolboy, climbing extensively both in the English Lake District and, during vacations, in the Alps; and by the time he reached his mid-twenties he was generally known as the most daring and accomplished young climber in England. Mallory served in France with the heavy artillery during the First World War and after demobilization returned to his teaching career, which soon expanded to include a position as lecturer in history at Cambridge. When the members of the 1921 Everest reconnaissance expedition were selected, however, he was the unanimous first choice of the organizing committee, and from then on, for the remaining three years of his life, his career was centered almost entirely on the struggle for the earth's summit. By this time he was already in his late thirties—scarcely a young age by ordinary athletic standards; but his climbing abilities were at their very peak, and he became, both physically and psychologically, the driving spirit of the three expeditions in which he took part. Between the actual attempts on the mountain he worked indefatigably on the organization and financing of the ventures, his activities including a lecture-tour of the United States during the winter preceding his death. He was survived by a wife, a son and two daughters—and a legend that bids fair to endure as long as Everest itself.

JOHN B. NOEL (1922, 1924) fell under the spell of Everest as early as 1913, when he was a junior officer in the British Army in India. Disguised as a native, he made an unauthorized journey through Tibet to within forty miles of the then unexplored mountain; and upon his return to England after the First World War he was one of the prime movers in the organization of the first expeditions. He was not a practiced climber and never went higher than the North Col. But he was an accomplished photographer and motion picture cameraman, and his pictorial records of the 1922 and 1924 expeditions have perhaps contributed more than any other factor toward making the Everest adventure known to the world.

EDWARD FELIX NORTON (1922, 1924) reached a height of over 28,100 feet on Everest in 1924, and no man since has gone higher and come back alive. Like so many other Everesters, he was an Army man. Born in 1884, he served in the First World War as a Major in the Royal Horse Artillery and by the time of the expeditions had risen to the rank of Lieutenant Colonel.

Since then he has held various Army posts of increasing importance, in England, India and elsewhere. In 1937-38 he was aide-de-camp to King George VI, in 1940-41 Acting Governor of Hong Kong, before the colony was captured by the Japanese. He was retired in 1942 with the rank of Lieutenant General. (It is interesting to note that Norton, like Mallory, was no youngster during his Everest days. Indeed, he was already forty years old when he made his great climb of 1924.)

NOEL E. ODELL (1924, 1938) has ranged all over the world as geologist, explorer, and mountaineer. Summoned from Persia to take part in the 1924 expedition, he was expected to function as scientist rather than climber; but his solitary search for Mallory and Irvine on the wild upper slopes of Everest marked him as one of the best mountain-men of his time. Nor did the years diminish his zest and ability. In 1936, in company with H. W. Tilman, he reached the top of Nanda Devi—still the world's record for a climbed peak; and in 1938, he returned to Everest after fourteen years, as a member of the last pre-war expedition. He has also climbed extensively in America, particularly in the Canadian Rockies.

HUGH RUTTLEDGE (1933, 1936) was born in 1884 and was therefore too old for active high-climbing on the two expeditions of which he was leader. As a young man he had climbed extensively in the Alps, and his subsequent twenty-four years (1909-32) with the Indian Civil Service gave him a wide and thorough knowledge of the Himalayas. In recent years, back in England, he has devoted much time to writing.

EDWARD OSWALD SHEBBEARE (1924, 1933), though not a high-climber, did invaluable work as transport officer on two expeditions and on the 1933 venture was second in command to Ruttledge. A lifelong member of the English Civil Service, he was with the Indian Forest Department from 1906 until 1938, when he became Chief Game Warden of Malaya. He was interned by the Japanese when they overran the Malay Peninsula in 1942.

Eric Earle Shipton (1933, 1935, 1936, 1938) has been on more Everest expeditions than any other man. Born in 1907, he lived in Kenya, East Africa, as a young man, first as a planter and then as a member of the Consular Service; and during this period he made notable ascents of the great African peaks of Kenya, Kilimanjaro, and Ruwenzori. In the Himalayas, in addition to his Everest ventures, he has climbed and explored on Kamet, on Nanda Devi, and in the Karakoram, and is perhaps the outstanding exponent of exploratory, as opposed to record-setting, mountaineering. From 1940 through 1942 he served as British consul in the remote city of Kashgar in Chinese Turkestan.

Francis Sydney Smythe (1933, 1936, 1938), who usually shortens his name to *Frank S.*, is, on the record, the foremost of contemporary mountaineers. A key man on three Everest expeditions, he shares the world's altitude climbing-record with Norton, Harris, and Wager. In 1930, as a member of the Swiss Kanchenjunga Expedition, he reached the summit of Jonsong Peak, and in 1931 the crest of Kamet—each of these feats establishing a new mark for the highest peak yet climbed to the top. Born in 1900, Smythe was educated as an electrical engineer and for a brief period in the 'twenties served in that capacity with the R.A.F. In recent years, however, he has devoted most of his time to climbing and exploration. He is the author of many mountaineering books, and his photographs of mountain scenery rank among the finest in their field. As a colonel in the British Army during the Second World War, he was for some time in charge of the training of mountain troops in the Canadian Rockies.

THEODORE HOWARD SOMERVELL (1922, 1924) has lived a life of remarkable variety and interest. Born in 1890, he attended Cambridge, subsequently studied medicine, and served in France from 1915 through 1918 as a captain in the Royal Army Medical Corps. At the time of his selection for the Everest expedition of 1922, he was on his way to becoming an outstanding London surgeon. Traveling through India in that year, however, he was so appalled by the living conditions of the people that he decided to become a medical missionary, and for the next twenty-three years he served on the staff of the London Mission Hospital in Travancore. One of the outstanding climbers of his day, Somervell reached 28,000 feet on Everest in 1924. In addition to his medical and mountaineering activities, he is an accomplished amateur painter and musician.

HAROLD WILLIAM TILMAN (1935, 1938) was born in 1898, fought as a very young man in the First World War, and was twice wounded. Like Harris and Shipton, he has lived in Kenya Colony, where he was a planter from 1919 to 1933, and like them, too, he began his high-climbing career on the great African peaks. In 1934 he and Shipton made a remarkable exploration of the theretofore unknown approaches to Nanda Devi, and two years later, after the intervening Everest reconnaissance of 1935, he and Odell reached Nanda Devi's summit— an altitude record for a climbed peak that still endures. A strong advocate of small and simply run expeditions, Tilman was leader of the last Everest attempt, in 1938. During the Second World War he returned to the British Army as a major.

LAWRENCE RICKARD WAGER (1933) is a geologist and teacher. Born in 1904, he studied (like so many Everesters) at Cambridge and subsequently accepted a professorship at Reading University. He had done much climbing in the Alps, but it was his work as geologist for the British Arctic Air Route Expedition in 1930-31 that particularly recommended him for a place in the Everest party in 1933. In 1935-36 he was back in the Arctic, as leader of the British East Greenland Expedition, and since then has been professor of geology at the University of Durham.

FRANCIS EDWARD YOUNGHUSBAND unquestionably deserves a place of honor in any roster of Everesters, even though he never laid eyes on the mountain. Born in 1863, he entered the Army by way of Sandhurst and was sent out to India in 1890. During the years that followed he took part in many frontier campaigns and made several adventurous journeys into inner Asia, of which the most famous was the 1904 military mission to Lhasa, that established the first official contact between Tibet and the outside world. One of the first dreamers of the Everest dream, he was the principal organizer of the earlier expeditions and served for many years as chairman of the Mount Everest Committee. A geographer, scientist and prolific writer, he was also longtime president of the Royal Geographical Society, and was knighted in recognition of his services to the Empire. Younghusband was a deeply religious man—in many ways a mystic—and in 1936 founded an organization known as the World Congress of Faiths. He visited the United States several times, both on behalf of the Congress and on extensive lecturing tours. He died in 1942 at the age of seventy-nine.

Appendix III

Glossary of Mountaineering Terms

(F indicates French derivation, G German, W Welsh)

arête, F.—a ridge

belay—securing of a rope by hitching it over a projection or passing it around the body

bergschrund, G.—a large crevasse separating the main portion of a glacier from its upper slopes

bivouac—a temporary camp

cairn—a pile of stones set up to mark a summit or route

chimney—a steep, narrow cleft in a rock wall

col, F.—a pass, or the low point of a ridge

cornice—a projecting mass of snow, as on a ridge

couloir, F.—a gully

courte-échelle, F.—clambering on the body or head of another climber

crampons, F.—climbing irons. Iron or steel frames, with projecting spikes, that are attached to the soles of the boots for use on steep snow or ice

crevasse, F.—a deep crevice or fissure in a glacier, caused by its downward movement

cwm, W.—a hollow in a mountainside; a deep ravine

gendarme, F.—a rock tower, usually on a ridge

glissade, F.—sliding down a snow-slope

ice-fall—the steepest section of a glacier, usually taking the form of a wildly jumbled mass of ice

moraine—rock and debris carried down by a glacier

névé, F.—a snowfield lying above the snow-line, usually the source of a glacier

pitch—a short, steep section of rock

rappel, F.—roping down. The maneuver of letting oneself down
    a steep place by means of a supplementary rope
scree—small stones and rock debris, usually found in the form
    of slopes at the foot of steep rock faces
sérac, F.—a tower of ice, usually found on glaciers
snow-bridge—an arch of snow joining two sides of a crevasse
traverse—the horizontal or diagonal crossing of a mountain-
    side. Also the crossing of a peak or pass from one side to the
    other.
verglas, F.—thin veneer of ice on rock

Appendix IV

Reading List

Books dealing with Mount Everest fall into two large cate-
gories: those which are entirely, and those which are only
partly, concerned with it. Also, much material on the mountain
is to be found in alpine and geographical journals and other
more general periodicals.

The following list includes all the books from which excerpts
have been taken for this anthology, plus several others not represented; and, taken together, these constitute most of what has
been written about Everest, in English and in book form.
Books marked with an asterisk are stories of personal experience
by men who have actually been to the mountain.

Books Wholly About Everest

* *Mount Everest: the Reconnaissance, 1921*, by Lt. Col. C. K. How-
    ard-Bury and others. London, Edward Arnold & Co.; New
    York, Longmans, Green & Co. 1922.
        Official account of the preliminary expedition of 1921.

* *The Assault on Mount Everest, 1922*, by Gen. C. G. Bruce and others. London, Edward Arnold & Co.; New York, Longmans, Green & Co. 1923.

    Official account.

* *The Fight for Everest, 1924*, by Lt. Col. E. F. Norton and others. London, Edward Arnold & Co.; New York, Longmans, Green & Co. 1925.

    Official account.

The Epic of Mount Everest, by Sir Francis Younghusband. London, Edward Arnold & Co. 1927.

    A resumé of the expeditions of 1921, 1922, and 1924.

* *The Story of Everest*, by Capt. John Noel. Boston, Little, Brown & Co. 1927.

    Account of the same three expeditions by the photographer of the 1922 and 1924 exploits.

* *Attack on Everest*, by Hugh Ruttledge. New York, Robert M. McBride & Company. 1935. (Published in England as *Everest —1933.*)

    Story of the 1933 venture recounted by its leader, with one chapter by Frank S. Smythe.

* *Camp Six*, by Frank S. Smythe. London, Hodder & Stoughton. 1937.

    Personal story of the 1933 attempt.

* *Everest: the Unfinished Adventure*, by Hugh Ruttledge. London, Hodder & Stoughton. 1937.

    Official account of the 1936 expedition.

Everest, the Challenge, by Sir Francis Younghusband. London and New York, Thomas Nelson and Sons, Ltd. 1936.

    A discussion of the various expeditions, through 1936.

* *First Over Everest: the Houston-Mount Everest Expedition, 1933*, by Air-Commodore P. F. M. Fellowes and others. London, John Lane, 1933.

    Story of the first flight over the mountain.

Books Partly About Everest

* *After Everest*, by T. Howard Somervell. London, Hodder & Stoughton. 1936.

    Reminiscences of a famous Everester, who was also for many years a medical missionary in India.

* *The Making of a Mountaineer*, by George I. Finch. London, Arrowsmith. 1924.

> Climbing experiences in many ranges and over many years.

* *Upon That Mountain*, by Eric Shipton. London, Hodder & Stoughton. 1943.

> Story of many far-flung climbing adventures in Africa and the Himalayas.

* *The Adventures of a Mountaineer*, by Frank S. Smythe. London, J. M. Dent & Sons, Ltd. 1940.

> High points in the author's distinguished career.

* *The Spirit of the Hills*, by Frank S. Smythe. London, Hodder & Stoughton. 1935.

> Essays on the philosophy of mountaineering.

George Leigh-Mallory, by David Pye. London, H. Milford. 1927.

> A memoir.

The Romance of Mountaineering, by R. L. G. Irving. London, J. M. Dent & Sons, Ltd. 1935.

> A history and discussion of the sport in all its aspects.

Ten Great Mountains, by R. L. G. Irving. London, J. M. Dent & Sons, Ltd. 1940.

> Stories of the attempts on the world's most famous peaks.

The Mountain Way, edited by R. L. G. Irving. London, J. M. Dent & Sons, Ltd.; New York, E. P. Dutton & Co., Inc. 1938.

> An anthology of mountain writing.

Mountains and Men, by Leonard H. Robbins. New York, Dodd, Mead & Co. 1931.

> Tales of the great ascents (through 1930) by a popular American writer.

High Conquest, by James Ramsey Ullman. Philadelphia and New York, J. B. Lippincott Company. 1941.

> History and discussion of mountaineering, with accounts of the most famous climbs.

* *God Is My Co-Pilot*, by Col. Robert L. Scott. New York, Charles Scribner's Sons. 1944.

> The adventures of a U. S. Army flier during the Second World War.

References to Everest and the Everest expeditions are to be found in all geographical and mountaineering periodicals. The most detailed accounts of the various attempts—usually by the participants themselves—appear in *The Alpine Journal* (London) and the *Himalayan Journal* (Calcutta).

Index

403

INDEX